THE Shaw Festival

L.W. CONOLLY

THE Shaw Festival

THE FIRST FIFTY YEARS

OXFORD
UNIVERSITY PRESS

OXFORD
UNIVERSITY PRESS

Oxford University Press is a department of the
University of Oxford. It furthers the University's
objective of excellence in research, scholarship,
and education by publishing worldwide. Oxford
is a registered trade mark of Oxford University
Press in the UK and in certain other countries.

Published in Canada by Oxford University Press
8 Sampson Mews, Suite 204,
Don Mills, Ontario M3C 0H5 Canada
www.oupcanada.com

**Library and Archives Canada
Cataloguing in Publication**
Conolly, L. W. (Leonard W.)
The Shaw Festival : the first fifty years / Leonard
W. Conolly.

ISBN 978-0-19-544611-1

1. Shaw Festival (Niagara-on-the-Lake, Ont.)–History.
2. Theater–Ontario–Niagara-on-the-Lake–History.
I. Title.

PN2306.N5C65 2011   792.09713'38   C2010-907492-0

This book is printed on permanent (acid-free) paper ∞
Printed and bound in the United States of America.

1 2 3 4 — 14 13 12 11

Book designed by Scott McKowen
www.punchandjudy.ca

COVER: TARA ROSLING IN *SAINT JOAN*, 2007, PHOTO
BY DAVID COOPER. THIS PAGE, AND OVERLEAF: THE
SHAW FESTIVAL THEATRE, PHOTOS BY DAVID COOPER.
TITLE PAGE: ILLUSTRATION BY SCOTT MCKOWEN.

CONTENTS

ACKNOWLEDGEMENTS

Many people have been extraordinarily generous in helping me write this book. Kathryn Harvey and her staff in Archival and Special Collections in the McLaughlin Library at the University of Guelph have been accommodating beyond the call of duty in facilitating my work and the work of Scott McKowen in the archives of the Shaw Festival. We are particularly grateful for the Library's generosity in scanning scores of images used in the book. At the Festival itself I have received nothing but gracious and helpful responses to my many requests for information and guidance. I owe particular gratitude to Calvin Rand, Christopher Newton, Jackie Maxwell, Colleen Blake, and, in the Festival Library, the indefatigable Nancy Butler and Faye Goodwin. In delving into my constant enquiries (always, so far as I could tell, cheerfully), Nancy Butler probably learned more about the Shaw Festival than she ever needed or wanted to know. The Festival's Odette Yazbeck, Jenniffer Anand, Valerie Taylor, Eda Holmes, Jerry Doiron, Sarah Lynch, Janet Hanna, Joanna Falck, and Rita Brown have also been extremely helpful in many and varied ways. Jean German's careful reading of the text and her several corrections and valuable suggestions were especially helpful. This book has also benefited enormously from the talents of designer extraordinaire Scott McKowen and the editorial skills and panache of Jennie Rubio at Oxford University Press. The help of Katie Scott at OUP, and Janet Straker at Punch & Judy Inc., has also been invaluable. International Shaw Society stalwarts Richard and Lori Dietrich provided inimitable hospitality in their lakeside Florida home while I was writing the early chapters of the book, and gallantly protected me (and my wife Barbara) from alligators and less conspicuous reptiles. Less exotic, but still very much appreciated, hospitality has also been provided by the Warden and Fellows of Robinson College, Cambridge. My colleagues in the English Department at Trent University have likewise been warmly supportive. My graduate students at Trent have politely listened to my accounts of some of the research challenges inherent in writing a book of this kind, and one of them, Christopher Gray, kindly helped by trolling through Toronto newspapers published during the Festival's inaugural year. Jay Tunney provided encouragement and empathy when he had much more important things on his mind, and Michel Pharand rescued me from more egregious errors than I care to contemplate. Much appreciated invitations to give talks about the Festival at the Shaw Society in London, the Bernard Shaw Summer School in Carlow, Ireland, the Shaw Guild in Niagara-on-the-Lake, and at University College Dublin, helped give a firmer focus to the book. Closer to home, my family has provided, as on many previous book-writing adventures, its usual and always welcome blend of practical support and down-to-earth reminders of the existence of other worlds and other responsibilities. My sincere thanks to one and all.

The publication of *The Shaw Festival: The First Fifty Years* has been made possible by a generous grant from The 1916 Foundation in Montchanin, Delaware.

IAN RICHARDSON AND CAROLE SHELLEY IN *MAN AND SUPERMAN* BY BERNARD SHAW, 1977. DIRECTED BY TONY VAN BRIDGE, DESIGNED BY BRIAN JACKSON, LIGHTING DESIGNED BY JOHN STAMMERS, MUSIC BY DENNIS PATRICK. PHOTO BY ROBERT C. RAGSDALE.

PREFACE

The motivation for this book is very simple. It is based on my conviction, developed over many years of theatre-going in several countries – but primarily in Canada, the United States, and Great Britain – that the Shaw Festival is one of the great theatre companies of the English-speaking world, and that its history, therefore, is worth recording and discussing.

My aim has been to write a comprehensive and balanced history of the Festival from its unlikely and tenuous beginnings in 1962 to its fiftieth anniversary season in 2011. By "balanced" I mean that I have not glossed over those times in the Festival's history that have been problematic artistically or financially or in terms of the Festival's sometimes stormy relationship with the local community of Niagara-on-the-Lake. I believe, however, that such times are far outweighed by Festival successes and achievements. I also believe that the successes and achievements can be better understood, appreciated, and celebrated in the full context of the many challenges encountered by the Festival over the years.

During the Shaw Festival's first half century there have been some four hundred Festival productions involving more than two thousand actors, directors, designers, stage managers, technical directors, musicians, choreographers, and administrative staff. Not to mention countless volunteers. There have also been seven artistic directors of the Festival, not including Maynard Burgess, who directed the Festival's first two plays in 1962, but did not have the full range of artistic responsibilities that the term "artistic director" normally signifies. Four of the seven artistic directors (Barry Morse, Tony van Bridge, Richard Kirschner, and Leslie Yeo), for a variety of reasons, served only for one season. Building on the original vision of founder Brian Doherty, the history of the Shaw Festival has, then, been strongly shaped by just three artistic directors: Paxton Whitehead, Christopher Newton, and Jackie Maxwell, who, collectively, have been responsible for forty-two of the Festival's fifty seasons.

While artistic directors cannot and should not take sole responsibility for a company's successes or failures, their authority and influence in a theatrical structure like that of the Shaw Festival are such that it seems to me appropriate to structure the history of the Festival around their terms as artistic directors. The general structure of this book, therefore, is chronological, with each chapter focused on an artistic director. The exceptions to this are Tony van Bridge, whose one season as acting artistic director is covered under the Paxton Whitehead chapter (chapter 4), and Richard Kirschner and Leslie Yeo, who are covered jointly in chapter 5. Within the overall chronological framework there are topic-related sections, such as that on the controversy-filled plans for the Festival Theatre (chapter 4), or on Christopher Newton's "Risk" series of plays (chapter 6).

The core of each chapter, however, is, as it should be, discussion of the plays produced under the leadership of each artistic director. Nearly all of the plays produced in the Festival's fifty seasons are mentioned, some, admittedly, by the briefest of references, others by thumbnail sketches. Many of the Festival's greatest successes are, however, discussed more fully. Through quick reference to the index, it should be possible for readers to remind themselves of productions they recall only dimly, or relive vividly remembered ones, or learn something of productions they missed, perhaps to their regret, perhaps not. The photographs chosen so expertly by

the book's designer, Scott McKowen, will help bring productions to life more effectively than my (and others') words alone can manage. These images are mostly the work of two legendary Canadian theatre photographers. Robert C. Ragsdale created most of the images through the 1979 season; David Cooper has been the company photographer since 1980. Cooper shoots "on the run" at each production's dress rehearsals, with an assistant providing a second camera angle – some 14,000 frames per season.

A confession, however, is in order. In the final chapter there is some discussion of the 2011 season. The fact is, however, that in order to be ready for the beginning of the fiftieth anniversary season this book had to go to press many weeks before the season even began. Whatever assessments are reflected, then, in comments on the 2011 season are based on the plays themselves or on what Jackie Maxwell and others said when the season was announced in September 2010. It will have to be left to a future assessment to gauge how the season actually worked when the plays got on their stages. By the time you are reading this you may have already come to some conclusions of your own.

It is important to stress that this book is *a* history of the Shaw Festival. I make no claims for it as *the* history. There are many ways of telling a story, and I hope and expect that in the fullness of time there will be other histories of the Festival. Although, for example, I firmly believe in the international quality of Shaw Festival productions, I make no attempt to argue the case for this belief by drawing comparisons with similar companies in England or Australia or the United States – or, indeed, in Canada. And, speaking of Canada, while a discussion of the place of the Shaw Festival in the panorama of Canadian theatre would be intriguing and, no doubt, revealing, such a discussion does not form part of this book.

This story of the Shaw Festival is told by many voices. I have been attending Festival productions for thirty years, but in no sense is this book an account of Leonard Conolly's personal journey through any part of the Festival's history. Having said that, and bearing in mind that I have no particular political, theoretical, or cultural axe to grind, it is inevitable that my own biases and values, however obliquely and benignly expressed, are present throughout the book, perhaps in ways that I don't fully understand myself. I have, after all, made decisions about how to structure the book, what aspects of the Festival's history to emphasize, what plays to focus on, and – crucially – what other voices to include. Those voices, I hope, are varied enough to give different, sometimes conflicting, perspectives on Festival strategies, productions, controversies, and so on. In theatre history, as in any other kind of history, there is no absolute truth, only different ways of struggling to define truth.

The sources outlined at the end of this book give some sense of the range of voices to be heard. They include, of course, the artists – especially the artistic directors – who make the Shaw Festival plays live so vibrantly on stage; Festival volunteers, who made the whole thing possible in the first place and continue (through the Shaw Guild) to provide invaluable support; the critics, who labour in a much maligned but, at its best, honourable profession and whose thousands of reviews of Festival productions I have referred to and quoted from extensively; and the audiences, without whom the Shaw Festival would not exist. As regards the audience voice, I hope, dear reader, that the statistics I frequently give about box office returns on productions do not impose themselves *too* tediously. They are, after all, a crucial indicator of the most important theatrical bottom line – ticket sales.

In the interests of providing a text uncluttered by scholarly protocols (i.e., hundreds of footnotes), I have refrained from providing exact references for sources of information and for the many quotations in this book. I will be happy, however, to provide details to any interested readers (lconolly@trentu.ca).

Many Shaw Festival staff and company members have been generous in their support and guidance of the writing of this book, but their involvement has never been intrusive. Unless otherwise indicated, all opinions and judgments in the book are my own, and do not reflect any kind of Shaw Festival official position. And, of course, any errors of fact are both deeply regretted and entirely my own responsibility.

The experience of writing this book has increased both my knowledge and understanding of the Shaw Festival. It is a pleasure and a privilege to share this experience with readers, many of whom, I hope, will also share my immense admiration of all that has been accomplished in fifty years of outstanding playmaking in Niagara-on-the-Lake.

THE SHAW FESTIVAL AT A GLANCE

1962   "Salute to Shaw" opens at the Court House Theatre on June 29 with four staged readings of the *Don Juan in Hell* scene from Shaw's *Man and Superman*, followed on July 27 by four performances of Shaw's *Candida*. The all-amateur season is produced by Brian Doherty, and directed by Maynard Burgess.

1963   "Salute to Shaw" turns professional and becomes the Shaw Festival, with Andrew Allan as the first artistic director. The all-Shaw season runs from July 10 to July 28.

1965   The season includes the first non-Shaw play at the Shaw Festival, Sean O'Casey's *The Shadow of a Gunman*. Founder Brian Doherty defines the mandate of the Festival as "Shaw and his great contemporaries."

1966   The Festival receives its first government grant ($10,000 from the Ontario Arts Council).

1966   Barry Morse succeeds Andrew Allen as artistic director.

1966   The last all-Shaw season (*Man and Superman*, *Misalliance*, and *The Apple Cart*).

1967   Paxton Whitehead succeeds Barry Morse as artistic director.

1967   First touring production of a Shaw Festival play (*Major Barbara* in Winnipeg and at Montreal's Expo 67).

1969   Marigold Charlesworth becomes the first woman to direct a play at the Shaw Festival, Part I of Shaw's *Back to Methuselah*.

1970   Alan Bennett's *Forty Years On* (1968) is the first contemporary play produced at the Festival.

1971   Shaw's *The Philanderer* is the first Festival production to tour outside of Canada when it plays in Rochester, N.Y.

1972   The season opens with George S. Kaufman's and Edna Ferber's *The Royal Family*, the first time a non-Shaw play has opened the season.

1973   Opening of the Festival Theatre. The first play produced there is Shaw's *You Never Can Tell*.

1975   Tony van Bridge serves one season as acting artistic director while Paxton Whitehead takes sabbatical leave.

1975   *Leaven of Malice* by Robertson Davies is the first Canadian play produced at the Festival.

1978   Richard Kirschner succeeds Paxton Whitehead as artistic director. Kirschner is given the title Producer, a new position that combines artistic and administrative responsibilities.

1979   Leslie Yeo serves one season as guest artistic director, pending the arrival of Christopher Newton as artistic director.

1979   Shaw's *Village Wooing* is the first Festival lunchtime production.

1980   Christopher Newton becomes artistic director.

1980   The Festival acquires the Royal George Theatre. The first production there is *Puttin' on the Ritz*, a miscellany of the music and lyrics of Irving Berlin.

1981   Head of Design Cameron Porteous redesigns the Court House Theatre from a proscenium to thrust stage configuration.

1983   Noel Coward's *The Vortex* launches the Festival's Risk Series at the Court House Theatre. The series runs until 1990.

1984   François-Louis Tilly's *Delicatessen* launches the Toronto Project at Toronto Free Theatre. The project runs until 1988.

1985   The Academy, the Festival's training and education centre, is founded.

1986   The Festival celebrates its twenty-fifth anniversary with a production of the full-length *Back to Methuselah*, Shaw's epic five-part play.

1988   The Festival participates in the Olympic Arts Festival in Calgary with a production of *You Never Can Tell*.

1988   The Directors Project is launched with a production of act one of Merrill Denison's *Contract*.

1990 A series of renovations at the Royal George Theatre is completed. Designed by Cameron Porteous, renovations include installation of an orchestra pit and a permanent proscenium arch.

1996 The Reading Series is launched with a staged reading in the Royal George Theatre of Herman Voaden's *Murder Pattern*.

2000 The Festival's mandate is expanded to include plays written *about* the period of Shaw's lifetime.

2000 The Musical Reading Series is launched with Cole Porter's *What a Swell Party* and Vernon Duke's *Sadie Thompson* in the Royal George Theatre.

2003 Jackie Maxwell becomes artistic director.

2003 Michel Marc Bouchard's *The Coronation Voyage* is only the second Canadian play presented in the Festival Theatre (after *Leave of Malice* in 1975).

2004 Opening of the Donald and Elaine Triggs Production Centre.

2005 *Gypsy*, book by Arthur Laurents, music by Jule Styne, and lyrics by Stephen Sondheim, is the first musical presented in the Festival Theatre.

2009 The Studio Theatre, the Festival's fourth performance space, is inaugurated with John Osborne's *The Entertainer*.

GEORGE DAWSON WITH THE ENSEMBLE IN *THE CORONATION VOYAGE* BY MICHEL MARC BOUCHARD, TRANSLATED BY LINDA GABORIAU, 2003. DIRECTED BY JACKIE MAXWELL, SET DESIGNED BY KEN MACDONALD, COSTUMES DESIGNED BY WILLIAM SCHMUCK, LIGHTING DESIGNED BY ALAN BRODIE, ORIGINAL MUSIC COMPOSED BY ALLEN COLE. PHOTO BY DAVID COOPER.

CHAPTER I   BEGINNINGS: "SALUTE TO SHAW," 1962

NIAGARA-ON-THE-LAKE IN THE 1960S   There are many accounts of what a pleasant town Niagara-on-the-Lake was in the early 1960s. One resident recalled walking with her children around town; chatting to a few other people on the street; and shopping at the drugstore, the five-and-dime store, the shoe store, or the hardware store. This "lazy, quiet, little town," as she described it, was ideal not just for shopping, or chatting on the street, but for playing golf (maybe on North America's oldest public golf course), going to church (perhaps at St Mark's, one of the oldest Anglican churches in Ontario), walking by the lake, or simply enjoying the town's rich historical heritage (as the first capital of Upper Canada, or as the site of key battles during the War of 1812). Another long-time resident who grew up in the town recalled in a 1991 interview what "a great town it was to grow up and be a kid in," and how "everything was here for the townspeople…barber shops, cobblers, affordable clothing stores." Niagara-on-the-Lake as it was in the early 1960s probably wouldn't have been named "The Prettiest Town in Canada" (as it was in 1996), and certainly not the liveliest. For those who enjoyed a sedate and unhurried life, Niagara-on-the-Lake was the place to be.

But not all residents saw it this way. Dorothy Middleditch, one of the many volunteers whose tireless support made the Shaw Festival possible, found Niagara-on-the-Lake "quite a dead little town." Yes, there were the churches, but if you weren't involved with one of those, "there wasn't anything else." Tim Devlin, who played Marchbanks in *Candida* in the inaugural season of the Festival in 1962, thought the town "very seedy and run down…grand old estates decaying and collapsing." It was, he said, "like *Gone with the Wind* after the war." And Christopher Newton, subsequently to become the Festival's artistic director, but in 1964 in town for only a few weeks as an actor (and living at the Anchorage Hotel for $35 a week), remembers a "sort of sense that the town had not come to life, that it was sort of drifting around in some other world." "There didn't seem to be anything happening here," so he and other actors headed to Buffalo or "even Niagara Falls" on days off "for some excitement."

CALVIN RAND   Calvin Rand, an American citizen who was living in Niagara-on-the-Lake as a landed immigrant, and commuting to his job as a philosophy professor at the University of Buffalo, agreed that a "torpor" had overcome the town. It wasn't just quiet and laid-back, but – he agreed with Tim Devlin – "seedy in spots" and "just plain dull." The military presence, such as the regimental camps each summer on the Commons, which had long enlivened the town ("the pipe and bugle bands, the weekend parades, the socializing between soldiers and townsfolk"), had diminished. There were no steamers from Toronto anymore, no trains. Niagara-on-the-Lake, Rand feared, "was becoming a backwater," and the steady improvements in the 1950s and early 1960s to the Queen Elizabeth Way (so-named in 1939) from Toronto to the Niagara Peninsula appeared to Rand to seal the town's "doom," making it possible to bypass "the old train and shipping routes entirely."

BLUEBELL LUNCH, QUEEN STREET,
NIAGARA-ON-THE-LAKE, IN THE EARLY
1950S. PHOTO COURTESY JIM SMITH.

CORNER OF QUEEN AND WELLINGTON
STREETS – SITE OF THE FUTURE SHAW
FESTIVAL THEATRE – AS SEEN FROM
A TOWER BUILT FOR AN INTERNATIONAL
BOY SCOUT JAMBOREE ON THE COM-
MONS IN 1962. PHOTO BY JIM SMITH.

BRIAN DOHERTY AND CALVIN RAND
IN 1964; DOHERTY IN FRONT OF THE
COURT HOUSE THEATRE IN THE EARLY
1970S.

BRIAN DOHERTY ´Coincidentally, one of Rand's neighbours was having the same misgivings about Niagara-on-the-Lake. Brian Doherty had trained as a lawyer in Toronto, where he had practised law before joining the Royal Canadian Air Force (RCAF) in 1941. After five years of active service, he retired from the RCAF as a wing commander and returned to Toronto. But in 1955 he moved his practice to Niagara Falls and his home to Niagara-on-the-Lake. Much about the town impressed him – its beauty and charm, its fine homes, its long-standing heritage. But all of this, Doherty sensed, was under threat from the torpor and economic decline that Rand was witnessing.

Doherty knew that other residents shared his concern, so on a cold February evening in 1962 a group of like-minded citizens met in the home of one such concerned citizen, Jean Marsh (then Jean Usher), who was to become another important volunteer for the Shaw Festival. No one came to the meeting with a specific agenda for revitalizing Niagara-on-the-Lake, but the discussion soon turned to theatre.

That theatre so quickly came up wasn't surprising. While law was Brian Doherty's profession, theatre was his passion. His comedy, *Father Malachy's Miracle*, had run on Broadway in 1937–38 for a respectable 125 performances, and in the 1940s he had produced shows in New York, including *Macbeth*, starring Michael Redgrave, and Shaw's *John Bull's Other Island*, starring Micheál MacLiammóir. Doherty was on first-name terms with many other leading actors in London and New York, and sometimes found it hard to control his excitement when telling friends about them. One close friend, Norah Harris, remembers him beginning a story about Peggy Ashcroft with, "As I was saying to Pashy Eggcroft…" (Doherty's well-known fondness for a drink from time to time perhaps helped stimulate his enthusiasm on this and other occasions). In Canada Doherty had helped found the Red Barn Theatre at Jackson's Point, Ontario, and the New World Theatre Company in Toronto, which performed in cross-Canada tours. He had also served as an adjudicator for the Dominion Drama Festival. Added to Doherty's own passion for theatre was the presence at the February meeting of his New York actress friend, Peggy Meyer.

Accounts differ as to who said what at the meeting, but by Doherty's own account (in his 1974 book on the early years of the Shaw Festival, *Not Bloody Likely*), after he had said "Instead of worrying and criticizing, let's do something for the town we love, something we believe in," Peggy Meyer said "How about theatre?" The question prompted an immediate answer from Doherty – "Shaw! I suddenly exclaimed…Shaw would be wonderful."

The inspiration may have been sudden, but it was backed by Doherty's extensive knowledge and experience of Shaw's plays. In addition to his involvement in the Broadway production of *John Bull's Other Island*, Doherty had seen many of Shaw's plays in American touring productions in Toronto throughout the 1940s. He remembered in particular Gertrude Lawrence in *Pygmalion*, Katharine Cornell in *Candida*, and Raymond Massey in *The Doctor's Dilemma*. Even before the idea of a theatre festival in Niagara-on-the-Lake came up, Doherty said that productions such as these had convinced him that "Shaw was far from dead as far as Canadian audiences were concerned," and that he had even then begun to "explore the idea of a Shavian theatre" in Canada.

Other playwrights were, however, considered as the focus for a theatre event – Oscar Wilde, Eugene O'Neill, Somerset Maugham, even Christopher Marlowe among them. But none of these, Doherty concluded, "had produced enough truly great works to inspire a successful and continuing festival." Nor could any of them, in Doherty's view, match Shaw – "the greatest thing since uranium as a source of untapped wealth and power," he exuberantly told a journalist in 1963.

So Shaw it was. But the idea was one thing; implementing it was another. Doherty decided to call Calvin Rand for advice. Rand's own theatre experience, particularly in New York, where he had been an avid theatregoer for many years, was extensive, and he shared Doherty's view that if a theatre were to be established in Niagara-on-the-Lake it should be something more than "just another summer stock company" (Doherty's words) presenting "warmed-over Broadway shows" (Rand's words). What was needed, they agreed, was something "really professional, something like Shakespeare in Stratford," as Doherty put it. "We wanted a focus, we wanted a great playwright, we wanted an intellectual," Rand said. And now, with Shaw fulfilling those needs, Rand recognized that he was being given an opportunity "not just to see theatre, but to help make it."

And so he did. His involvement was crucial, as was Doherty's. But they couldn't do it alone. An organizing committee was established by Doherty with representation from local communities, and in April 1962 some thirty amateur actors from the area attended a meeting in the historic Court House on Queen Street at which Doherty explained the concept of a festival devoted to the work of Bernard Shaw. It was at that meeting, Doherty says in *Not Bloody Likely*, that "we decided to take the plunge." Doherty was ready and willing to be producer of an inaugural season, but who was to take artistic responsibility?

MAYNARD BURGESS The name that came up at that April meeting to assume artistic responsibility was Maynard Burgess. A personal friend of Doherty, Burgess had been both a professional and amateur actor in the United States (with several Broadway appearances in the late 1920s), Canada, and England, but was now an executive with a chemical company in Niagara Falls and artistic director of the Niagara Falls (New York) Little Theatre. Doherty phoned him, and Burgess agreed to organize a first season, no one really knowing if there would ever be a second season. The season was to be called not the Shaw Festival, but the less ambitious "Salute to Shaw."

The initial plans to have a six-week season, with performances on three days each week, were scaled back, but there was still much to be done. Burgess and Doherty would look after the choice of plays and casting (auditions were held at the Court House in late May), while Rand took responsibility for raising some money. Both were helped by many volunteers, among them Dorothy Middleditch, Jean Marsh, Barbara Trantner, Bas and Jean Mason, and Patricia Rand. It was to be an all-amateur event, so the financial needs were not great, but where would the event be held? There were no theatres in Niagara-on-the-Lake, and the only viable location, however inadequate, seemed to be the Court House itself.

THE COURT HOUSE But would the town council agree to the Court House being used as a temporary theatre? Well, yes, at least for 1962, but with no promises for future seasons (if there were any). Rarely, however, have actors, directors, and designers (not to mention audiences) had to cope with such an inadequate performance space. The theatre was to be located in the Assembly Room – the space still used by the Festival for the Court House Theatre – which was approached in 1962 through the main entrance to the building on Queen Street. On the right as the audience entered was the Lord Mayor's office; on the left was the town jail, used, as Calvin Rand recalls, "for drunks and other disturbers of the peace." The Assembly Room itself had a flat floor, with a small platform stage, and the only wing space was a small room on either side, formerly used as judges' chambers when court sessions were held there. Rudimentary lighting was installed for the first season, blackouts were fixed to the windows, and stacking chairs were borrowed for seats. The kitchen and part of the lobby were used as dressing rooms, separated from the audience at intermission only by a curtain.

The chairs were wooden, and when moved on the wooden floor created so much noise that before a play began, longtime Festival patron Mary Anne Seppala recalls, audience members were asked to "please sit still," an admonishment that couldn't always be honoured. The unexpectedly loud gun shots in *The Shadow of a Gunman* in 1965, for example, caused such a commotion, such shuffling and even tumbling of chairs, that the performance had to be halted until calm was restored. Early audiences were also invited to use their programs as fans, but they were so "wimpy," Seppala says, that people got into the habit of bringing their own fans.

Conditions inside were bad enough, but they were exacerbated by goings-on outside. The local fire siren was on the Court House roof, and "many a night," Calvin Rand recalls, it went off during performances, "with an earsplitting roar, causing actors to freeze in their stance until *minutes* later they could resume their roles." He also recalls a Court House neighbour who kept hunting dogs in his backyard that "barked all night long. Even with the windows closed you could hear the barking."

But the show, of course, went on – with interruptions for the next thirty years from the fire siren. But one night in 1993 the siren went off while Christopher Newton and Lord Mayor of Niagara-on-the-Lake Michael Dietsch were hosting Canadian Prime Minister Kim Campbell at a performance of *Candida*. Its use was discontinued thereafter.

PROGRAM COVER FROM THE FIRST
SEASON; YOUNG VOLUNTEERS ON THE
STEPS OF THE COURT HOUSE, 1962.

OPENING NIGHT *DON JUAN IN HELL*   Unlike the star-studded pomp and circumstance opening of the Stratford Festival in 1952, with Alec Guinness heading the cast of *Richard III*, directed by Tyrone Guthrie on a stage designed by Tanya Moiseiwitsch, in front of an audience of over one thousand people, the opening night of the "Salute to Shaw" on June 29, 1962, was a modest affair. Four amateur actors (Americans David Loveless, Mavis Corser, and Maynard Burgess, and Canadian Eric Davis) perched on stools on a bare stage, scripts on lecterns, and read the *Don Juan in Hell* scene from Shaw's *Man and Superman* to an audience of fewer than two hundred people – all sitting on uncomfortable chairs on an unraked floor. What's more, it was a stiflingly hot night, and there was no air conditioning in the Court House. This prompted Doherty to run up and down Queen Street with Calvin Rand and Dorothy Middleditch to commandeer as many electric fans as they could, spreading them around the theatre in a vain attempt to cool people down. "There seemed," Doherty recalled, "no end of torments." Even with the fans, it remained, in Rand's view, "unbearably hot" in the Court House. "To sit in there listening to Shaw for three hours was awful; I'll never forget it." At the end of the performance the audience, Rand said, "burst through the exit doors, many of them gasping and choking." He wondered how the Festival managed to survive that first night. It wasn't until the third season, in 1964, that an air-conditioning system was installed, but it was so noisy that it had to be switched off during performance.

According to Doherty, the audience enjoyed themselves on that first night anyway. "Laughter and applause echoed through the Court House," and, what's more, "they all expressed interest in our next play." Well, perhaps, but the critic for the *St Catharines Standard* didn't have much fun, troubled as he was by the "steamy heat," which created "a lethargy…that was a real drawback to full enjoyment of the Irish playwright's masterpiece." Still, on balance, the critic concluded that it was "a good beginning for this newest theatrical venture in the district."

That view, unfortunately, was not shared by *Toronto Star* critic Ralph Thomas, who belittled the company's attempt to cope with Shaw's "wordy piece of dialectical argument so misconceived and dull" that "the whole idea lost whatever charm it ever had." The four readers, he said, "stumbled through their scripts, grimacing like possessed children."

Grimacing or not, the actors did another three performances of *Don Juan in Hell*, on June 30 and July 13–14. They continued to battle with the difficult conditions in the theatre, while front-of-house staff had their own challenges. One of Dorothy Middleditch's jobs was to sell and take tickets at a table placed in the corridor outside the jail. One night, she recalls, just before a performance of *Don Juan in Hell*, "there was an awful commotion coming out of the jail, right next to my table. This voice was yelling and hoarse, and screaming 'Let me out, let me out.'" One of the police officers explained that it was a drunk they had found in the park and locked up. The screaming continued. "You can't have that man in there, we're doing *Don Juan in Hell* upstairs," Middleditch exclaimed, albeit wondering whether leaving the drunk there would enhance the sound effects for the show. But better judgment prevailed, and the police obligingly took their man to the St Catharines jail to scream at a safe distance from hell.

CANDIDA   In the meantime, preparations continued for the season's second show, *Candida*, which, unlike *Don Juan in Hell*, was to have a full production. Burgess had directed *Don Juan in Hell* and he also directed *Candida*, with set and costume designs for both productions by Alice Crawley and Louis G. Berai, respectively. Costumes and stage furnishings were mostly borrowed from local amateur theatre companies or Niagara-on-the-Lake residents. It was not uncommon for audience members to see a table or chairs or sofas that had come from their own homes.

There were a number of problems with casting *Candida*. Terry Cahill, who played Lexy, was still in high school, which complicated rehearsal schedules. Ted Forham, the actor who played Candida's father, came in as a late replacement for the original choice (Johnson Butler, a Thorold lawyer) and didn't have enough time to learn his lines. Barbara Ransom (Candida) recalls lines being written on different parts of the set to help him out. Ransom had some acting experience with the St Catharines Community Theatre and had recently won best actress award for her performance in *Desire under the Elms* at the Dominion Drama Festival in Montreal. Tim Devlin (Marchbanks), Jean Malloy (Miss Prossy), and David Michener (Morell) were all

well known for their work with local amateur theatres and operatic societies. Devlin initially got involved to help paint sets, but after hearing him read Marchbanks to support auditions for other roles, Burgess prevailed upon him to play the part.

Unlike Ted Forham, Tim Devlin did know his lines, but such was the enthusiasm of the prompter, Bonnie Clark, that whenever he took a pause she would shout out the line at a volume so high that it echoed round the theatre. "I was almost terrified to pause," he said. It had been the same in rehearsal: "I felt I was doing rap because I daren't leave a gap or she would be shouting the lines."

Despite the trials and tribulations of the "Salute to Shaw" season, Doherty was determined to carry on – and to do so on a professional basis. Because there were no salaries to pay, the expenses for the 1962 season had been modest – $2238.04 covered all promotion, production, and administrative expenses. Revenue from box office, advertising, and donations was $2382.00, generating a profit of $143.96. To boost the coffers, Doherty produced and directed a translation of Henri Ghéon's 1935 nativity play *Le Noël sur la place* (*Christmas in the Market Place*) in December in the Court House. But that production lost over $500. If a second season were to be presented on a professional basis, the financial scenario would have to alter significantly. Doherty was aware of the challenge and the risk, but, he argued, "if we expected to progress artistically, to improve our theatre facilities, and to put the Festival on a solid foundation, it was the only choice." "Dynamo Doherty," as he was known by his friends, would need all the energy he could muster to pull it off.

CHAPTER 2

ANDREW ALLAN, 1963–65

Artistic leadership, venue, money, name. All were pressing issues as Doherty and his colleagues contemplated the move to professionalism. For artistic leadership Doherty turned to Andrew Allan, acclaimed radio and television drama producer for the Canadian Broadcasting Corporation (CBC). Allan had minimal experience of live theatre, but this deficiency was balanced somewhat by the appointment of Sean Mulcahy as Allan's associate director. Mulcahy had worked with Allan in radio and television, but prior to that had acted in Ireland and England. Allan appealed to Doherty in part because of his commitment to the ensemble concept (unlike Stratford, the Festival couldn't afford stars – at least, not yet), and in part, as Mulcahy put it, because Allan's "gentlemanly" demeanour would be valuable in community relations in Niagara-on-the-Lake, many of whose residents were far from convinced that having a theatre company in town was a good thing.

This community skepticism about the Festival was reflected in the town council's reaction to Doherty's request to use the Court House for the 1963 season. The marked lack of enthusiasm from the council ("obstructionism" was Doherty's blunter way of describing it) prompted Doherty to consider moving the Festival to a high school auditorium in Niagara Falls. Doherty had a Niagara-on-the-Lake ally in the town mayor, Gary Wooll (who later became a Shaw Festival board member), but even Wooll cautioned Doherty not to be too ambitious. The danger, said Wooll (in a letter to Doherty on March 27, 1963), was that "the pleasant small town atmosphere which your group has enjoyed in the past" might be destroyed by too big an undertaking. The council vote, however, was close: a 3–3 tie that was broken in the Festival's favour by Wooll. But again, there was no commitment from council beyond three weeks in the summer of 1963, leaving the Festival's long-term plans precarious. Doherty's commitment to Niagara-on-the-Lake, however, remained firm. In 1965 he declined Toronto theatre impresario Ed Mirvish's offer to house the Shaw Festival at his Royal Alexandra Theatre, Doherty retaining faith both in the town and in his conviction that a brand-new theatre for the Festival was a desirable and feasible objective – a belief that was eventually justified, but not easily, and not for some years to come.

FINANCING   There was also a good deal of uncertainty about the financing of the Festival. The 1963 season achieved 95 percent attendance, but without Calvin Rand's personal support the payroll would not have been met. As Festival treasurer Jack Couillard put it, Rand was "our showbiz angel. Without Calvin there would have been no Shaw Festival." Rand's generosity encompassed Festival social events as well. Until the Festival Theatre opened in 1973, all opening night audiences as well as Festival actors and staff – some three to four hundred in all – were invited to a post-show party at his home on John Street. There was music and dancing, Rand recalls, as well as a tempting swimming pool that "people got into one way or the other, with or without clothes on." Rand remembers one actress going in one night "with just her hat on." It was fun, but it didn't pay the bills.

ALFRED GALLAGHER AND MOYA
FENWICK IN *HEARTBREAK HOUSE*
BY BERNARD SHAW, 1964. DIRECTED
BY ANDREW ALLAN, DESIGNED BY
LAWRENCE SCHAFER, LIGHTING
DESIGNED BY DONALD ACASTER.

OPPOSITE: MARY BENNING AND
NORMAN WELSH IN *HEARTBREAK
HOUSE*, 1964. PHOTO BY ROBERT
C. RAGSDALE.

The situation worsened in 1964, which ended with a deficit of nearly $9000. Rand blamed the selection of plays for that season: *Heartbreak House* and *John Bull's Other Island*. "It was very stupid that year to try to do two big, difficult, long plays. The audiences just did not turn out." The audience didn't turn out in significant numbers in 1965 either. The box office came in at only 63 percent, but for the first time the Festival received government support; the Ontario Arts Council awarded the Festival $10,000, enabling it to end the season with a surplus of $1564.63.

To bolster the business operations of the Festival, a full-time business manager and publicity director, Ray Wickens, was appointed in 1965. Wickens, an actor who also had some administrative experience (he was with the Red Barn Theatre in Jackson's Point prior to being hired by Doherty), moved into a newly acquired small office on Queen Street, further reflecting the Festival's transition to a stronger professional structure, though like the theatre the company played in, the office found for Wickens was hardly state-of-the-art. "I had this tiny little office," he recalled, "with no bathroom." "I had to go to a little Chinese restaurant down the road and make a deal with them that I could use their bathroom when I needed it. But I said 'I'll be in to buy tea every day,' because I'm a great tea drinker, so that was alright, and occasionally I used to eat there as well."

MANDATE CHANGE   It was also decided that a name-change should accompany the move to professional status. The temporary-sounding "Salute to Shaw" was replaced by the more confident "Shaw Festival," the name that has been used ever since. In his three seasons as artistic director, Allan honoured the new name by selecting plays almost exclusively by Shaw. There was just one exception, a play by Shaw's friend and fellow Dubliner, Sean O'Casey. The O'Casey play, *The Shadow of a Gunman*, set in 1920 during the Irish "troubles" and directed by Mulcahy (who also played the lead role of Donal Davoren), was part of Allan's final season in 1965. Its production marked the first time that a non-Shaw play had appeared at the Festival. This was done with Doherty's support, as he now expanded the Festival's mandate to include plays by "Shaw and his great contemporaries."

While well received ("a shouting, cheering, stamping roar of approval greeted the opening performance," according to one report), the production of *The Shadow of a Gunman*, as Doherty anticipated, raised questions about the Festival's mandate. For critic Robert Fulford, O'Casey was "the most neglected great man of the modern English-speaking theatre," and "it might be worth considering the idea of incorporating [him] into the Festival permanently." But maybe, said fellow Toronto critic Herbert Whittaker, the Festival was thinking of a broader reach. "Will the admission of O'Casey open the way to such other talented sons of Eire as Wycherley, Sheridan, O'Neill, Wilde, and Behan?" Whittaker wondered (generously granting American playwright Eugene O'Neill honorary Irish citizenship, based, no doubt, on his Irish heritage). "Or will it remain with Shaw's contemporaries and go through the glorious roster of the Abbey Theatre?" Judging by the all-Shaw season that followed in 1966 (under a new artistic director), the answer to Whittaker's questions was no, but 1966 proved to be the last ever all-Shaw season at the Festival. There is nothing to suggest that in selecting *The Shadow of a Gunman* Allan was consciously and deliberately pushing the boundaries of the mandate – the selection had more to do with Mulcahy's Irish interests and enthusiasms – but, in effect, the Festival had taken the first step in expanding its mandate.

Of the productions of the Shaw plays that Allan chose (*You Never Can Tell*, *The Man of Destiny*, *How He Lied to Her Husband*, and *Androcles and the Lion* in 1963; *Heartbreak House*, *John Bull's Other Island*, *Village Wooing*, and *The Dark Lady of the Sonnets* in 1964; and *Pygmalion* and *The Millionairess* in 1965), none received unqualified critical praise, though Whittaker, as always, tried to be as positive as possible. He was especially enthusiastic about *John Bull's Other Island*, the Festival's "finest hour" to date, with "intelligent and sympathetic direction" from Allan and a "completely satisfying" set design from Lawrence Schafer, a design "greatly enhanced," Whittaker added, by the lighting of Donald Acaster. Another designer, Martha Mann, was praised by critics for her "superbly designed" set for *You Never Can Tell* on the "tiny, inadequate stage" of the Court House, and even the curmudgeonly Nathan Cohen of the *Toronto Star* found kind words for Schafer's "handsome" set and "expressive" costumes for *Pygmalion*.

As regards the acting, some individual performances received high praise – Ian Thorne, for example, in *The Man of Destiny* ("brilliant as the young Napoleon") and Norman Welsh as Shotover in *Heartbreak House* ("always impressive and always believable"). But over the three seasons under Allan's direction, critics frequently used phrases such as "a definite lack of vitality" (*You Never Can Tell*), "woefully short on speed and finesse" (*How He Lied to Her Husband*), "lacking fluency and rhythm" (*Androcles and the Lion*). Not for the first time (or last), the harshest criticism came from Cohen, particularly for *Pygmalion*. Patronizing about the play itself ("a genial and intelligent little play that suffers by comparison to the film [*My Fair Lady*]"), he roundly dismissed the performances of the three leading actors: Anne Butler (Eliza) "has no authenticity in her Cockney accent and carriage [and] no truth in her metamorphosis"; Paul Craig (Higgins) "shows a startling disrespect for the English language he claims to venerate"; and Alfred Gallagher "acts the gentlemanly Colonel Pickering as if he were an undertaker."

In *Not Bloody Likely* Brian Doherty recognized "a dozen ways, large and small," in which Andrew Allan's three years at the Festival "set the pace, and set some standards as well for events and ideas, for patterns of growth and direction, that were to characterize the Festival through the following years of its remarkable growth." There had certainly been progress under Allan, but it had been more quantitative than qualitative. He took over the Festival as a nascent and fragile organization that had only eight amateur performances to its name. During his tenure there were eighty-one professional performances, and those initial four weekends of the 1962 season had expanded to six weeks by 1965. But, tellingly, Christopher Newton's 1964 experience had left him thinking that the Shaw Festival wouldn't last. Allan, Newton thought, didn't seem to be particularly interested in directing ("he sort of worked for a couple of hours in the afternoon and around 4:30 he would pop over to the Prince of Wales for a drink"), and Mulcahy's style of directing (he directed Newton in *Village Wooing*) was simply to "tell you what to do." To do Shaw's plays well, Newton believed, actors "need lots and lots of help from the director. We didn't have that, so we played the obvious."

The public explanation of Allan's and Mulcahy's departures from the Festival early in 1966 was that it was "due to a difference regarding the Festival's nature and artistic policy," but it wasn't so much a matter of policy as of artistic standards and leadership. There is little doubt that Doherty, Rand, and other board members were not satisfied with the quality of what Allan, and in turn Mulcahy, had brought to the stage. That speaks well of their ambitions and aspirations for the Festival, but it put considerable pressure on Allan's successor to meet their high expectations.

CHAPTER 3   BARRY MORSE, 1966

The Shaw Festival's second artistic director was the first member of the company to have actually met Bernard Shaw. Barry Morse was a student at the Royal Academy of Dramatic Art (RADA) in London when Shaw, one of RADA's governors, dropped in on rehearsals for a student production of *Androcles and the Lion*, in which Morse was playing the Lion. Shaw thought that Morse could benefit from some advice on how to play the part, so he "lay on his back on the floor and waved his arms and legs back and forth in the air to show me how I was to behave as the lion when he said he 'wants his tummy tickled.'" There had also been a Shaw connection for Morse when he auditioned for RADA. He chose the chaplain's speech from *Saint Joan*, the one after the chaplain has just witnessed Joan's execution, and one of the judges was Sybil Thorndike, who played Joan in the British premiere of the play in March 1924.

After RADA, Morse went on to a career in the British repertory theatre, BBC radio, and film. From 1951 he worked in Canada with CBC radio (where he met Andrew Allan), but his big break came with the ABC television series *The Fugitive*, in which he famously played Lieutenant Philip Gerard in pursuit of Richard Kimble (played by David Janssen), who has been falsely accused of murdering his wife. The series began in 1963, and was still running when Brian Doherty invited Morse to become artistic director of the Shaw Festival.

Morse agreed because he could fit in his television commitments around the Festival's still relatively short summer season, and although his tenure as artistic director turned out to be short lived, his one season had an impact out of all proportion to the brevity of his stay. For Doherty, "working with Barry Morse was like going over Niagara Falls in a barrel," and in one season, said Doherty, "Morse transformed the Festival forever." Calvin Rand agreed: "The big year, the year that really made the Shaw Festival, was Barry Morse's one year in 1966."

Telling the press that he had "high hopes for the future of the Shaw Festival and the possibility of a new theatre of unique design for it," Morse embraced his new job with gusto. He describes in his autobiography, *Remembering with Advantage*, how he set about energizing the Festival and attracting an outstanding company of actors for the 1966 season:

> We began an exciting round of cajolery, blandishment, arm-twisting, foot-licking, exploiting old friends, inflammation of total strangers, and the outlay of almost everything *except* money. The fever was catching: all manner of theatre workers, some eminent, some novices, were willing to throw in their lots with us under working conditions and for rewards which, in most cases, were infinitely lower than they could reasonably expect in their normal working lives. This was the grandest kind of largesse, the richest subsidies any theatre venture could ever have. Their names are a luscious litany to remember – Zoe Caldwell, Pat Galloway, Betty Leighton, Susan Clark, Tom Kneebone, Leslie Yeo, Hugh Webster, Norman Welsh, and a young man of sonorous voice and twinkling-solemn manner named Paxton Whitehead (who would himself have a fine future with the Shaw) – and many, many more – fine troupers all!

In his own account (in *Not Bloody Likely*) of Morse's success in attracting accomplished actors to Niagara-on-the-Lake, Brian Doherty adds Henry Ramer, Sandy Webster, and Patrick

Boxill. Many of those named by Morse and Doherty made a major contribution not only to the 1966 season, but to many more seasons to come (Paxton Whitehead and Sandy Webster in particular, but also Betty Leighton, Patrick Boxill, Norman Welsh, and Leslie Yeo).

The "working conditions" that Morse refers to were, of course, those in the Court House Theatre, not just the stage itself but the dressing rooms, which remained where they had been from the beginning, in the kitchen and in part of the theatre lobby. There were no showers, no washrooms – actors had to dash round to the public washrooms in the entrance hallway, which were off-limits to them during intermission, once the audience was seated – and privacy was in short supply in the cramped space. These were, Morse justifiably complained, "conditions for which the average factory owner would probably be sent to jail if he housed his workers in anything similar."

Andrew Allan's associations with the CBC had helped calm local nerves about the traditional disreputable image endured by the acting profession (quite unjustifiably, of course), and Barry Morse's presence also helped the cause. While a much more flamboyant personality than Allan, Morse had stature and fame (he was one of the best-known faces on television) that made him a prized presence in social circles that otherwise were not enamoured of the Festival. Dorothy Middleditch was aware that those associated with the Festival – actors in particular – were considered, as she put it, "a bunch of weirdos." There was, she said, "a great deal of antagonism towards us." Morse's few weeks in town could not entirely dispel these attitudes, but he tempered them as best he could.

Morse's season consisted of three plays, *Man and Superman* (without the *Don Juan in Hell* sequence), *Misalliance*, and *The Apple Cart*. The season ran for nine weeks, the longest so far, and there were sixty-one performances (close to a 50 percent increase over the previous season). Morse's own involvement was to act in (Tanner) and direct *Man and Superman* and also direct *Misalliance*. Apart from selecting it, he was not much involved with the third show, *The Apple Cart*, which was directed by Edward Gilbert, with Paxton Whitehead as Magnus.

MAN AND SUPERMAN, 1966   Although *Toronto Telegram* critic McKenzie Porter declared the season, "under the galvanic direction of Barry Morse," an "artistic and commercial triumph," some of the reviews, particularly of *Man and Superman*, were mixed. Morse himself said that "we had a far from enthusiastic press." The problem with *Man and Superman* was, in part, that Morse tried to do too much. "It was," according to Calvin Rand, "a bit of a disaster" because not only did Morse direct it and play a major role in it, he also worked closely with Lawrence Schafer on the design, and, says Rand, "also swept the floor and painted the walls." Morse thought the walls of the theatre needed painting because the existing "public-urinal green" made them look "bleakly unpromising." Cast, crew, and volunteers, led by Morse, spent the night before the first performance painting the auditorium, and finishing touches weren't completed until the audience had started to arrive the next evening for the opening.

Morse was also determined that the season's opening would not go unnoticed by the Niagara-on-the-Lake community, so he arranged with local military personnel for a rocket to be fired from the roof of the Court House to mark the opening-night performance of *Man and Superman*. Prior to that, Morse had set up an outdoor press conference by the clock tower on Queen Street to show off the antique car he had borrowed for the show. He drove the car along Queen Street and promised that it was the car that would be driven on the Court House stage. It was left to company manager Ray Wickens to figure out how to get the car up the stairs and on to the stage, but it happened. "I guess it's one of those things where the impossible can become possible," Wickens said.

Rand could not help but admire Morse's "spectacular" commitment to all aspects of *Man and Superman*, but in Rand's view Morse's acting suffered: "He didn't know his lines and his timing was right off...," says Rand.

I remember going back to see him right after the opening, and he asked me, "What did you think? What did you think?" I guess he could tell what my reaction was. "Well...," I said, "You really tried hard," and he went into a fury. He said, "Is that all you can say, that I tried hard? Wasn't I magnificent?" I said, "Well, it's going to get better, isn't it?" And he turned on his heels. But it did get better."

Unfortunately, some influential critics didn't come back after opening night to see the improvements, so while there was certainly some praise for *Man and Superman* – "uproariously funny from start to finish," said one critic – Nathan Cohen again dampened everyone's enthusiasm with his judgment that the production was "a mundane, mirthless and puny effort."

MISALLIANCE, 1966   There was less unevenness, however, about *Misalliance*. Morse didn't give himself a part in this show, so was free to concentrate on directing it, which by all accounts he did exceptionally well, with an outstanding performance from Zoe Caldwell as Lina Szczepanowska, supported by strong performances all round. Looking back on the production in 1997, Rand judged that "it was just about the best ensemble piece the Shaw Festival has ever done." Leslie Yeo, who played Tarleton, recalled standing-room-only audiences for the show, "the first big sellout success" the Festival had enjoyed. The headline for an enthusiastic review in the *St Catharines Standard* was "Cheers, Roars, Foot-Stomping Greet Sparkling Shaw Comedy."

THE APPLE CART, 1966   Both *Man and Superman* and *Misalliance* ran for twenty performances. *The Apple Cart* got twenty-one. Like *Man and Superman*, *The Apple Cart* has a fairly large cast (fifteen actors), and one of them, Sandy Webster (who played Pliny) described what a hard time they had fitting onto the small stage. The production was, nonetheless, Webster claimed, "tremendously well received," helped by positive reviews from the Toronto press – particularly for the performances of Whitehead (Magnus) and (again) Zoe Caldwell (Orinthia), hailed by *Toronto Telegram* critic Ron Evans as "surely the most lovable, lunatic, versatile, melodious, seductive, sophisticated, ironic, and irresistible woman in the English-speaking theatre." Praise from the influential U.S. weekly *The Saturday Review*, whose drama critic happened to be in the area and popped in to see *The Apple Cart*, was also helpful. His enthusiasm for the production brought curious Americans to town – Webster counted car licence plates on Queen Street from some twenty-five American states – but few of them could get tickets for the sold-out show.

The overriding sense at the Festival and in the press was that the 1966 season was the most successful in the Festival's brief history. And the 98 percent box office sales figure was compelling evidence to back up general impressions. But Morse made it clear towards the end of the season that he would not return as artistic director in 1967. By then he had learned that *The Fugitive* television series would end in 1967, so one reason for his decision was that he felt he needed more flexibility to pursue other film and television work. It was also very clear to Morse that if the Festival wanted to progress to a higher level of achievement it desperately needed a new theatre. The Stratford Festival had built and opened its new theatre after only four seasons in its famous tent. The Shaw Festival had now completed five seasons in the ill-equipped Court House Theatre, and, despite much discussion, there were no tangible signs of a new theatre. For Morse, another season in those conditions was not appealing.

And so Morse returned to Hollywood to conclude his search for the elusive fugitive Kimble, and the Festival began a different kind of search for a new artistic director who could build on Morse's success.

CHAPTER 4

PAXTON WHITEHEAD, 1967–77

AN EVOLVING MANDATE   Paxton Whitehead was a British-trained actor who had worked in British repertory theatre and with the Royal Shakespeare Company before making his Broadway debut in 1962 in Ronald Millar's play *The Affair*. In 1965 he made his Canadian debut at the Manitoba Theatre Centre in Shaw's *Heartbreak House* before moving to Toronto, where he met Barry Morse. Morse hired him for the Festival's 1966 season, when he played Octavius Robinson in *Man and Superman*, Lord Summerhays in *Misalliance*, and Magnus in *The Apple Cart*. When Morse decided that he would not return to the Festival after the 1966 season, he recommended that Whitehead succeed him. According to Calvin Rand, given Morse's recommendation, no one else was seriously considered for the position of artistic director. Whitehead was only twenty-nine years old when he took charge of the Festival, the youngest person ever to hold the position.

McKenzie Porter thought that Whitehead's performances in the 1966 season had shown "a flair and force that reveal a scholarly grasp of the paradox and profundity that teemed in the dome-like head of the late GBS." Even so, appointing someone so young and inexperienced was something of a gamble. And Whitehead did encounter problems. In his determined and laudatory initiatives to expand the mandate of the Festival, for example, his choice of plays convinced some critics that he was more interested in "lightweight" entertainment than the loftier ideals of theatre represented by Bernard Shaw.

The Shaw Festival began with the plays of Bernard Shaw as the raison d'être of its existence. Before Whitehead took over as artistic director only one non-Shaw play had been mounted at the Festival – Sean O'Casey's *The Shadow of a Gunman* in 1965. At that time founder Brian Doherty had redefined the mandate of the Festival as "Shaw and his great contemporaries," and Whitehead had publicly expressed the view when he was appointed in 1966 that the Festival mandate "should be free to range anywhere between the period 1890 and 1930, specializing in the theatre Shaw wrote for and about." He also realized that "we would run out of the major Shaw plays fairly quickly if we continued to do three or more a season." Building, then, on the O'Casey precedent, Whitehead adopted the policy of including a non-Shaw play in every season, beginning with Somerset Maugham's *The Circle* in 1967.

THE CIRCLE, 1967   *The Circle* was a fairly obvious and safe choice as Whitehead's first non-Shaw play. An amusing and gently satirical 1921 comedy of manners about the British upper classes, it emphatically lacks the intellectual bite and vitality of Shaw's plays. But under Whitehead's skilful direction, and with strong performances from Kate Reid (making her Festival debut) and well-known American actor Hiram Sherman in the lead roles, it was welcomed and enjoyed by Festival audiences during its run of twenty-nine performances (as was the 2007 revival at the Festival, in a much longer run). The production was enhanced by widely praised set and costume designs from Maurice Strike and Hilary Corbett (two young British-born designers who formed a remarkable partnership at the Shaw Festival for several seasons). The success of *The Circle* gave Whitehead both encouragement and motivation to further explore the plays of Shaw's contemporaries.

OPPOSITE: PAXTON WHITEHEAD AND LOUISE MARLEAU IN *THE PHILANDERER* BY BERNARD SHAW, 1971. DIRECTED BY TONY VAN BRIDGE, SET DESIGNED BY MAURICE STRIKE, COSTUMES DESIGNED BY TIINA LIPP, LIGHTING DESIGNED BY DONALD ACASTER. PHOTO BY ROBERT C. RAGSDALE.

Opening up the mandate made sense, but the decision created problems. Even with the mandate as defined by Whitehead (which he didn't in any case adhere to), the choice of plays was vast, and blending the selection of non-Shaw plays into the Shaw plays to create a tone, a balance, and a set of values that key constituencies (board members, audiences, critics) felt appropriate for the Festival was challenging. Doing this while also balancing the budget each season (which Whitehead generally succeeded in doing) made the challenge still more daunting.

"LIGHTWEIGHT" WHITEHEAD The "lightweight" charges against Whitehead began to emerge early on in his tenure, supported by productions such as a Feydeau farce, *The Chemmy Circle* (in a new translation for the Festival by Suzanne Grossman) in the 1968 season. Whitehead directed and acted in the play at a frenetic slapstick pace. He also directed and starred in another farce, Brandon Thomas's *Charley's Aunt* in 1974, and was again accused of going over the top, performing the title role in drag. By Herbert Whittaker's count, Whitehead devised and included "almost twice as much comic business as is needed for the purpose of maintaining steady laughter." And then there was *Thark*, the Ben Travers farce that Whitehead selected (and starred in) for what proved to be his final season at the Festival in 1977. Seeing Whitehead "mug and camp wildly" in his "so annoyingly broad" way in *Thark* pushed one critic to ask Festival publicists Michael Franks and Pamela Evans why the play had been chosen in the first place. The answer was as simple as it was compelling: "*Thark* was the season's biggest draw, helping to finance the other more adventurous, but less popular, productions." As it happens, it was also a production much admired by Christopher Newton, who, as artistic director, included many farces in the Festival's repertoire (see below, page 187).

Several comedies – as opposed to outright farces – of varying degrees of subtlety were also part of Whitehead's expanded mandate.

Hungarian playwright Ferenc Molnár's 1910 comedy *The Guardsman*, about a husband disguising himself as a military officer to seduce his own wife (1969 season), had the potential for broad farce. In this case, in a new translation by British playwright Frank Marcus, the play came across, said *Toronto Telegram* critic Ralph Hicklin, more as "a fresh, witty comedy" about marital trust than a *Charley's Aunt* kind of farce, and on this occasion at least there was no excess of comic business from Whitehead in the title role. (Whitehead was supported in his production of *The Guardsman*, somewhat improbably, by the Russian actress Lila Kedrova, who had won an Oscar as Best Supporting Actress in the film *Zorba the Greek* in 1964, opposite Anthony Quinn.)

Whitehead's choice of Alan Bennett's *Forty Years On* (1970 season) may have had as much to do with his friendship with the author (they had appeared together in the New York production of *Beyond the Fringe* in 1964) as its intrinsic merit, but the play's gentle debunking of British between-the-wars shibboleths appealed to Festival audiences (aided by the appearance in the play of seventeen local schoolboys). (*Forty Years On* was a North American premiere, New York producers having rejected it as "too British.")

NOEL COWARD And in the following season (1971) Whitehead brought Noel Coward to the Shaw Festival for the first time in a selection from his *Tonight at 8:30* cycle (directed by Eric House) – *We Were Dancing*, *Family Album*, and *Shadow Play* (all of which were to be revived by the Festival in subsequent seasons). "Swinging from the big, comfortable comic structures of Shaw's comedies over to the fragile, tinkling divertissements of Noel Coward," said Herbert Whittaker, "demands resources just as extraordinary as if the Shaw Festival were to suddenly plunge into *Ben Hur*." But designer Maurice Strike didn't have a *Ben Hur* space and *Ben Hur* resources to work with, so he devised a modest turntable to fit the Court House stage and accommodate the three different sets required by the Coward one-acts (winning a round of applause on opening night). The actors were well received, too, with special praise for prominent Broadway and Stratford actress Carole Shelley in the first of her three seasons at the Festival.

George S. Kaufman and Edna Ferber's *The Royal Family* (1972 season) about the famous American Barrymore family of actors, was also well received, with American star Ruth Nelson heading a cast that *Toronto Star* critic Urjo Kareda thought the best he had seen "for a long time."

ELIZABETH SHEPHERD AND NEIL
VIPOND IN *ROSMERSHOLM* BY HENRIK
IBSEN, 1974. DIRECTED BY TONY VAN
BRIDGE, DESIGNED BY TIINA LIPP,
LIGHTING DESIGNED BY AL ANDERSON.
PHOTO BY ROBERT C. RAGSDALE.

OPPOSITE: CANDACE O'CONNOR,
ALEXANDRA BASTEDO, AND LYNNE
GRIFFIN IN *THE ADMIRABLE CRICHTON*
BY J.M. BARRIE, 1976. DIRECTED BY
BARRY MORSE, DESIGNED BY MAURICE
STRIKE, LIGHTING DESIGNED BY
ROBERT BRYAN. PHOTO BY ROBERT
C. RAGSDALE.

***THE ADMIRABLE CRICHTON*, 1976**   Another first from the British repertoire of Shaw's contemporaries was a J.M. Barrie play, *The Admirable Crichton*, directed by Barry Morse in the 1976 season, the one and only season for which Barry Morse returned to the Festival after serving as artistic director for the 1966 season. *The Admirable Crichton* production was also notable for featuring Michael Ball (in the title role) in his Festival debut.

Another comedy (like *The Circle*) about class issues in post-Victorian England, *The Admirable Crichton* pleased audiences, but there were still more rumblings of discontent among the critics. Even the friendly E.H. Lampard of the *St Catharines Standard* seemed troubled by the lack of "any real substance" amid all "the good fun." Buffalo critic Roberta Plutzik also regretted the absence of any kind of "dramatic or emotional sustenance." Morse had tried hard to show the darker side of class prejudice and inequality in *The Admirable Crichton* by giving to the production what John Fraser (writing in the *Globe and Mail*) described as "a practically Chekhovian veneer" – which Fraser regretted, wanting (unlike some of his colleagues) more "frivolity and nonsense." But in expressing what he conceded was "a minority viewpoint," Fraser also noted that the Festival was "usually chided" for providing too much frivolity and nonsense.

"ADVENTUROUS" WHITEHEAD   It is worth recalling, though, the point made by the Festival in explaining and defending the choice of *Thark* in 1977 – that plays such as *Thark* helped to finance "more adventurous, but less popular, productions." And some of Whitehead's expanded-mandate selections – albeit a minority – certainly fit into the "adventurous" category. The 1971 season, for example, included a contemporary French play that entirely escaped the limitations of Whitehead's defined mandate, or, indeed, any other mandate that the Shaw Festival has ever adopted. Romain Weingarten's *L'Été*, previously produced in Germany, France, and Israel, and translated into English by Suzanne Grossman as *Summer Days* for its North American premiere at the Festival, was described, with good reason, in the season brochure as "the most unusual play ever produced by the Festival." Its cast of characters, the brochure advised patrons, included: "an articulate girl and her apparently inarticulate brother, each struggling with the discoveries of adolescence; a couple of sophisticated, incredibly vocal tom cats; Delilah, an amorous fly; and an unseen pair of lovers." Praised by scholars (such as Martin Esslin) and fellow playwrights (such as Eugène Ionesco) as one of the most important avant-garde plays of its time, *Summer Days* was altogether too bizarre for E.H. Lampard, who willingly confessed to being "dismayed and confused," but for others it was a memorable production, "an extraordinary evening of theater for which the Festival deserves high praise," said Terry Doran (in the *Buffalo Evening News*). New York critic Julius Novick was also happy to see a play such as *Summer Days* at the Festival. He found Festival audiences "rather stodgy," and thought that Whitehead's "willingness to take chances augurs well for the Shaw Festival's immortal soul."

And then there was another mandate-contravening adventure in the 1973 season, William Golding's *The Brass Butterfly*, a comedy (based on his short story "Envoy Extraordinary") about political intrigues and struggles at the court of a Roman emperor that Golding had written for British actor Alastair Sim in 1958. The play was "hard to get airborne" said one headline, a cool reception that captured overall audience and critical reaction.

Well within the mandate, but still perhaps deserving of the "adventurous" designation was the Festival's first Ibsen play, *Rosmersholm*, which Whitehead chose for the 1974 season. Directed by Tony van Bridge, the production didn't have the strong cast that Whitehead had frequently assembled for Festival productions, and five performances (including the scheduled opening) had to be cancelled because of the illness of Neil Vipond, who played Rosmer. And when the show did finally get underway, there was a "restlessness" in the audience that E.H. Lampard took to be a reflection of the difficulty of this "most obscure" play, "full of abstractions."

Whitehead found other ways as well to use the extended mandate to bring audiences to the Festival – Micheál MacLiammóir's one-man show about Oscar Wilde in 1968, Tony van Bridge's one-man show about G.K. Chesterton (performed in St Mark's Church) in 1970, and *Sisters of Mercy: A Musical Journey into the Words of Leonard Cohen* in 1973.

In Whitehead's ten seasons of programming of non-Shaw plays, it is difficult to discern any pattern, consistency, or governing principle in his choices. He blurred or ignored the mandate with *Summer Days* and *The Brass Butterfly*, both of which were written after Shaw had died, and neither of which had anything in particular to do with Shaw's lifetime. And when he stayed

MARTHA HENRY; DOUGLAS RAIN IN *ARMS AND THE MAN* BY BERNARD SHAW, 1967. DIRECTED BY EDWARD GILBERT, SET DESIGNED BY MAURICE STRIKE, COSTUMES DESIGNED BY HILARY CORBETT, LIGHTING DESIGNED BY CHRISTOPHER ROOT. PHOTOS BY ROBERT C. RAGSDALE.

within the mandate his preferences did indeed, as was often noted, veer towards the lightweight. On the other hand, he reached out to an ever-increasing audience, and, as Calvin Rand stressed when Whitehead left the Festival, he assiduously protected the bottom line of the budget.

WHITEHEAD AND SHAW

Paxton Whitehead expanded the mandate of the Shaw Festival into many new areas – music, farce, one-person shows, contemporary plays, European and American classics – but the plays of Bernard Shaw remained at the core of his Festival repertoire. In all, Whitehead included twenty-three plays by Shaw in his ten seasons as artistic director, twenty-five if *Five Variations of Corno di Bassetto* (a selection of Shaw's music criticism) and *GBS in Love* (a selection of Shaw's correspondence with Alice Lockett, one of his early loves) are counted. By contrast, there were sixteen non-Shaw plays. Of the Shaw plays, Whitehead himself acted in eleven and directed or co-directed six. Edward Gilbert and Tony van Bridge were Whitehead's most frequent choices as directors of other Shaw plays. Maurice Strike (sets) and Hilary Corbett (costumes) were far and away his preferred designers.

In his first six seasons Whitehead had to fit all plays, including Shaw, into the cramped confines of the Court House Theatre. After the opening of the long-awaited Festival Theatre in 1973 (and the retention of the Court House Theatre), Whitehead had more (and improved) options for his programming of Shaw's plays. He was able, for example, to mount in his final season in 1977 the most impressive Shaw selection to date – sixty-nine performances of *Man and Superman* (including fourteen with the *Don Juan in Hell* scene) and thirty-seven performances of *The Millionairess* in the Festival Theatre, and, in the Court House Theatre, thirty-one performances of *Widowers' Houses* and thirty-eight performances of *Great Catherine*.

ARMS AND THE MAN, 1967   There were several Shavian highlights under Whitehead's leadership, beginning with the play that opened his first season as artistic director on June 21, 1967 – *Arms and the Man*, directed by Edward Gilbert. This was the Festival premiere of Shaw's satire on militarism, his first commercial success when performed at the Avenue Theatre in London in 1894. In a packed Court House Theatre, Herbert Whittaker sensed from the moment that he saw Maurice Strike's design of elaborate and richly painted sets and meticulously detailed furnishings that the Festival was striving for higher standards in its productions of Shaw. The cast – led by Whitehead as the bumbling Bulgarian officer Sergius, Douglas Rain as his pragmatic Swiss rival Bluntschli, and Martha Henry as the romantic dreamer Raina (Festival debuts for both Rain and Henry) – gave performances that convinced Whittaker there was indeed a "real advance" in production qualities for Shaw. Whittaker particularly noted Whitehead's "daringly underscored" Sergius, and praised the balance that he maintained with Rain and Henry. This production of *Arms and the Man* also marked the Festival debut of Heath Lamberts (as the servant Nicola), an actor who in subsequent years was to take the Festival by storm.

HEARTBREAK HOUSE, 1968   In many respects a more challenging play than *Arms and the Man*, *Heartbreak House* was another early Shavian success under Whitehead. The second Festival production of the play (Andrew Allan had previously directed it in 1964), its large cast and set again posed difficulties in the Court House, but Whitehead knew the play well from having performed in it at the Manitoba Theatre Centre in 1965. In the Court House production he chose to reprise his MTC role as Hector Hushabye (played by Christopher Newton in Allan's production). Rather than directing it himself, Whitehead brought in a director from England, Val Gielgud, well-known not only as actor John Gielgud's brother, but also as Britain's leading radio and television drama director. Like former Festival artistic director Andrew Allan, Val Gielgud had relatively little experience of live theatre, but Whitehead provided him with a strong cast. It included British actor Bill Fraser (Boss Mangan) who had recently played in a major London revival of *Heartbreak House*, and experienced Stratford Festival actors Tony van Bridge (Shotover) and Frances Hyland (Lady Utterword) – both making their Shaw Festival debuts. But Whitehead's biggest coup for the production was Jessica Tandy, who, among many other acting accomplishments, created the role of Blanche Dubois in the original Broadway production of Tennessee Williams' *A Streetcar Named Desire*.

Calvin Rand remembers the day when Whitehead heard that Tandy would come to play Hesione Hushabye in *Heartbreak House*: "I was in the front office and Paxton was in the back – there were only two offices – and I heard this great whooping, yelping, howling, and he came rushing out and he said 'I've just got Jessica Tandy to agree to play in *Heartbreak House*.'"

Tandy's presence in the cast helped persuade leading New York critics that a trip to Niagara-on-the-Lake was worth their while. Dan Sullivan, for example, came to see *Heartbreak House*, and liked what he saw. Yes, he told his *New York Times* readers, the Court House Theatre wasn't quite up to Broadway standards – "The cast dresses behind curtains strung on a clothes-line; the audience sits on bridge chairs fitted out with blue pillows; you can't enter the auditorium once the curtain is up because the floor creaks" – but the production itself "would be worth going to London to see." He praised the acting of Tony van Bridge and Jessica Tandy, but applauded as well Maurice Strike's set, which "does wonders in the tiny space assigned." (The production survives in a recording by Caedmon Records, and in excerpts used in the Festival's 1968 fundraising film "The Want of a Suitable Playhouse.")

There was, perhaps, a slightly condescending note in Sullivan's view that "to come across a really elegant production of *Heartbreak House* in this setting is a little like finding a Watteau at a country auction," but his prediction that "ten or fifteen years from now [the Shaw Festival] will doubtless be a really big-time operation, a twin of Stratford and not just a kid cousin" was as well-intentioned as it was well-judged.

STARS Whitehead had made up his mind from his first season that it was in the Festival's best interest to bring as many prominent actors – British, Canadian, America, European – as could be afforded to the Festival. Their presence, he argued, would raise both the quality of productions and the profile of the Festival, particularly within the audience-rich American border states. Jessica Tandy was undoubtedly one of the best-known actors Whitehead attracted to the Festival, but he had already embarked on his strategy in his first season in 1967, bringing America actor Larry Gates and British actress Renée Asherson to the Festival. They were hardly superstars, but they helped make the 1967 *Major Barbara*, said one critic, a "resounding success," with Gates as Andrew Undershaft and Asherson as Lady Britomart.

After Jessica Tandy, Whitehead's next big coup was to lure British actor, singer, and comedian Stanley Holloway to the Festival in 1970. Internationally recognized for his Broadway and film performances as Alfred Doolittle in *My Fair Lady*, Holloway (aged seventy-nine) played Burgess (Candida's father) in *Candida*, gaining plaudits from Hamilton critic and academic Berners Jackson for "gambolling" through his part "with an astonishing verve and sprightliness." Canadian actress Frances Hyland, who made her professional debut playing Stella in the 1949–50 London premiere of *A Streetcar Named Desire* directed by Laurence Olivier, and went on to become a regular at the Stratford Festival, was Candida in that production in a cast that also included Tony van Bridge and Jennifer Phipps.

Whitehead brought Stanley Holloway back to the Festival in 1973 to play the Waiter in *You Never Can Tell*, the inaugural production in the Festival Theatre. Directed by Edward Gilbert, Holloway again received plaudits – "his performance in the showy role is remarkably free of trickery or affectation, is never rushed or forced, and evinces humility and wisdom," said Herbert Whittaker. But an even bigger Shavian impact by visiting stars was in the offing.

Following a well-received but relatively low-key debut in Noel Coward's *Tonight at 8:30* in 1971, British-born Carole Shelley returned to the Shaw Festival in 1977. A familiar figure on Broadway following her debut there in the original 1965 production of Neil Simon's *The Odd Couple* as Gwendolyn Pigeon (she also appeared in the same role in the film and television ser-ies based on the play), Shelley had also won acclaim at the Stratford Festival for her Rosalind in *As You Like It* in 1972. She received a Tony nomination in 1975 for her role as Jane in the Broadway premiere of Alan Ayckbourn's *Absurd Person Singular*, and subsequently won a Tony in 1979 as Best Actress for her performance as Mrs Kendal in Bernard Pomerance's *The Elephant Man*. (And in later years continued to star in film, on television, and on stage – most prominently, perhaps, in the 2003 Broadway musical *Wicked*.)

While Carole Shelley was making her name on Broadway, Ian Richardson was establishing himself as one of the leading actors of England's Royal Shakespeare Company. His performance in the title role (and also as Bolingbroke) in the RSC production of Shakespeare's *Richard II* on Broadway in 1975 was widely praised, but, like Stanley Holloway, Richardson's appearance in

My Fair Lady gave him even greater prominence, his performance as Higgins in the 1976–77 Broadway revival of the musical earning him a Tony nomination. In his later career Richardson became a major television star, best known as the Machiavellian politician Francis Urquhart in the BBC television series *House of Cards*.

My Fair Lady closed in New York on February 20, 1977. Soon after, Richardson and Shelley were in Niagara-on-the-Lake rehearsing the roles of John Tanner/Don Juan and Ann Whitefield/Doña Ana in *Man and Superman* (directed by Tony van Bridge), which opened in the Festival Theatre on May 26 (previews began on May 13).

And once *Man and Superman* was underway, Richardson and Shelley began rehearsals for their roles as the Doctor and as Epifania Ognisanti di Parerga (the title role) in *The Millionairess*, which opened (also in the Festival Theatre) on July 12 (previews from July 7).

THE MILLIONAIRESS, 1977   *Toronto Star* critic Gina Mallet, intent on out-curmudgeoning her curmudgeonly predecessor Nathan Cohen at the *Star*, didn't like *The Millionairess*. She described the play as having "the consistency of spaghetti…ideas and characters are introduced, and we are lured into interest, only to have them suddenly dropped from sight." She also thought that Carole Shelley was miscast as Epifania. Other critics, however (all male), were bowled over by Shelley, who achieved, said *Toronto Sun* critic McKenzie Porter "a glorious clarity of meaning and a dazzling iridescence of wit" in a performance "never excelled by other women at this Shavian shrine." Richardson was praised too in helping "build *The Millionairess* into a milestone on the onward and upward march of one of the best festivals in English-speaking theatre" (Porter's assessment), but this show was Carole Shelley's, not Ian Richardson's.

MAN AND SUPERMAN, 1977   *Man and Superman*, on the other hand, was a collective triumph, led by director Tony van Bridge, who, remarkably, also played the Mendoza/Devil role in the play. Most of the sixty-nine performances were of the shorter version of the play, but fourteen included the *Don Juan in Hell* scene, which gave the play a running time of five-and-a-half hours. The opening performance of the full version, at a matinee on July 17, 1977, received an astounding eight-minute standing ovation (probably a Festival record). Critic Jamie Portman found the whole experience "spellbinding"; the "abiding memory," he said, "will be its sustained brilliance." In one of the best compliments the Shaw Festival (and Shaw) had so far received, Portman wrote that "a production like this reminds us how starved we are in the modern theatre for the type of glorious indulgences in language and dizzily somersaulting ideas so typical of Shaw in his heyday." "This," he concluded, "is theatre worth flying across an ocean to experience."

OPPOSITE: CAROLE SHELLEY, TONY
VAN BRIDGE, IAN RICHARDSON, AND
NORMAN WELSH IN THE *DON JUAN IN
HELL* SCENE IN *MAN AND SUPERMAN*
BY BERNARD SHAW, 1977. DIRECTED
BY TONY VAN BRIDGE, DESIGNED BY
BRIAN JACKSON, LIGHTING DESIGNED
BY JOHN STAMMERS, MUSIC ARRANGED
AND RECORDED BY DENNIS PATRICK.
PHOTO BY ROBERT C. RAGSDALE.

THIS PAGE: TONY VAN BRIDGE;
GILLIE FENWICK, STUART KENT, AND
ELIZABETH SHEPHERD; ELIZABETH
SHEPHERD AND HEATH LAMBERTS IN
TOO TRUE TO BE GOOD BY BERNARD
SHAW, 1974. DIRECTED BY DOUGLAS
SEALE, SET DESIGNED BY MAURICE
STRIKE, COSTUMES DESIGNED BY
HILARY CORBETT, LIGHTING DESIGN-
ED BY DONALD ACASTER. PHOTOS
BY ROBERT C. RAGSDALE.

Praise for Richardson himself was virtually unqualified. Mackenzie Porter could wax lyrical about Carole Shelley in *The Millionairess*, but he had a hard time finding adequate superlatives for Richardson's performance in *Man and Superman*. Like Jamie Portman, he settled on "spell-binding" as the word that best described how Richardson handled Shaw's language in the play: "a constant flow of exquisitely turned phrases cascade from Richardson's lips, and fly, dancing and sparkling like wind-driven spume, out to the audience." The evening was "spent in the company of a genius," an "intellectual and artistic feast that will nourish minds throughout the season." Richardson's was a bravura performance that, like Ben Carlson's in the same role many years later (in 2004), triggered audience applause in the middle of scenes, like arias in opera.

TOO TRUE TO BE GOOD, 1974   No other Shaw productions under Whitehead could quite match the 1968 *Heartbreak House* and the 1977 *Man and Superman*, but several came close, including *Too True to Be Good* in 1974. A difficult play, with its bizarre opening act featuring a human-sized microbe, *Too True* worked because the accomplished design team of Maurice Strike, Hilary Corbett, and Donald Acaster came up (in the Festival Theatre) with "witty sur-real settings…breathtaking costumes…and impeccable lighting," and because of the all-round strength of a cast that included Tony van Bridge, Heath Lamberts, and Domini Blythe. In their hands, under the direction of British director Douglas Seale, the production, in Herbert Whittaker's view, "came close to being a model for what the Shaw Festival should be trying to accomplish." An "awfully problematic play" gave "an exceedingly satisfying evening" of theatre.

MRS WARREN'S PROFESSION, 1976   And so did *Mrs Warren's Profession* in 1976, with Kate Reid in the title role. Reid had made her Shaw Festival debut in 1967 in Maugham's *The Circle*, and then spent several seasons playing leading roles at the Stratford Festival and on Broadway. Leslie Yeo directed *Mrs Warren's Profession*, handed the job by Whitehead because (according to Yeo) Reid had a reputation for giving directors "a hard time," and Whitehead knew that Yeo and Reid were personal friends. Whitehead needn't have worried. Reid was, Yeo said, "absolutely superb." The critics agreed, and so, it seems, did audiences, regularly giving standing ovations to Reid and the cast (which included Roberta Maxwell as Vivie Warren and Barry Morse as Sir George Crofts).

In one respect, however, Yeo did have to humour Kate Reid. During rehearsals, she preferred not to take director's notes in front of the rest of the cast. Instead, she invited Yeo to her house the morning following rehearsal. The first time that he arrived, he went in though a slightly ajar front door and heard her call "Come in, I'm in the bathroom." He found her in the bath. She invited him to make himself comfortable on the toilet seat and give his notes. The same routine was followed for the full three weeks of rehearsal.

KATE REID IN *THE APPLE CART* BY BERNARD
SHAW, 1976. DIRECTED BY NOEL WILLMAN,
DESIGNED BY MAURICE STRIKE, LIGHTING
DESIGNED BY DONALD ACASTER. PHOTO
BY ROBERT C. RAGSDALE.

OPPOSITE: ROBERTA MAXWELL AND BARRY MORSE IN *MRS
WARREN'S PROFESSION* BY BERNARD SHAW, 1976. DIRECTED
BY LESLIE YEO, SET DESIGNED BY ROBERT WINKLER, COSTUMES
DESIGNED BY HILARY CORBETT, LIGHTING DESIGNED BY
ROBERT BRYAN. PHOTO BY ROBERT C. RAGSDALE.

TERENCE KELLY AND PAUL-EMILE
FRAPPIER; JAMES VALENTINE IN *THE
ADMIRABLE BASHVILLE* BY BERNARD
SHAW, 1974. DIRECTED BY STEPHEN
KATZ, DESIGNED BY MARY KERR,
LIGHTING DESIGNED BY AL ANDERSON.
PHOTOS BY ROBERT C. RAGSDALE.

OPPOSITE: 'WENNA SHAW IN *FANNY'S
FIRST PLAY* BY BERNARD SHAW, 1973.
DIRECTED BY TONY VAN BRIDGE,
SET DESIGNED BY MAURICE STRIKE,
COSTUMES DESIGNED BY HILARY
CORBETT, LIGHTING DESIGNED BY
DONALD ACASTER. PHOTO BY ROBERT
C. RAGSDALE.

THE PHILANDERER, 1971 The quality of Whitehead's own acting was also a factor in the success of his productions of Shaw's plays. Whitehead's comedic talents were best showcased in *The Philanderer* in 1971. As Leonard Charteris he "vivified" the production, wrote New York critic Julius Novick:

> There is something very subtly preposterous about Mr Whitehead's Charteris: his long legs, his nervous movements, his heroic nose, his toothy grimace of a smile, his adenoidally vibrant voice, are all excessive to just the right degree, suggesting keenness and fatuity at the same time. And, like all really fine comic actors, he does not simply mug and do bits in a vacuum; his effects are rooted in the nature and situation of the character.

The *Toronto Sun* agreed, and astutely captured the compelling physicality of Whitehead's performance, describing his Charteris as "shrinking hideously from the truth, jack-knifing his way across the stage in a split second, betrayed constantly by a face that won't obey orders." This was, said the *Sun*, "a major piece of acting."

There were personal bouquets for Whitehead as well for his portrayal of Valentine in *You Never Can Tell* in 1973, and as Sergius in *Arms and the Man* in 1976, and he earned respect, if not always critical or popular approval, by making sure that lesser-known Shaw plays were included in his seasons. *O'Flaherty, V.C.* (1971 season), a short comedy about recruiting soldiers in Ireland in the First World War, was dismissed by some as "a beastly bore." But it needn't be, as other productions have shown (including a Shaw Festival revival in 1983). An even more obscure Shaw play, *The Admirable Bashville*, Shaw's own blank verse adaptation of his 1885 novel about boxing, *Cashel Byron's Profession*, was included in the 1974 season. The choice "does the Shaw Festival credit in that it celebrates Shaw, both great and small works alike," wrote one critic. The "credit," however, was decidedly qualified: "if there are many more like *The Admirable Bashville* at the bottom of Shaw's barrel, let them stay there, please." And so, as far as the Festival is concerned, it has. There have been no revivals. *Press Cuttings*, on the other hand, has been revived twice (1991, 2006) since its 1971 premiere at the Festival. A short suffragette comedy banned in England when Shaw wrote it in 1909 because of its allusions to prominent public figures, *Press Cuttings* was on the same bill as *O'Flaherty, V.C.* and a forgettable Max Beerbohm play (*A Social Success*), so perhaps benefited by comparison.

There were, inevitably, setbacks and disappointments in Whitehead's handling of Shaw's plays. After the big success of *Heartbreak House* in 1968, expectations were high for 1969, but both of the Shaw plays that season – *The Doctor's Dilemma* and *Back to Methuselah (Part I)* – were let-downs. Dan Sullivan's colleague from *The New York Times*, Clive Barnes, came up to Niagara-on-the-Lake to see *The Doctor's Dilemma*, but the production didn't show the company at its best. Whitehead cast himself as the talented but charlatan artist Louis Dubedat, but played it for more laughs than the part can reasonably sustain. It was, Calvin Rand recalled, "terrible, a great disappointment." Barnes was inclined to blame the play, not the players, but Nathan Cohen, true to character, went for the jugular. Like Barnes, Cohen didn't care much for *The Doctor's Dilemma* either ("the animus against the doctors which permeates the play is forced, clumsily inserted and heavy-handed"), and it couldn't be rescued by this "humdrum and glutinous" production.

Back to Methuselah was hampered from the beginning by technical problems. Director Marigold Charlesworth decided to do the first scene, the Garden of Eden, on audio tape, but the sound system in the Court House wasn't up to the task. On opening night, one review noted, "the audience was forced to sit through three quarters of an hour of unintelligible talk." Improvements were made, but the show never really recovered from the disastrous start.

SHAW IN THE FESTIVAL THEATRE The opening of the Festival Theatre in 1973 helped the company bypass Court House Theatre deficiencies, but, ironically, the first two Shaw productions in the new theatre have to be included among the disappointments of Whitehead's term as artistic director. With the rush to get the theatre ready for the opening of *You Never Can Tell* on June 20 (with previews from June 12), inadequate attention was paid to the play itself. Even the combined and trusted talents of Whitehead (playing Valentine, the dentist), Gilbert (director), Strike (set design), and Corbett (costume design) and the talents of Stanley Holloway (the Waiter) couldn't pull the production much above what Clive Barnes thought "good enough for an everyday

provincial repertory, but perhaps not good enough for an international festival." There was more time to prepare for *Fanny's First Play*, which previewed in the Festival Theatre from August 8, but that production too failed to stir much excitement. It is, in fact, a play much better suited to the Court House, where it has been done for the two Festival revivals in 1987 and 2001.

As Whitehead gained more experience of having two quite different theatres at his disposal, so he learned how to balance productions between them. His choice of plays for the 1977 season, and where he put them, showed how the two theatres could best be used to Shaw's advantage: two plays (*Man and Superman* and *The Millionairess*) in the Festival Theatre that could exploit and benefit from the big stage and attract larger audiences; two plays (*Widowers' Houses* and *Great Catherine*) better suited to the more intimate Court House and likely to have minority appeal.

A second theatre also gave Whitehead much more flexibility with the scheduling of plays. In the early years of the Festival, plays were given sequentially. In 1971, however, Whitehead decided to experiment with what he called a "modified repertory system." In that season, and in 1972, he had pairs of plays running concurrently (e.g., in 1972, *Getting Married* and *Misalliance*). In 1973 he moved to a full repertory system, so that, as he explained, "people can come for a few days and see a roster of what we do, rather than having to make five visits in order to see everything." Openings, then as now, had to be staggered, but the structure adopted by Whitehead has remained in place since 1973.

By the time he left the Festival after the end of the 1977 season, Paxton Whitehead had achieved a great deal with the plays of Bernard Shaw. True, there had been some disappointing productions. True, he hadn't tackled some of the major plays: no *John Bull's Other Island*, no complete *Back to Methuselah*, no *In Good King Charles's Golden Days*. And it was left to Tony van Bridge (in Whitehead's 1975 sabbatical year) to bring back *Pygmalion* to the Festival (first seen in 1965) and to premiere *Caesar and Cleopatra*. The biggest and most surprising omission was *Saint Joan*, which after sixteen seasons still hadn't been seen at the Festival. But Whitehead and the Shaw Festival were leaders in keeping the plays of Shaw alive on the stage in the 1970s, supported only sporadically by other companies as Shaw went through one of his periodic spells in the theatrical doldrums on the world stage. That was, and is, an achievement worth celebrating.

EARLY TOURING

"I did want to get the word out about the Festival," Paxton Whitehead said, and the ideal opportunity occurred in his very first season, the year of the 1967 International and Universal Exposition in Montreal, or Expo 67 as it was popularly known. Invited by Edward Gilbert, artistic director of the Manitoba Theatre Centre in Winnipeg (where Whitehead had made his Canadian acting debut), to take an MTC-Shaw Festival co-production to Expo, Whitehead "leapt at the opportunity," seeing it, as he put it, as an excellent way "to propagate the faith of the Shaw Festival."

***MAJOR BARBARA* AT EXPO 67** The play chosen was *Major Barbara*. Directed by Gilbert, with Whitehead playing Adolphus Cusins, the production ran for thirty-one performances at the Festival in August and September before moving to Montreal where it ran at Expo (in the Théâtre Port-Royal, Place des Arts) for eight performances, opening on September 16. It then headed back west to Winnipeg, where it opened at the Manitoba Theatre Centre on October 3 and ran for twenty-two performances.

Jennifer Phipps, who played Rummy Mitchens (the beginning of one of the longest and most distinguished acting careers in the Festival's history), found the switch from the tiny Court House stage to the much bigger stage of the Place des Arts challenging, but it had its amusing aspects as well. The worry was that the "tiny little set" from the Court House simply wouldn't work on the "very long, very wide stage" at the Place des Arts. So the "brilliant idea" was "to make things bigger, so it would look as if they filled the stage." Thus "the cannon was twice as fat as it had been in the Court House, so that the two actors who were sitting on the Court House cannon quite comfortably with their legs dangling on either side, now had their legs spreadeagled." And the Salvation Army table was now made twice the size as well, so Phipps

PAXTON WHITEHEAD AND IRENA
MAYESKA; LARRY GATES IN *MAJOR
BARBARA* BY BERNARD SHAW, 1967.
DIRECTED BY EDWARD GILBERT,
DESIGNED BY MAURICE STRIKE, LIGHT-
ING DESIGNED BY CHRISTOPHER ROOT.

OPPOSITE: IRENA MAYESKA AND ROY
COOPER IN *MAJOR BARBARA*, 1967.
PHOTOS BY ROBERT C. RAGSDALE.

found herself talking to Snobby Price (played by Eric House) "right down this enormous six-foot or eight-foot table." Phipps went into the auditorium to watch those parts of the play she wasn't in, and found much of it "hysterically funny." "You can't make the actors any bigger, and if you make the set bigger the actors look smaller. They were like tiny, wee ants walking around this enormous set" – Lilliputian actors on a Brobdingnagian set.

But the audiences and critics loved it anyway. "The capacity audience," said the *Montreal Star*, "went on applauding long after the cast stopped taking curtain calls," stimulated "by two principal reactions – the clarity and smoothness of Mr Gilbert's production and the amazing topicality of Shaw's text."

The designer charged with the daunting task of moving the set of *Major Barbara* from the Court House to the Place des Arts was a young British designer who had only recently arrived in Canada. His name was Maurice Strike, who designed the sets for all three plays in the Festival's 1967 season, and stayed with the Festival for the next decade.

The tour of *Major Barbara* to Montreal and Winnipeg heralded many more tours during Paxton Whitehead's period as artistic director. Venues in Canada included Ottawa, Kingston, Toronto, and Halifax (and several other Maritime towns on a 1974 tour of *The Devil's Disciple*). And in the United States the Festival visited Rochester, Washington DC, Detroit, New Haven, Ann Arbor, Cambridge, and Philadelphia.

IN THE UNITED STATES The Rochester visit was brief – just two performances of *The Philanderer* in June 1971, directed by Tony van Bridge, designed by Maurice Strike, with Whitehead as Leonard Charteris – but it was a significant milestone for the Festival as it marked the first time that the company had performed outside of Canada. The occasion was welcomed and celebrated in Rochester, which declared the week of the visit "Shaw Festival and Ontario Week," brought in the Fort Henry Guard from Kingston for downtown performances, and hosted receptions and parties throughout the week.

The American performance that Whitehead was most proud of, however, was the 1972 *Misalliance* that went to the John F. Kennedy Center for the Performing Arts in Washington DC, directed by Whitehead himself, with another set design by Strike. Whitehead thought the opening night on June 26 was "the best thing" he had seen the company do. It was, he said, "stunning to watch," and the critics agreed. Frank Getlein in the *Washington Star* described the production as "gorgeous." "The players are superb, the setting and costumes [designed by Hilary Corbett] imaginative and appropriate." It was, Getlein declared, "top-quality Shaw... an intellectual treat of the highest order."

Calvin Rand was in Washington for the production and attended one of the receptions for the company. It was held, he remembers, "in an apartment building called Watergate." Nine days before *Misalliance* opened, five men broke into the Democratic Party National Committee headquarters in the building, with consequences that brought down a President. "I remember," Rand says, "our hosts or a few people murmuring about a break-in...just casual conversation."

Another memorable visit to the United States took place in 1975 when the Festival's production of *The Devil's Disciple* (co-directed by Whitehead, who also played Burgoyne, and Tony van Bridge) took part in bicentennial celebrations in Philadelphia and Washington. The Fort Henry Guard was again prominent, this time with ten members of the Guard helping to fill the stage as officers and soldiers of the British army. A "rousing, invigorating production, full of excitement and thrills, and rich satisfying laughter," said Julius Novick in *The New York Times*. And, appropriately for the bicentennial celebrations, the right side wins in Shaw's play.

Whitehead's enthusiasm for a Shaw Festival presence in the United States was such that he seriously considered establishing a permanent winter base there. Early in 1977 he was invited by Festival enthusiast (and subsequently founding President of the International Shaw Society) Richard Dietrich, then a professor at the University of South Florida, to visit Tampa to look at local theatres. Among the possible locations was the 1400-seat Tampa Theatre, built in 1926 as a movie theatre, and being restored by Tampa City Council. But Whitehead, possibly deterred by the size of the house and the absence of backstage space and flytower, and not finding any other available theatre suitable, dropped the idea.

Tours were undertaken in eight of Whitehead's eleven years at the Festival (including the post-season tour of *The Devil's Disciple* in 1975, Whitehead's sabbatical year). Provincial and federal government grants made the tours financially viable, and the company benefited not only

from higher profile in many parts of Canada and the United States, but also, of course, from longer seasons (earlier starts or later finishes) that provided extra income for company members. That early commitment from Whitehead to "get the word out about the Festival" was fulfilled to everyone's benefit. (See Appendix C for full list of all Shaw Festival tours.)

A NEW THEATRE

There was little argument from anyone, least of all Paxton Whitehead, that a modern, well-equipped theatre was the highest of all priorities for the Shaw Festival. Improvements had been steadily made in the Court House Theatre – air conditioning, semi-comfortable cushions for seats, increased seating capacity, risers for better sight lines – but backstage facilities for actors remained far below adequate, and designers, especially set designers, were constantly struggling to fit the plays of Shaw and his contemporaries onto the tiny stage. This problem was one of the reasons that *Saint Joan* was not attempted at the Festival in the early years.

"THE NIAGARA THEATRE"   Initiatives to build a new theatre began as early as 1964. The 1964 Festival brochure contained an announcement for "The Niagara Theatre." It was to be "a beautiful, intimate, modern but Colonial style Theatre," overlooking the Niagara River, near Fort George. Ambitiously conceived as "a unique cultural and entertainment centre" that would house "music and the other arts" as well as the Shaw Festival, construction was expected to begin in the summer of 1964. The estimated total cost of the building was $500,000, and a Building Fund Campaign had an "immediate objective" of $250,000. "Substantial contributions from interested citizens, business and corporations" were encouraged as "essential to the success of this campaign."

Audience members in the 1964 season received copies of a hand-written letter by Brian Doherty that encouraged them to join "the swelling host of 'Angels'" who were supporting a new theatre, but, unfortunately, the host did not swell sufficiently to move things forward. The idea was not abandoned, but 1967 – Canada's Centennial Year – was adopted as a more realistic date for a new theatre.

SITES AND DESIGNS   Centennial Year, however, came and went, and still there was no new theatre. There was consensus within the Festival around Whitehead's view – expressed when he was appointed – about the size of the theatre, which Whitehead thought should be "no larger than 700 or 750 seats," and that it should be a proscenium design, "as suits the plays of Shaw and his contemporaries." And size and style would be determining factors in cost. But – crucially – after the initial confidence about a site near Fort George had dissipated, there was no firm sense of where the theatre should be located. Indeed, the differences of opinion within the community of Niagara-on-the-Lake about location were held and expressed so passionately that one reporter described the controversy as generating "the hottest time in the old town since the Americans burned it in 1813."

Calvin Rand (Chair) and his colleagues on the Board of Directors could not be faulted for their diligence in exploring potential sites for the theatre. Numerous possibilities were considered, including two – in St Catharines (Rodman Hall) and Queenston Heights (on property owned by the National Parks Commission) – that weren't even in Niagara-on-the-Lake. Possibilities closer to town included a site near the old Department of Defence firing range on Lakeshore Road, and another federally owned site on the Commons, east of the eventual location. In Niagara-on-the-Lake itself Butler's Barracks (at John and King streets), Queen's Royal Park (on the lake at the foot of King Street), and a property previously run as a school for mentally handicapped children (now the Riverbend Inn) were looked at, while one of the most creative (and unlikely) ideas was to buy a building that had housed a 372-seat auditorium at Expo 67 in Montreal and transport it to Niagara-on-the-Lake (by road and/or water).

Various architectural plans were developed while locations were being considered. Among the more intriguing (some might say bizarre) was one presented to the board on June 6, 1968. It showed "a sphere suspended in an egg-like outer shell which would be a transparent plastic material, all to be supported by a series of conical wing shapes." Calvin Rand hesitatingly described this "a fascinating approach to theatre."

JAMES VALENTINE, STUART KENT, TONY VAN BRIDGE, ALAN SCARFE, AND NORMAN WELSH WITH THE ENSEMBLE IN *THE DEVIL'S DISCIPLE* BY BERNARD SHAW, 1974. DIRECTED BY BRIAN MURRAY, DESIGNED BY ROBERT DOYLE, LIGHTING DESIGNED BY LYNNE HYDE. PHOTO BY ROBERT C. RAGSDALE.

Later in 1968 the Festival selected the Queen's Royal Park as the preferred location for the new theatre and formally sought to buy or lease the site. There were immediate public protests about the loss of picnic areas and the town's only public beach. The request was unanimously rejected by the town council on September 10, 1968, and Mayor Walter Theobald warned of "problems with taxpayers" over the potentially "hot issue" of the new theatre. How right he was, but even the mayor could not have predicted just how hot the issue would become.

"A BEDRAGGLED BANNER ACROSS THE MAIN STREET" Public concern about the location of a new theatre broadened into questions about whether the Shaw Festival was a valuable asset to the town at all. The writer of one long letter to the *St Catharines Standard* yearned for the halcyon days when there were soldiers in town. They "ate in our restaurants, drank in our hotels, bought gifts for their families from our merchants, attended our [movie] theatre, and patronized our gas stations, taxis, carnivals, and ball games." The soldiers were, "on the whole," "an orderly bunch," and "they made our town boom." Shaw Festival patrons, on the other hand, come to the Court House Theatre, "spend the next three hours being 'cultivated,'" and then leave – and "we probably won't see them again until next year." What little money they spend, claimed the writer, "goes to the Shaw Festival 'coffer,' which itself leaves for other places." What did the town have to show for hosting the Shaw Festival? Just "a bedraggled banner across the main street."

There was an immediate and vigorous response from the Festival to those charges in a speech by Calvin Rand to the Rotary Club of St Catharines. He went armed with statistics from a recent Festival audience survey that showed an economic impact on the town from Festival patrons (accommodation, food, and services) at a healthy $385,000 a season. And that didn't include money spent by actors and technical and administrative staff who lived in the town. Rand reported that the Festival was operating in the black, but barely; even if it sold 100 percent of tickets in the Court House Theatre it could earn only two-thirds of operating costs, the remainder coming from government grants and fundraising.

FORT MISSISSAUGA The Festival needed as much public understanding and support as it could get: more trouble was brewing. The attempt to secure the Queen's Royal Park site having failed, the Festival considered other options, settling this time on the golf course at the west end of the town, a site owned by the Canadian government. The government planned to develop the site as a national park around the ruins of Fort Mississauga, completed in 1814 in anticipation of possible future conflicts with the United States. Viewing the Shaw Festival as an appropriate partner, the government offered to lease some five acres of land adjacent to the Fort to the Festival (for $100 a year) for a new theatre. The golf course would move to other federal land on the Commons along Queen's Parade.

The Shaw Festival board authorized negotiations with the government on May 26, 1969, but, somewhat disquietingly, there were two dissenting votes. Further evidence of differences of opinion within the Festival's own ranks came with the resignation of the President and several other members of the Women's Committee, a group whose volunteer work was essential to the Festival's social activities. The view of those who resigned was that the area around Fort Mississauga should be left as open space, golf course or not. But the golfers themselves weren't too happy either about losing the course that had been located there for over ninety years. Calvin Rand walked across the course one day with a government official and received an "intense glare from a nearby resident, nine iron firmly in hand," while Brian Doherty, on a similar trek, had to be even more vigilant when confronted with an "upraised putter."

Political action was taken as well. A petition against locating a theatre on the Fort Mississauga site was presented to the Town Council. It had 1273 signatures. (The population of Niagara-on-the-Lake in 1969 was just under 3000.) Another petition, signed by twenty-four business owners in the town, also objected. Concerned not so much by the loss of open space as lost opportunities for their businesses, they wanted the new theatre in, or close to, the town core. Under pressure, the town council turned up the heat on the federal government, but the minister responsible for the offer to the Shaw Festival, Jean Chrétien – future Prime Minister of Canada – refused to budge. When his letter confirming the government's decision to lease the Fort Mississauga site to the Shaw Festival was read to the council, an "explosive" Mayor Theobald declared that he was "thoroughly disgusted" with Chrétien's response.

ENTRANCE TO THE COURT HOUSE THEATRE, 2010. PHOTO BY DAVID COOPER.

The Festival, however, encouraged by public support from the National and Historic Parks Branch of the Canadian government, persevered, and commissioned plans for the theatre. But the controversy wouldn't go away. An editorial in the *St Catharines Standard* on July 5, 1969, condemning the government and the Festival for engineering "the loss forever of this unique open lakeshore area" was endorsed by several letters to the editor, and soon there were signs that the government was beginning to waver. When another federal minister – Gérard Pelletier, Secretary of State – landed at the Niagara District Airport later in July en route, ironically in the circumstances, to see a Festival production (*The Doctor's Dilemma*), he was greeted by a delegation that presented him with a dossier of newspaper clippings of editorials, letters, and news stories opposing his government's plans. By late July the press was carrying rumours of a new plan, and a headline in the *Standard* on August 5, 1969, declared "Shaw Festival Loses Struggle for Lakefront."

The government now said that it would put on hold plans to move the golf course to the Commons, and meanwhile offered the Festival a site known as the old military grounds, near where John Street meets the Niagara Parkway. In another editorial (August 6, 1969) the *Standard* celebrated this "eminently satisfactory" resolution of the dispute, and called on everyone involved to "rally round the Festival authorities, and bring the new theatre into reality as soon as possible."

It was a classic case of wishful thinking.

BEHIND THE COURT HOUSE Disappointed by losing the Fort Mississauga site, the Festival administrators chose not to consider the now preferred government site, but to look to their own backyard instead, so to speak. In January 1970 the Festival asked the town council for a long-term lease on the land directly west and south of the Court House, encompassing what was then known as market square, though no longer used as such. The idea was to build the new theatre on that site, linked to the Court House itself, so that the Festival would have two adjoining theatres. Council was favourably disposed to the concept, since it continued to bring Festival patrons into the centre of town, with all the attendant benefits for local businesses.

Negotiations with the town council were laborious but cordial, and by early summer agreement had been reached for a long-term lease on the property needed for the new theatre and for ongoing use of the Court House Theatre itself. The Festival had by then requested, received, and reviewed architectural proposals for the new theatre, and had selected a design by Ron H. Thom, well-known as the architect for Massey College in the University of Toronto and for the founding colleges of Trent University in Peterborough, Ontario, but with no previous experience in theatre design.

Estimated to cost $2.5 million, Thom's design was widely reported and discussed in August 1970. It called for an 850-seat theatre, with one balcony, a proscenium arch, and a fly tower no higher than the tower on the Court House. A box office, snack bar, workshops, dressing rooms, offices, and Green Room were included, and a glassed-in terrace would be located at the rear of the theatre. In a public presentation about the theatre on August 10, 1970, Calvin Rand welcomed and praised Thom's design as "a vital and visual element in the centre of Niagara-on-the-Lake," but also recognized the Achilles heel of the plan, conceding that there was no room for parking in the cramped site. He calculated, however, that there were "small lots behind stores and hotels, on the streets, and around two nearby parks" that could accommodate some 1200 to 1300 cars.

That was all very well, but as knowledge of the Festival's proposal circulated around town, opposition to the downtown location grew. The Niagara Historical Society, for example, was concerned, as a *Niagara Advance* editorial expressed it on September 21, 1970, that "commercialism and the unwanted masses of hangers-on that pursue culture for other ends than cultural will change and even destroy the present colonial air of the town." Other groups and individuals urged that the "old world charm" and "gentle decay" of the town not be spoiled. Wary of the fate that had befallen Niagara Falls, residents of Niagara-on-the-Lake did not want their community to become, as one resident put it, "Coney Island."

So tension was again building. And things got worse when it was announced that the town council had agreed that the Shaw Festival, as a non-profit organization, should be exempt from paying municipal taxes. That news prompted a full-page protest in the *Niagara Advance* on

CLOCKWISE FROM TOP: ARCHITECT'S
SKETCH FOR A PROPOSED FESTIVAL
THEATRE ADJACENT TO THE COURT
HOUSE; SKETCH FOR THE AUDITORIUM;
FESTIVAL THEATRE ARCHITECT RON
THOM AND HIS ASSISTANT PETER SMITH,
IN 1972. SMITH WENT ON TO DESIGN
THE PRODUCTION CENTRE EXTENSION
TO THE FESTIVAL THEATRE SOME 30
YEARS LATER (SEE PAGE 254).

September 17, 1970, that challenged Council's decision on the grounds that the Festival "should carry all of its own cost and be no burden to the Taxpayers," and, moreover, that Bernard Shaw "was a Marxist and a Communist...an open admirer of Soviet Russia." The Festival responded with its own full page, arguing that "there is no need to go into the irrelevant remarks about Shaw being a Marxist or a Communist," and pointing out that the Stratford Festival and many other theatres across the country were exempt from property and other taxes. Exemption, however, required approval of the government of Ontario, which was denied in May 1971, leaving the Festival in the precarious position of having to negotiate an annual tax refund with the town council.

The bigger issue, however, was still the location of the theatre. Letters to the editor continued to appear in the local papers. A few welcomed development of the market square site, an area of town that, in the opinion of one writer, was "most appallingly run-down...a positive eyesore." But most were vehemently opposed. A crusading rhetoric pervaded many of them – a crusade to save "the historical core" of the town from the "infectious disease" of "Shawitis." "We who love this town know that Niagara-on-the-Lake is more important than Shaw," wrote one resident. "The gradual conversion of its core to a parking lot" must be resisted, added another. The Festival was condemned as a "colossal organization that interferes everywhere in the life of our citizens." A "Save-Niagara Fund" was established to support legal challenges to the site, a fund that the local bank declined to handle, diplomatically maintaining neutrality in the dispute.

From Rand's point of view, once the lease with Council had been agreed, and architectural drawings had been commissioned, it was "practically impossible" to move the theatre to another site. But delays were costing money, and even Rand's firm but tactful diplomacy did not seem capable of winning over the tenacious opposition.

RESOLUTION As 1971 was drawing to a close it was very difficult to see how the controversy could be resolved. But – astonishingly – by the end of a meeting of town council on December 29, a meeting described by the press as "a model of cooperation and understanding," agreement had been reached between the Council and the Festival for an entirely new site. And just a few weeks later (March 7) a headline in the *Advance* declared that "Only One Resident Still Opposes Site of Shaw Festival."

The deadlock was resolved by the Festival's general manager Tom Burrows. Burrows had come to Niagara-on-the-Lake from Yale University, where he had worked as Managing Director of Theatre Operations in the Yale School of Drama. Burrows was rapidly immersed in the politics of the theatre site, and soon became familiar with the key players in Niagara-on-the-Lake and Ottawa. He addressed the parking problem by reaching an agreement with St Vincent de Paul Church to build and maintain a parking lot for shared use, and negotiated with the federal government for more parking spaces on the opposite side of the road, at the corner of Wellington and Picton Streets. Both parking lots were just a few minutes' walk from the Court House Theatre.

Burrows then arranged a private meeting with the two leading opponents on town council of the market square site at the home of board member Henry Wiens. He confidently put the parking solution to them, but they still refused to withdraw their opposition. What happened then was as spontaneous as it was crucial. As Burrows describes it,

> I looked at Henry and looked at these two men. "Well, what if we build the theatre there [on the Wellington/Picton site]?" "Yeah." That was it, just that simple – I mean not that simple, because this had dragged on for a year and we had been over and over and over it. But I had never mentioned that [site] before. I said, "I don't know what it will take, but if I can get three acres, will you support it?" "Yes."

It was an audacious move by Burrows, because neither board chair Calvin Rand nor architect Ron Thom knew anything about it. Conversations and meetings rapidly ensued. The Mayor and board members jointly and successfully lobbied Ottawa for the new site. Thom began adapting the market square design to the site, and calculating the additional cost of the parking lot ($200,000, bringing the total cost of the project to close to $3 million). Wellington Street residents were consulted and promised a 100-feet separation between their homes and

the parking lot. Formal approval was unanimously given by town council and the Festival board. Fundraising efforts were accelerated. The lone opponent – who argued before the Ontario Municipal Board that "the project would destroy parkland, would not fit in with the historical background of the town, would create traffic problems, and would conflict with the use of adjacent land occupied by Niagara hospital" – was overruled by the board at its hearing in Virgil on March 6, 1972.

GROUNDBREAKING Such was the speed of this final phase of the Festival Theatre saga that only four months after Tom Burrows' conversation with the two recalcitrant councillors the official groundbreaking ceremony for the new theatre took place. Monday April 17, 1972, was a bright, sunny day, but a biting wind met participants and guests on the steps of the Court House. After remarks by Paxton Whitehead, the procession walked behind the Welland Police Pipe Band to the new site, where musical responsibilities were taken over by the Canadian Brass. After speeches and the handing over of a $500,000 federal government cheque to Calvin Rand, Brian Doherty, who had kept a low profile during the arguments about the new theatre – his flamboyance and plain-talking perhaps not being considered assets in tense times – proudly turned the first sod to begin construction of the theatre. Then Reverend Hugh Maclean of St Mark's Church gave an invocation that while avoiding any mention of Shaw, called for much that Shaw would have welcomed, including a world "where evil and poverty shall be done away with." Ceremonies concluded with a wine and cheese reception given by the Festival's Women's Committee, the very committee whose leaders had resigned three years earlier in protest against the selection of the Fort Mississauga site for the theatre.

OPENING NIGHT Fourteen months after the sod turning, on June 12, 1973, the opening day of the theatre, new sod was still being laid. But the 800 guests who snacked on liver paté, crabmeat canapés, stuffed mushroom caps, breaded shrimps, Swedish meatballs, and breaded drumsticks – washed down by local champagne – were oblivious to the last-minute hustle and bustle outside and inside the theatre.

The opening play was Shaw's *You Never Can Tell*, but the star and the centre of attention was the theatre, not the play. Among the accolades was Clive Barnes's description of it in *The New York Times* as "the loveliest in North America," but the most eloquent tribute to what Ron Thom had achieved came from the *Toronto Star*:

> Beautifully proportioned and superbly detailed, the new Festival Theatre gives its lucky audiences room to admire, room to wander, and, most important, room to think. It is an environment which leaves a dimension for the intellect, for words, ideas, and reflections.

Many famous people came to the Shaw Festival in the inaugural season of the Festival Theatre. Ontario Premier William Davis officially opened the theatre on June 12; Canadian Prime Minister Pierre Trudeau escorted Indian Prime Minister Indira Gandhi on June 20; and Queen Elizabeth and the Duke of Edinburgh attended a special performance of *You Never Can Tell*

on June 28. Calvin Rand and Brian Doherty were on hand to proudly greet them all. Rand lived on to help create and celebrate many more significant moments in the history of the Festival, but Doherty died in Niagara-on-the-Lake on October 30, 1974, four months after being admitted to the Order of Canada for his services to theatre. He is buried in the family plot in Mount Hope Cemetery in Toronto, and a memorial service for him was held in the Festival Theatre on November 3, 1974. A bronze bust of Doherty by Niagara-on-the-Lake artist Jacobine Jones was placed in the lobby of the Festival Theatre in June 1973 as part of the opening celebrations for the new theatre. Calvin Rand was similarly honoured when a bust by American sculptor Mary DeWitt Smith was installed in the lobby on September 30, 2008.

AN EMERGING CRISIS

After two years' experience of running both the Court House and Festival Theatres, Paxton Whitehead felt that he needed time to reflect on where the Shaw Festival was heading. The board agreed to his request for a sabbatical, during which, he said, he would "examine the principles and values of the Shaw Festival." One of the key issues for Whitehead concerned the "international" aspirations of the Festival. The Festival should, Whitehead told the board, "draw on the best Canadian artists available," but should also use artists "from elsewhere," both to enhance the quality of Festival productions and to raise its international profile.

NATIONALIST SENTIMENTS   In promoting internationalism for the Festival, however, Whitehead was swimming against a rising tide of nationalism in Canadian theatre. He had been present at a meeting held in Brian Doherty's home in Niagara-on-the-Lake in 1971 attended by playwrights and by officials from the Canada Council and the Ontario Arts Council, the Festival's main sources of government support. At that meeting the councils were urged to consider implementing incentive programs to encourage Canadian theatres to produce more Canadian plays, perhaps even to implement a "minimum content" rule of Canadian plays to be eligible for funding.

TONY VAN BRIDGE, ACTING ARTISTIC DIRECTOR, 1975   Those kinds of nationalist feelings had no perceivable impact on Whitehead's subsequent programming, but the season that acting artistic director Tony van Bridge organized in 1975 at least made a nod towards feelings in the wider Canadian theatre community by including the first Canadian play ever produced at the Festival. Robertson Davies' *Leaven of Malice* had flopped on Broadway in 1960 (then with the title *Love and Libel*), but van Bridge, who had been in the Broadway production, believed the play deserved another chance. It didn't.

The Festival production of this satire on small-town Ontario hypocrisy and smugness, directed by van Bridge himself, was sympathetically reviewed by *Toronto Star* critic Urjo Kareda (who went on to become a major force in the development of Canadian plays as artistic director of Toronto's Tarragon Theatre). Kareda's support of *Leaven of Malice* was, however, very much a minority viewpoint. Calvin Rand, privately, was blunt in his judgment that *Leaven of Malice* was a "terrible" play that the Festival should never have produced. Several critics agreed. Among the most outspoken was Clive Barnes, whose *New York Times* review called the whole thing "jejune nonsense," and, for once, Barnes was even critical of designers Maurice Strike ("ugly" set) and Hilary Corbett ("hideous" costumes).

The failure of *Leaven of Malice* (critically and at the box office) overshadowed the rest of van Bridge's 1975 season. The two big Shaw plays were *Pygmalion* and *Caesar and Cleopatra* (a Festival premiere). *Pygmalion* was a disappointment, with a general consensus that neither Elizabeth Shepherd (Eliza) nor Powys Thomas (Higgins) was much more than adequate. Shepherd got off to a grumpy start to the run when she accused the opening night audience of being "the worst and most insensitive I have ever played to." At curtain call she "stared crossly" at the audience, some of whom, she charged, were "inebriated." "You could smell the stuff coming across to the stage," she told a reporter. *Caesar and Cleopatra*, directed by Douglas Seale, fared better, graced with a "glorious Cleopatra" (said both Urjo Kareda and Herbert Whittaker) in Domini Blythe, and, as described by Whittaker, a powerful set by Leslie Hurry "of glowing colour and mysterious depths, of towering shapes and exquisite gauzes."

Whittaker thought that the production of *Caesar and Cleopatra* was a turning point for the

Festival, one that would allow it to "cast aside the minor label of summer theatre it has worn and take its place with the country's major festivals." But in reality van Bridge's season was a different kind of turning point, one that marked the beginning of the end of Paxton Whitehead's term as artistic director and a period of turmoil and uncertainty about the Festival's future.

When he took the job of acting artistic director, Tony van Bridge said that he didn't see his task as "sweeping with a new broom since the old broom has its full complement of bristles." He didn't go into the 1975 season with great expectations, and he didn't come out of it with a great deal of satisfaction. He wrote in his 1995 memoirs (*Also in the Cast*) that the season "went well enough, but it could have been better," and he said that he "learned quite a lot," particularly that "office drudgery is quite foreign to a mind that is absorbed in playing and directing, and that one discipline can suffer at the hands of the other."

What also suffered was the budget. The Festival incurred a loss of over $300,000 on the 1975 season, a massive blow after several deficit-free seasons. The Festival was also carrying a capital debt of $500,000 from the new theatre. This meant that when Whitehead returned from his sabbatical he was faced with serious financial concerns as well as how to respond to pressures to "Canadianize" the Festival.

CANADIAN CONTENT After the debacle of *Leaven of Malice* Whitehead was in no mood to attempt more Canadian plays, insisting that the financial risk was simply too great for the Festival, and that the smaller alternate theatres in Toronto were far better positioned to support Canadian playwrights. Nor did Whitehead want to be restricted to Canada in his choice of actors. He said that when he cast a play he always looked first at Canadian actors, but if he couldn't find the quality he wanted, he absolutely insisted on the freedom to look elsewhere.

The ensuing debates about Canadian plays and Canadian actors at the Shaw Festival (debates in which *Toronto Star* critic Gina Mallet took a particularly aggressive stance against the Festival) were inflamed by Whitehead's decision to bring British star Ian Richardson to the Festival in 1977 to play John Tanner in *Man and Superman*. Ronald Bryden, who was later to become Literary Advisor to the Festival, but was then writing for *Maclean's* magazine, praised Richardson as "after [John] Gielgud the finest virtuoso speaker in the British theatre," but he also accused the Festival of pandering to American tourists, who "don't give a damn for Canadian content." In the same article (*Maclean's*, July 25, 1977), Bryden reported that the Canada Council had "issued an ultimatum" to Whitehead to "upgrade his Festival's quality, its content of Canadian plays and players, or the Council would start thinking of reducing its subsidy." That ultimatum infuriated executive director Richard Kirschner, who accused the Council of already having unfairly treated the Festival by giving more generous subsidies to other performing arts organizations in Canada and now was guilty of "gross interference" in the Festival's artistic management. According to Kirschner, the Council had pressed for a new artistic director as well as lobbied for particular Canadian plays and actors. "It's a scandal reaching critical proportions," Kirschner alleged. One Canada Council official was reported as saying that the Festival "cannot expect more liberal tax subsidies until it does more to promote Canadian playwrights rather than concentrating on an Irishman's plays," a comment that prompted advice from one newspaper to have Shaw "posthumously declared an honorary Canadian citizen."

Attacked from one side by cultural nationalists, Whitehead was also being pummelled from another angle by critics such as Herbert Whittaker who charged him with being "a bit lightweight." What we have, said Whittaker, is a situation in which "one of our two major theatres" (the other, of course, being the Stratford Festival) is "behaving like a straw hat theatre," mounting attractive but "glib" productions.

So having been under siege for some years from the local community about where the Festival Theatre should be located, the Festival now found itself under siege from critics and funding agencies for its artistic policies and the quality of its productions.

Whitehead had his supporters, among them Southam News critic Jamie Portman, whose reviews were carried in papers across the country. Portman characterized Whitehead's critics as "purists, idealists, and academic theorists," and praised the Festival for resolutely pursuing its unique mandate, and for "unabashedly and unrepentantly embracing the entertainment aspect of theatre." For this, said Portman, the Festival "should be honoured rather than chastised."

The Festival board remained supportive of Whitehead during the controversy – at least publicly – and invited him to plan the 1978 season. But Whitehead was aware (as he recalled

in an interview in 1997) of growing board dissatisfaction with the low level of Canada Council support, and with his reputation (fair or not) for favouring the "frivolous" over the serious in his programming.

RESIGNATION, 1977 Whitehead decided that it was time to go. His resignation was announced by the Festival on August 24, 1977. The appreciation of Whitehead's contribution to the Festival expressed by Calvin Rand in the press release was genuine and fully supported by the record. The steady and consistent growth in the length of each season, the increased international reputation of the Festival, the tours, the new theatre – all achieved, said Rand, with responsible budgeting. Only two of Whitehead's ten seasons ended with deficits (small ones of $11,000 in 1973 and $7000 in 1974), and box office achieved "a phenomenal average" of 90 percent over those years. (On another occasion, Rand described Whitehead as "one of those amazing artistic directors who was very stingy with the buck.")

The press release ended with the announcement that *Thark*, a farce by British playwright Ben Travers, would be held over for an extra week of performances. Appropriately, some of his critics might have thought, Whitehead's final appearance at the Festival was as Captain Edstaston in *Thark* at the Festival Theatre on October 9, 1977.

CHAPTER 5   TRANSITION: RICHARD KIRSCHNER, 1978, AND LESLIE YEO, 1979

RICHARD KIRSCHNER   Five days after Whitehead's resignation, the appointment of his successor was announced: Richard Kirschner. Not only was the rapidity of the decision surprising (as with Whitehead's appointment, there was no formal search process), but a radically different leadership structure was also precipitously put in place. Kirschner's title was Producer, which, as Calvin Rand explained in a press release on August 29, 1977, meant that Kirschner would have "the overall responsibility for both artistic and administrative direction of the Festival." This was, Rand conceded, "a major change in policy for the Shaw Festival," but one which was "appropriate, at this stage of our development, in order to foster growth and expansion of the Festival and provide greater service to the Canadian Arts community."

Kirschner had been appointed executive director of the Festival in January 1976, having previously served as managing director of the Annenberg Center in Philadelphia and program director for the First American Congress of Theatre in New York. During his twenty months at the Festival before he succeeded Whitehead, Kirschner had helped secure federal and provincial government grants to eliminate the capital debt on the Festival Theatre and to reduce the operating deficit, but he had also experienced – and protested against – pressure from the Canada Council to "Canadianize" the Festival.

His specific task now was – somehow – to maintain the core mandate and artistic policies pursued by Whitehead, while responding to the concerns of the Canada Council and others who were demanding more Canadian content at the Festival. Thus, said the August 29th press release, "individual artists will be selected on the basis of talent and suitability for the job," but the Festival will, "in employment practices," at the same time "provide first opportunity for Canadians." And while Kirschner and the board reconfirmed the Festival mandate of producing the plays of Shaw and his contemporaries, there would, "from time to time," be plays from outside the mandate. These would include "a new Canadian play," to be commissioned "during the course of this next season" – a promise that would go unfulfilled.

Kirschner lost no time in promoting the Festival's revised agenda. He told Gina Mallet that he would initiate "a major commitment to developing Canadian talent," that "Canadian actors will be first choice," and that he had in mind "a couple of Canadian playwrights" (unnamed) to approach with commissions for new plays. His commitment to Canadian actors didn't prevent him, however, from telling Mallet that he wanted to bring Norwegian film star Liv Ullmann to the Festival to play the lead in Shaw's *Saint Joan*.

Ullmann never came, but Canadian actors did – to the extent that the 1978 company, for the first time in the Festival's history, was all-Canadian, headed by Kate Reid, Frances Hyland, and – making his first appearance at the Festival – Douglas Campbell.

Kirschner also seemed determined to distance himself and the Festival even further from Whitehead by selecting a season that had a "heavyweight" rather than "lightweight" feel about it. Of the four plays chosen by Kirschner, only the Victorian melodrama, *Lady Audley's Secret*, could be said to be undemanding. He put that in the Court House Theatre, and in the Festival Theatre he scheduled *Heartbreak House* (with Douglas Campbell as Shotover), *Major Barbara* (with Janet Amos as Barbara), and Ibsen's *John Gabriel Borkman* (with Campbell and Frances Hyland as the Borkmans and Kate Reid as Ella Rentheim). No Whitehead "frivolity" here.

But not many audience members, either. *Lady Audley's Secret* was a popular hit, but despite the acting talent that Kirschner had assembled, the three Festival Theatre plays fared badly at the box office, particularly the dour Ibsen tragedy about a disgraced financier whose lust for money and power ruins the lives of those around him. The *Borkman* production incurred a loss of $103,000, the season overall lost more than $200,000, and the accumulated operating deficit rose to $460,000.

Well before those final figures were known, however, Kirschner had shocked everyone by resigning. Anticipating financial problems with the season, the board had told Kirschner early in 1978 to reduce costs, a directive that Kirschner took to be a vote of no confidence. In a terse statement on March 5, 1978, Calvin Rand announced that Kirschner would leave the Festival in December, though he would stay in his position throughout the 1978 season. It was left to Kirschner to tell the press what – from his point of view – the problem was. It was, he said, lack of money "to operate a first-class quality theatre." "Without adequate funds to finance future seasons," he said, "I would have no choice but to curtail the quality and scope of our program. I am unwilling to preside over such an operation." Kirschner didn't spell it out, but he was not-too-subtly criticizing the board for failing to raise enough money to cover the costs of the season he had planned.

There were different perspectives on the Kirschner situation. In retrospect, Calvin Rand later reflected, it was clear that the board had allowed itself to be "talked into" appointing Kirschner without sufficient thought, and had too easily gone along with his ideas to "really sock it to the critics and do a heavy, serious, weighty season." *John Gabriel Borkman* in particular, Rand thought, "was awful, an absolute disaster," and Rand also thought that Kirschner's policy of hiring only Canadian actors backfired badly when it became clear that actors accus-

tomed to working with new plays in Toronto's small alternate theatres just couldn't cope with major roles in classical plays in the large Festival Theatre. It was, Rand concluded, all in all "a terrible season."

The crisis that had been developing towards the end of Paxton Whitehead's term as artistic director had, then, been deepened, not alleviated, by the appointment of Richard Kirschner.

LESLIE YEO The Festival's press release on March 5, 1978, announcing Kirschner's resignation also said that a search committee for his successor had already been set up and was "currently considering candidates." Three months later (on June 12, 1978) the Festival announced that the search for Kirschner's successor had successfully concluded with the appointment of Christopher Newton, artistic director of the Vancouver Playhouse. Because of Newton's other commitments, however, the appointment wasn't effective until January 1, 1980, leaving the Festival in a quandary about the 1979 season.

In the meantime, Kirschner was still in charge of the 1978 season. Among the actors that he hired was Leslie Yeo, who played Boss Mangan in *Heartbreak House*. In hiring Yeo, Kirschner unwittingly both solved the problem of the 1979 season and hastened his departure from the Festival.

Yeo was no stranger to the Festival. He had acted in *Man and Superman* and *Misalliance* in 1966, in *The Circle* in 1967, and in *Arms and the Man* and *The Apple Cart* in 1976, the season in which he also directed *Mrs Warren's Profession*. Although British-born and trained, Yeo had some thirty years of acting and directing experience in Canadian theatre – including running his own professional company in Newfoundland for several years in the 1950s – and on this basis he seemed to Newton to be the obvious choice to take charge of the Festival pending his own arrival. Thus, on Newton's advice, Rand announced on July 26, 1978, that Yeo had been appointed "guest artistic director" for 1979.

This meant that the Festival now had a producer (Kirschner), a guest artistic director (Yeo), and an artistic director designate (Newton).

To reduce the crowd at the top, Rand asked Yeo to assume responsibilities as guest artistic director prior to the end of the 1978 season, and negotiated an early exit with Kirschner. Yeo, whose appointment was approved by the board on July 25, 1978, then set about planning the 1979 season in consultation with, but not under the direction of, Newton. Unlike Tony van Bridge, who deliberately avoided any innovations during his term as acting artistic director for the 1975 season, Yeo made it clear that he wanted to leave his mark on the Festival. Being a stop-gap artistic director was "a thankless job," Yeo told Rand: "If I make a great success, you can't keep me on, but I don't intend to sit here with a holding pattern, because that's not the way I'm made." He was not, he said, "an interim sort of guy."

When Yeo outlined his plans to the press in September 1978 he was adamant that "one thing is certain about next season," and that was that the Festival "will be carefully budgeted for a profit." He had several strategies to achieve that profit. One was to reverse the reversal that Kirschner had put in place. Yeo wanted the Festival "to entertain rather than educate." "Heavier work" (an oblique reference to Kirschner's choice of plays for 1978) was "for another year," and even then, in Yeo's view at least, such plays should have "a limited number of performances." Yeo also significantly increased the number of productions in the season, from a previous maximum of five to seven in 1979, and – his major innovation – he introduced lunchtime theatre to the Festival.

Yeo's 1979 season was unveiled on October 2, 1978. It consisted of three Shaw plays: *You Never Can Tell* (the Festival's third production of the play), *Captain Brassbound's Conversion* (a Festival premiere), and *Village Wooing* (the Festival's second production, and its first-ever lunchtime show). There were also two Shaw-related shows: Jerome Kilty's *Dear Liar*, based on the correspondence of Shaw and actress Mrs Patrick Campbell, and a one-man portrait of Shaw by Michael Voysey, *My Astonishing Self*, performed by Donal Donnelly. The two non-Shaw plays were Emlyn Williams' 1940 play about the education of a young Welsh miner, *The Corn is Green*, and Noel Coward's *Blithe Spirit*, the first full-length Coward done at the Festival.

Yeo directed *Blithe Spirit* and *The Corn is Green*, while Tony van Bridge (*You Never Can Tell*), Douglas Campbell (*Dear Liar, Captain Brassbound's Conversion*), and young Edmonton director Scott Swan (*Village Wooing*) handled Shaw. Like Kirschner, Yeo eschewed

imported stars, although Irish actor Donal Donnelly was a familiar figure on Broadway in the 1960s and 70s (in, for example, the plays of Brian Friel and, for a three-year run, in Anthony Shaffer's *Sleuth*). Donnelly directed himself in *My Astonishing Self*.

In the 1979 season brochure Yeo described his season as offering "the widest range of emotional and intellectual appeal," and promised Festival audiences "some of the finest summer entertainment in North America." For the most part, audiences liked what Yeo gave them.

The lunchtime experiment, for example, was successful, eliciting critical praise for the show's two actors (Merrilyn Gann and Jack Medley) and drawing an 85 percent box office. The two full-length Shaws also did well. Critic Jamie Portman found van Bridge's direction of *You Never Can Tell* "too often heavy-fisted and obvious" in a production that has "all the sensitivity of a sledgehammer." But that didn't seem to bother audiences, who bought 90 percent of tickets for the run (fifty-five performances) in the Festival Theatre. The less familiar *Captain Brassbound's Conversion* had a shorter run (thirty-five performances), but it achieved an impressive 81 percent box office, also in the Festival Theatre.

But the big box office hit of Yeo's season was *Blithe Spirit*, which filled nearly 98 percent of the Court House Theatre for its fifty-one performances – even though critics were lukewarm about the production ("almost worth the jaunt" to Niagara-on-the-Lake, was Ray Conlogue's muted praise in the *Globe and Mail*). *Blithe Spirit* went off on its own jaunt at the end of the season, touring to upstate New York, more than a dozen communities in Ontario, and to Montreal.

Yeo had promised a profit, and he delivered it – sort of. In a press release on October 1, 1979, Yeo had predicted ("promised" was his word) that "when the final count is made in December, the Festival will end up with the largest one-year surplus in its eighteen-year history." What the final count showed, however, was a season deficit of over $175,000, bringing the Festival's accumulated deficit at the end of the year to $635,901. Nonetheless, Yeo's one-season achievement was considerable. Box office revenue hit a new record level of over $1.4 million, representing 81 percent of total box office potential, and came in at over $200,000 above budget. The budget problems related not to box office, but to increased administrative expenses and shortfalls in fundraising and government grants.

Leslie Yeo had done all that could reasonably be expected in his one season at the helm. There had not been a great deal of critical acclaim for his season, but he had halted the box office hemorrhaging, and morale at the Festival had bounced back after the problems of 1978. New board Chair Jack Mackenzie (who had replaced Calvin Rand in 1978) had good reason to thank Yeo at the end of the season for the box office success and for "encouraging marvellous enthusiasm on the part of performers and staff."

There remained, however, huge artistic and financial issues for Yeo's successor to address. Whither the Shaw Festival under Christopher Newton's leadership? No one could be sure (including Newton), but the beginnings were far from auspicious.

CHAPTER 6   CHRISTOPHER NEWTON, 1980–2002

UNCERTAIN BEGINNINGS   A search committee – chaired by Calvin Rand – to find someone to replace Richard Kirschner was set up by the executive committee of the board on February 27, 1978. Unlike previous searches, this one started with a list of names of possible candidates, all of whom were Canadians or had substantial experience of working in Canadian theatre. Rand and Festival board chair Jack Mackenzie were given a mandate to consult within the Canadian cultural community on possible candidates, and to approach some of them directly to determine their interest in the position of artistic director of the Shaw Festival. The search committee gave a progress report to board members on May 27, 1978, informing them that an offer had been made to a candidate, but not naming the candidate, who, the board was advised, might not in any case be available until 1980. Just over two weeks later, on June 12, 1978, the candidate was identified as Christopher Newton (though his appointment was not formally approved by the board until July 25, 1978).

Newton's extensive and accomplished experience in Canada was outlined in the press release announcing his appointment. British-born, he had done graduate work in English Literature in the United States, and then had begun an acting career with the Canadian Players and, briefly, with the Shaw Festival (in 1964). In 1968 he became founding artistic director of Theatre Calgary, before his 1973 appointment as artistic director of the Vancouver Playhouse, which, said the press release, he "totally restructured," including the creation of a professional acting school. Newton had also worked on the Theatre Advisory Board of the Canada Council, a valuable asset for the Festival in light of the Council's lack of enthusiasm for the Festival's work under Paxton Whitehead.

Newton's commitments to the Vancouver Playhouse meant that he could not take up his appointment at the Shaw Festival until January 1, 1980. Mackenzie expressed delight, nonetheless, that "a man whose initiative and drive, both as an actor and director, have been instrumental in the development of the regional theatre movement in Western Canada" would be coming to the Festival. Mackenzie was confident that Newton's "intelligence and sensitivity will successfully mould the artistic future of the Festival."

It had taken less than two months to select and appoint Newton, but he wasn't as easy a catch at it might have seemed. Newton recalls being visited by Rand and Mackenzie at the Vancouver Playhouse. He was playing Malvolio in *Twelfth Night* at the time, "a rather exotic Malvolio in lederhosen." He was "getting out my lederhosen" when Rand and Mackenzie appeared in his dressing room to ask if he would "take over the Festival." The answer was no. Newton told them that in his view "all of the energies of the Festival had gone into making the new theatre and they had sort of lost their way in what they were actually putting on in the theatre." And besides, he was "very happy" in Vancouver. And so "they asked me again," and the answer was still no. And then they asked a third time.

The persistence of Rand and Mackenzie paid off to the extent that Newton agreed to visit Niagara-on-the-Lake. He "walked around" the Festival Theatre and "became disgusted" with the gardens, and it was "actually looking at the gardens and realizing that something could be done with them" he said, "that caused me to say 'yes'."

Newton also realized, of course, that "something could be done" with the Festival itself. Indeed, something *had* to be done if, as Newton (and many others) believed, it had "lost [its] way." But what? And how? And how quickly?

"A GOOD COAT HANGER"   Newton had over eighteen months to think about what he would do at the Festival, but one thing that he didn't need time to figure out was his antipathy towards Shaw himself – or at least to the Shaw he had experienced in Britain and North America. It didn't seem a good strategy for a prospective artistic director of the Shaw Festival to tell the chair of the board and the chair of the search committee that he felt this way about Shaw, but when asked by Rand and Mackenzie if he liked Shaw's plays, Newton, "without missing a beat," Mackenzie recalled, replied "Not very much." Newton had seen several Shaw plays at the Shaw Festival and thought them "terrible." "They were all sung or treated as bad Oscar Wilde," he said. Newton later told Shaw Festival literary advisor Dan Laurence that he had sat through too many productions of Shaw's plays "hearing simply the wash of syllables, devoid of passion, devoid of meaning, comforting an audience with flippancy and easy attacks on obvious targets." Something had to be done to make Shaw dangerous again, to get beyond the laughs, to create not comfort in the audience, but discomfort. Newton had reassured Rand and Mackenzie that he wasn't proposing to eliminate Shaw from the Shaw Festival (though he did subsequently raise the possibility of changing the Festival's name to the Niagara-on-the-Lake Festival), but his plays had to be presented to modern audiences in "a more profound manner."

The best Newton could initially say for Shaw was that he was "a good coat hanger" for other playwrights of the Festival mandate period, but Newton wasn't sure yet what coats could or should be hung on it. As Newton saw it, the Festival's mandate was supposed to be "Shaw and his contemporaries," so for his first season with the Festival he "threw caution to the wind" and said "let's see what comes of all this."

CHRISTOPHER NEWTON, 1980.
PHOTO BY DAVID COOPER.

NEWTON'S FIRST SEASON, 1980   An eclectic array of plays, with no obvious focus, Newton's first season consisted of a record ten productions: three Shaws (*Misalliance*, *The Philanderer*, and *Overruled*), a Chekhov (*The Cherry Orchard*), a French farce (Feydeau's *A Flea in Her Ear*), a musical (an Irving Berlin compilation of music and lyrics titled *Puttin' on the Ritz*), a Brecht (*A Respectable Wedding*), a Hungarian comedy (*The Grand Hunt*, by Gyula Hernády), a one-man show (Heath Lamberts in *Gunga Heath*), and a Canadian play (John Bruce Cowan's *Canuck*).

Just as Newton wasn't sure what would come from the season, so audiences, board members, and critics weren't sure what to make of it. In some ways, apart from the sheer size of the season, there was nothing especially new about it. Shaw was now, for the first time, in a minority (three plays out of ten), but three Shaws wasn't a significant reduction from previous seasons. As for the non-Shaw plays, there had been farce before (including Feydeau), there had been musicals, one-man shows, Canadian content, and European plays (including the esoteric *Summer Days* in 1971). But there were some hidden surprises in the season, surprises – shocks more than surprises to some – that marked profound change in the Festival's values.

The season began in the Festival Theatre conventionally enough with three well-known plays: *Misalliance*, *The Cherry Orchard*, and *A Flea in Her Ear*. Newton directed *Misalliance* himself (the first Shaw play he had ever directed), and brought Carole Shelley back to the Festival to play Lina Szczepanowska – a clear, though perhaps unintended, link with the Whitehead years. Shelley was supported by another link to the Festival's past, the experienced Sandy Webster as Tarleton. Set designer Cameron Porteous, on the other hand, was a newcomer – a migrant with Newton from Vancouver, one of a group of Newton's Vancouver colleagues who, as tensions around Newton's leadership grew, came to be known as the "Vancouver mafia." It was during rehearsals for *Misalliance* that Newton discovered sex in Shaw ("when in doubt, look for the sex," he told his actors). This, coupled with "some uproarious stage business," helped "blow away the tedium" from a play that has more talk than action, said Mackenzie Porter, and heralded a "fresh approach to Shavian comedy" at the Festival. Don Rubin (*Canadian Theatre Review*) detected a fresh approach as well, though he thought it came from textual insights rather than stage business, Newton's handling of the text delving into "the dark places…the magic places" of the play. Audiences were given a "profound Shaw," a Shaw deeply concerned with human relationships, Rubin said. That wasn't a universally held view of the season's opening play (Ray Conlogue of the *Globe and Mail* found the whole thing "lethargic"), but the disagreements were largely carefully considered critical differences of opinion, very different in tone from some criticism Newton would soon encounter.

Romanian director Radu Penciulescu's *Cherry Orchard* similarly divided the critics – "fractionalized and often self-contradictory…impossible to judge what the director has in mind," concluded Frank Rich in *The New York Times*; a "flawless" cast that allows you to "listen to the heartbeat of the play," countered Jacob Siskind in the *Ottawa Journal*. Don Rubin argued that the politically charged adaptation of *The Cherry Orchard* by left-wing British playwright Trevor Griffiths skewed the play, but all (or nearly all) was forgiven by the ending created by Penciulescu and designer Astrid Janson. As the axes were heard chopping down the cherry trees, "the lace set begins, piece by piece, to fall as well, leaving behind it only an empty and pathetic theatre stage." This was, Rubin wrote, "a stunning vision…with an intelligence clearly controlling it all."

But the third Festival Theatre play, *A Flea in Her Ear*, directed by Derek Goldby like "a speeded-up comic opera" was, with only a few exceptions, a critical success, and certainly a box office winner.

So far, so good – or so bad, depending on expectations and perspectives. There had been nothing in the opening shows to suggest radical change. Newton wasn't taking any serious risks in the Festival Theatre, on which the Festival heavily depended for box office revenue. The smaller Royal George and Court House theatres were, however, another matter.

The Royal George plays began on June 24 with a preview performance of Irving Berlin's *Puttin' on the Ritz*, directed by Don Shipley. There were mixed reviews again of this assemblage of Berlin's music and lyrics, performed by four singers and three musicians. Significantly, however, Clive Barnes, who didn't care for the "gimmicky" production that became "tiresome and tiring," nonetheless thought that the important thing about this innovative, unconventional show was "not how well it was done, but that it was done at all." "Times," he said "are changing in Niagara-on-the-Lake, and the Shaw Festival is clearly on the move." But where to?

***A RESPECTABLE WEDDING*, 1980**   One answer – a bombshell of an answer – was provided across the street at the Court House Theatre the next night, June 25, when previews began of Brecht's *A Respectable Wedding*, a 1919 satirical farce by Shaw's German Marxist contemporary that Newton had staged in Vancouver in 1979. The play mocks bourgeoisie pretensions, especially those surrounding marriage, exposing (in Brecht's view) its hypocrisy, sentimentality, and shallow idealism. The wedding day for the pregnant bride and her groom turns from the hoped-for happiest day of their lives to a day in hell. Aggression, hostility, and lust trump joy and celebration.

In tune with much that Shaw believed and expressed about marriage in his prefaces and plays (*Getting Married*, for example, which Paxton Whitehead had directed at the Festival in 1972), *A Respectable Wedding* was bound to be intrinsically offensive to some, but Newton and director Derek Goldby wanted to make sure that the farcical elements (e.g., chairs breaking when people sit on them) didn't override the play's biting satire. Thus a notice in the lobby of the Court House advised audience members that the production "contains scenes and dialogue that may offend some people. It is not suitable for children."

Indeed it wasn't. One scene in particular provoked the biggest furore ever experienced at the Festival. Goldby had the bridegroom, laughing hysterically, thrust under his drunk and prostrate bride's wedding gown with the neck of a wine bottle.

The response was predictable. Joan Draper, a long-time Festival volunteer, who found the play "ragged and startling" and "didn't enjoy it personally," still thought it "not to be missed."

It was, she said, "well worth attending a performance to see the audience response." "The hissing sound produced by the intake of breath [in response to the crude language] became part of the sound effects," and the rape scene with the wine bottle regularly caused "a stampede out of the theatre by a number of patrons." At the first preview the stage manager's report records that about a dozen people left during the rape scene, and at least that many during the curtain call. One group was lead out by Patricia Rand, wife of the chair of the search committee that had recommended Newton's appointment. Box office staff – not used to this kind of thing – were told to advise ticket holders who asked for a refund *before* the show that they would get one (a cheque in the mail – "do not give them cash"), but those who left *during* the performance were out of luck. "It will be up to you to handle the situation as diplomatically as possible," the staff were unhelpfully advised.

"It had to be done," Newton said. "We had to make a statement." And it was a statement that was welcomed as well as repudiated. The production was a "masterpiece," said Doug Bale in the *London* [Ontario] *Free Press* (a city and a newspaper hardly known as Marxist sympathizers). "That is not to say that you will necessarily like it. You may hate it. It is not a play to bring your children to, nor your stuffy uncle, nor your pious and elderly maiden aunt." But, Bale concluded, in a not-too-subtle knock at the Festival's pre-Newton reputation (and with a nod to a famous French *bon-mot* about the Charge of the Light Brigade, "c'est magnifique, mais ce n'est pas la guerre") – "c'est magnifique, mais ce n'est pas fluff."

The three other productions in 1980 at the Court House Theatre were placidly received by comparison, but they weren't without problems from the point of view of an increasingly nervous board. *Canuck*, by British Columbia playwright John Bruce Cowan, first published in 1931, was the Festival's second venture into Canadian drama, and, like the first (*Leaven of Malice*, by Roberston Davies, in 1975), a flop. Shaw's *The Philanderer*, directed by another Vancouver migrant, Paul Reynolds, with Newton in the title role, was mauled by the critics, and there were reports of some audience members walking out in boredom. And the minor Shaw piece *Overruled*, about two married couples enamoured with each others' spouses, a lunchtime production also directed by Reynolds, was dismissed variously as "trivial," "tedious," and "leaden."

The final production of Newton's inaugural season was another risky venture. *The Grand Hunt*, a 1975 play by the little-known Hungarian playwright Gyula Hernády (translated by Suzanne Grossmann), deals with the even less familiar subject of the politics of the Hapsburg Empire. The risk was reduced by limiting the run to just fifteen performances (though they were in the Festival Theatre), and bringing in the experienced John Hirsch (soon to become artistic director of the Stratford Festival) to direct the play. Not a box office success, the production still served the valuable purpose of continuing to expand the boundaries of the identity of the Shaw Festival. *The Grand Hunt*, said one critic, was "quite out of character for the Shaw Festival, and it's about time." Newton emphasized the point about the Festival's identity by taking *The Grand Hunt* on a post-season tour to Ottawa and Seattle.

Attendance for the 1980 season dropped from the 1979 figure of 83.5 percent to 81 percent, which, given the addition of the Royal George Theatre for 1980, was neither surprising nor alarming. The bigger issue was Newton's future at the Festival. Newton had quite intentionally alienated some segments of the Festival's audience base, and he had made it very clear that provocation – intellectual, moral, political – was central to his sense of what the Shaw Festival should be. Could he find the audience to support this vision? Would the board give him the time to do it? Was he really committed to the struggle?

THE PAVILION CONTROVERSY

At a meeting of the board's Artistic Relations Committee on October 5, 1980 – the last day of the 1980 season – Newton explained that he didn't think he could achieve his objective of redefining the Festival without the creation of a permanent acting ensemble. Forty of the fifty-eight actors in the 1980 season (and all twelve of the season's directors and designers) were new to the Festival. At the annual meeting of the Festival on January 23, 1981, having had time to reflect on the 1980 season (of which, he said, he was "very proud"), Newton elaborated on his objectives. In addition to reiterating his strong preference for an ensemble rather than a star-oriented company, he explained that he believed that "producing theatre for sheer entertainment is robbery," and that "we must remember that Shaw was a revolutionary." "We must look at the Festival's development with this in mind," he said. He also made it clear that in his view the typical Festival audience lacked sophistication. He wanted to "turn around at least 15 percent" of the present audience, so that they can "help us educate others who come here as to what theatre is about and what it is they are seeing: entertainment provided by a good theatre company versus merely entertaining theatre."

Newton's 1981 season would test the viability of these objectives, but planning that season was complicated by uncertainty about the Festival's access to the Court House Theatre, scheduled to undergo renovations. This uncertainty created headaches that Newton didn't need, not just the headaches about planning the season, but headaches – migraines might be a better word – about Festival-community relations. The troubles caused by disagreements about the location of the Festival Theatre in the 1960s and early 1970s were about to start all over again.

In the summer of 1980 the Festival board became aware that a major renovation of the Court House was planned as a Niagara-on-the-Lake bicentennial celebration project (the town was founded in 1781). This would mean that the Court House would not be available to the Festival for the 1981 season, and perhaps not for any subsequent seasons unless the Festival was prepared to make a significant investment in the costs of including an ongoing theatre facility as part of the renovations. (As things turned out, $1.7 million worth of renovations – completed by November 1984 – were carried out without disruption to the Festival's access to the Court House, and without cost to the Festival, but also without any permanent theatre facilities in the building.)

But even if the Festival remained in the Court House (with its approximately 380 seats), the Festival would not have sufficient capacity in its three theatres, Newton argued, to meet the heavy demand for tickets in July and August each year. At a board meeting on August 15, 1980, Newton proposed, therefore, that the Festival consider erecting what he described as "a temporary (or completely moveable) tent-like structure of steel and canvas." Known formally as a "pavilion," but in most subsequent public discussions as the "tent," the structure that Newton had in mind would, he estimated, cost about $400,000 with a seating capacity of about 650 and a thrust stage. That would generate, Newton calculated, something like $550,000 a season in box office revenue, compared to about $340,000 a season at the Court House. The location would be adjacent to the Festival Theatre on the Commons, land owned by the federal government and operated by Parks Canada. Parks Canada had been approached with the idea, and "the reaction appeared favourable." It would be possible, Newton assured the board, to have the structure in place for the 1981 season and would serve the Festival's needs for the foreseeable future.

The idea of an additional performance space on the Commons wasn't new. An amphitheatre structure had been included in a development study conducted for the Festival by Lett/Smith Architects in 1979, a study that had also included consideration of a 500-seat studio theatre added to the north end of the Festival Theatre. Nothing had come of those proposals, but the board now gave approval for Newton to explore the idea of a Commons pavilion.

He did, and by the following January Newton's assistant, Paul Reynolds, had a slide presentation of the new theatre ready for the board and the Town Council. By then it was clear that planning approvals could not be concluded in time for the tent to be ready for the 1981 season, but, fortunately, renovations to the Court House had been delayed so it was available as usual to the Festival for the upcoming season. And it did prove possible for Cameron Porteous's design for a thrust rather than proscenium stage in the Court House Theatre – a design that allowed Newton much more flexibility with his programming – to be implemented in time for the opening performance there on July 4, 1981 (*In Good King Charles's Golden Days*, directed by Paul Bettis).

There was a full discussion of the tent project at a board meeting on April 24, 1981. Costs were rising – now up to $700,000 (and would continue to rise to over a million dollars) – but the Province of Ontario had committed $250,000 to the project, and the federal government seemed likely to provide support as well. The board therefore "approved in principle" moving ahead with the plans.

There had still been little public involvement or consultation about the proposal, however. Public meetings were being scheduled, but Reynolds knew that trouble was brewing. He told the board in May that he was already aware of "strong criticism" in the community of a plan that would use up more of the Commons space.

WENDY THATCHER; ROBIN CRAIG AND
JACK MEDLEY; HEATH LAMBERTS AND
BARRY MACGREGOR IN *TONS OF MONEY*
BY WILL EVANS AND VALENTINE, 1981.
DIRECTED BY DEREK GOLDBY, DESIGNED
BY GUIDO TONDINO, LIGHTING DESIGN-
ED BY NICK CERNOVITCH. PHOTOS BY
DAVID COOPER.

The 1981 Festival brochure described the tent project as "an exciting expansion" that would coincide with the Festival's twenty-first anniversary season (1982). The tent was necessary, the brochure explained, because incorporating a theatre into the Court House renovations would be "prohibitively expensive." Based not on the famous Stratford Festival tent, but on the more recent Théâtre du Bois de Coulonge in Quebec City, the Shaw Festival tent, patrons were told, would "evoke the historic tents which dotted the Commons many years ago."

But if the Festival thought that this nostalgic appeal to the town's military past would soften resistance they were much mistaken. In June and July letters critical of the Festival once more began to fill the pages of the local press. Some prominent Festival supporters were among the most vocal opponents. Patricia Rand wrote to the *Niagara Advance* on June 24, 1981, to praise the views across the open Commons and to urge that "nothing should be built" to destroy them. And then Jean Marsh, who had hosted the meeting in February 1962 at which the Festival was conceived, wrote to say that she was "saddened, embarrassed, and now disgusted by the burgeoning mess our once pleasing little theatre has become."

There was some support for the tent – an editorial in the *Niagara Falls Review*, for example, on July 22, 1981 – but the Festival was now in damage control mode about what one writer called this "monument to artistic director Christopher Newton." Reynolds conceded that "an undercurrent of mistrust and misunderstanding" had grown between the Festival and the town. He expected to have things thrown at him, he said, as he walked down Queen Street. Newton said that two actors had been "ragged" in the street.

And so it went, back and forth, just as it had a decade and more ago, but the Festival was very much on the defensive against well-organized groups such as CASE (Citizens Against Shaw Expansion) and ACTION (Associated Townspeople in Old Niagara). Newton wrote to the *Niagara Advance* with a plea that the proposal for the tent theatre be discussed "in a civilized fashion," and when the national press started to take an interest he complained to the *Globe and Mail*'s Ray Conlogue that the controversy went beyond simply the issue of the tent theatre. "There's a faction," he said, in Niagara-on-the-Lake that "hates the Festival absolutely, and writes filthy letters to the editor about it." Another faction was opposed to him personally, he claimed, "and what they see as the avant-garde direction I'm leading the Festival in." In an interview with the *Toronto Star*'s Gina Mallet, Newton described Niagara-on-the-Lake and its small-town conservatism as "the kind of space I ran away from" [in England]. The *Toronto Sun*'s McKenzie Porter (who lived in Niagara-on-the-Lake) weighed in with an assault on the "tacky tent." He sympathized with citizens who feared the loss of land on which they "have walked their dogs, ridden their horses, and romped with their children for 200 years." And, inevitably, Porter glumly predicted, "vendors of hamburgers, ice cream, and stuffed toys will want to set up their stands around the tent," adding to "the several schlockshops and greasy spoons" on Queen Street.

It was a no-win situation for the Festival and for Newton. The board met on August 17, 1981, and issued a press release on August 21. The release stated that the board remained committed to "a low-cost, portable theatre structure" as a cost-effective alternative to returning to a renovated Court House, but the proposal to locate the structure on the Commons was withdrawn. Other possible sites in Niagara-on-the-Lake would be investigated, the board said. They were, but priority soon moved to negotiations with the town for ongoing use of the Court House for the 1982 season and beyond. Once that was confirmed, the addition of more seats to the Royal George Theatre was seen as the best means of increasing the overall seating capacity in the Festival's theatres.

Newton was, to put it mildly, annoyed and depressed by the row over the tent. In his interview with Gina Mallet in August 1981 he said that he wasn't convinced that the Festival had a viable economic base for what he wanted to achieve, in which case his interest in carrying on beyond his initial three-year contract was "moot."

Newton also added, ominously, that the hostile reaction to *Saint Joan* in his 1981 season (see below), following on the similar reaction to *A Respectable Wedding* in 1980, had left him wondering not so much about whether what he was doing was worth doing, but whether he was doing it "in the wrong place."

MORE TURBULENCE

With one or two exceptions, the consensus seemed to be that Newton hadn't handled Shaw particularly well in his first season, either as director of *Misalliance* or as artistic director in his choice of the other Shaw plays (*The Philanderer* and *Overruled*) and their director (Paul Reynolds). For the 1981 season Newton nonetheless kept himself and Reynolds as directors of two Shaw plays – *Saint Joan* and *The Man of Destiny* – but brought in a young director named Paul Bettis to direct the third Shaw play, *In Good King Charles's Golden Days*. Both *Saint Joan* and *In Good King Charles's Golden Days* were Festival premieres.

The Man of Destiny, a short play about Napoleon and "A Strange Lady" he meets on one of his campaigns, was well received in its lunchtime slot at the Royal George, well enough to set Reynolds off on a multi-year relationship with Shaw's one-act plays at the Royal George. *In Good King Charles's Golden Days* was also well received, Bettis drawing from a strong cast the energy and conviction essential for this notoriously talky play to succeed. Notable among that cast were two actors making their Shaw Festival debuts in 1981 and who stayed on to become core members of the Festival acting ensemble – Goldie Semple and David Schurmann.

SAINT JOAN, 1981   It was remarkable that the Shaw Festival was in its twentieth season before *Saint Joan*, one of Shaw's greatest plays, was produced. Previous artistic directors had not thought the play workable on the small Court House Theatre stage, but even when the Festival Theatre became available none of the artistic directors who had access to that space – Paxton Whitehead, Tony van Bridge, Richard Kirschner, and Leslie Yeo – took it on. To a greater extent than any other Shaw play, *Saint Joan* is dominated by one character, and no director will attempt the play without being confident that he or she has the right Joan.

Newton was not only confident that he had the right Joan (Nora McLellan), but also the right designer (Cameron Porteous), the right space (the Festival Theatre), and the right idea about what to do with the play. His confidence was sorely challenged by the controversies that erupted around the production.

The problems began even before *Saint Joan* opened. The play concludes with an Epilogue, in which Joan returns in a vision to the Dauphin (now the King) twenty-five years after her death, and the consequences of her life (and death) are discussed with the King and Joan's friends and enemies. About halfway through rehearsals, Newton decided that the Epilogue was redundant. In his view it added nothing to what has already been said in the play. So he cut it from the production. What Newton hadn't reckoned with, however, was the Shaw Estate, which held copyright on Shaw's plays in Canada (which didn't expire until 2000, fifty years after Shaw's death). The Society of Authors, representing the Shaw Estate, was advised by the Estate's Literary and Dramatic Advisor, the formidable Shaw scholar Dan H. Laurence, not to approve Newton's decision. To cut the Epilogue, Laurence said, was "a violation of the integrity of the work," and he insisted (through the Society of Authors) that it must be restored, or the licence to do *Saint Joan* would be revoked.

Newton was not amused, and he was initially adamant that the production would go ahead as he had planned it. Eventually, however, he complied (he really had no choice) with Laurence's directive – but on his own terms. *Saint Joan* began previews on May 7, 1981, and opened on May 27. Audiences were intrigued and, no doubt, puzzled by a note in the program:

> In compliance with the edict from the Society of Authors, the Epilogue to *Saint Joan* will be performed at the end of the evening for those who wish to see it. At the conclusion of the main action there will be a ten-minute intermission. The Epilogue lasts approximately twenty-five minutes.

The curious who stayed (more than half of the audience did so on opening night, somewhat lower numbers for subsequent performances) witnessed the actors – still in costume – read the Epilogue from lecterns. And although Newton included the Epilogue reluctantly, once the decision was made to do a pared-down performance he and the actors took it seriously. Many audience members were moved by the simplicity of the staging, particularly at moments when, as characters removed themselves from Joan's presence, they blew out candles on their lecterns. Shaw scholar Stanley Weintraub recalls a standing ovation at the performance he attended.

It wasn't, however, the best of ideas for the Festival to have its strong-willed artistic director at loggerheads with the equally strong-willed (and strong-voiced) advisor to the Shaw Estate. A generation separated Newton and Laurence by age, and there were distinct cultural differences between them deriving from their British and American backgrounds. Moreover, Laurence – a passionate and world-renowned Shavian – was well aware of Newton's ambivalence about Shaw. Some kind of rapprochement was needed, and it came from Newton's strategically astute decision to offer Laurence the position of Literary Advisor to the Festival. Laurence accepted (at a salary of one dollar a year, plus expenses), and stayed with the Festival until 1990 (by then as Head of Extramural Studies). During that time the relationship between Newton and Laurence mellowed, and Laurence became a staunch supporter both of the Festival and of Newton's approaches to directing Shaw.

But in the early days of the 1981 season there were other problems with *Saint Joan*. The reviews ran the gamut from laudatory to scathing, with more low notes than high notes. Even reviewers who mostly applauded the production had major reservations about Nora McLellan's Joan. Jamie Portman, for example, praised Newton for fashioning "a bold, provocative, imaginative production, frequently bursting with colour and excitement," but McLellan was a "major stumbling block" to the complete success of the production. Portman thought she played a character with only two dimensions, "obstinance" in the early scenes and "hysterical obstinance" (like a "shrieking fishwife") in the trial scene before Joan is burned at the stake. Other critics commented on ways in which the earthy, colloquial simplicity of McLellan's Joan stripped the character of any sense of spiritual depth or engagement. "One had the feeling," said Bob Pennington in the *Toronto Sun* (in an otherwise positive review of "a must for every theatregoer of intelligence") "of listening to a shrew in a domestic squabble rather than witnessing a cerebral, theological duel to the death with her inquisitors."

McLellan herself had been surprised to be offered the part by Newton. She had spent one season at the Festival (1980, in *Overruled* and *A Respectable Wedding*), but she was known more as a singer than an actor. She concluded that Newton had cast her because he wanted "a very unorthodox reading," which she provided, she said, by portraying Joan as a "nasty peasant girl, not a saint." That upset people, and the show "was universally panned," but she didn't regret the experience – "Chris is a risk taker, that's what I appreciate."

In any case it was Newton himself who took the brunt of the *Saint Joan* criticism. And it was harsh. Gina Mallet in the *Toronto Star* was convinced after *Misalliance* and now *Saint Joan* that "Newton does not have the capacity to be a worthy interpreter of Shaw's plays." *Village Voice* agreed, and went further: "As for Mr Newton, the Shaw Festival should either fire him or change its name – or, ideally, hire a co-director who likes and understands Shaw, and leave Mr Newton free to do what he does well." The *Christian Science Monitor* joined in: "Sad to say, nowhere in the production does Mr Newton give us a sense that he has understood the play. What we have is a stew of traditional (and mostly dull) performances framed in a clichéd avant-gardist theatrical staging. It's not good visually and is unusually gimmicky." And the biggest "gimmick" of all, according to the *Christian Science Monitor* theatre critic Thor Eckert, was the "flagrantly gratuitous male nudity."

The nudity in *Saint Joan* confirmed the worst fears of those audience members who objected to the sex in *A Respectable Wedding* the previous season. Newton introduced the nudity in the scene in *Saint Joan* where the French army is waiting for the wind to change so that they can cross the River Loire to relieve the English siege of Orléans. It wasn't Shaw's idea, but Newton thought it entirely natural that while soldiers have nothing to do but wait, and they are close to water, "they wash, simply because they may not get another chance." And so in the Festival production Newton had a young soldier naked in the river while his officer (Dunois) shaved. "I loved this little scene," Newton recalled some years later. "It was about soldiers and war.... The scene remained true to the words the actors say, true to the ideas, and most important of all, close to a modern audience."

A Buffalo radio station questioned the "necessity for a nude young man who wielded his towel with less dexterity than Sally Rand did her fan" (Sally Rand was an American burlesque dancer famous for her ostrich feather fan dance), and there were more – and predictable – protests from Festival theatregoers.

Things calmed down as other, somewhat less controversial, more lighthearted, shows opened in 1981 – *The Magistrate*, an 1885 farce by Shaw's contemporary Arthur Wing Pinero;

Tons of Money, a 1922 British farce; and *The Suicide*, a 1930 Russian comedy by Nikolai Erdman, this one with sufficient political bite to have caused its suppression in Stalin's Russia (an unemployed worker thinks it better to commit suicide than live under communism). And, as a follow-up to *Puttin' on the Ritz* in 1980, Newton selected a pocket-sized musical for the Royal George Theatre, *Rose Marie*.

CAMILLE, 1981 But the last show to open in 1981 (at the Festival Theatre on August 14) again set the Newtonian cat among the Festival pigeons. The play was *Camille*, by British playwright Robert David MacDonald, a multi-layered and provocative work (that Newton had first staged in Vancouver in 1976) about the consumptive courtesan who appears in Alexandre Dumas *fils*' 1848 novel *La Dame aux Camélias* and Verdi's 1853 opera *La Traviata*.

In stark contrast to the romantic and melodramatic nineteenth-century image of Camille, MacDonald presented the harsh social and sexual realities of the real-life model for Dumas' Camille, a woman named Marie Duplessis (played in the Festival production by Goldie Semple). Audiences were advised that there would be nudity and coarse language in the play, but many were shocked by the scene in which Camille fully disrobes in a crowded ballroom to reveal her naked body to her young lover (played by Joseph Ziegler) – and even more shocked by another scene in which her patron (played by Michael Ball, who had also been in the Vancouver production) forces her to suck his deformed foot to bring him to orgasm. It was not, Ball recalled in a 2010 interview, "a play for the faint of heart," but whatever the public reaction, Newton remained proud of *Camille* for the way in which, in his judgment, the acting company became a true ensemble, showing not just confidence in each other, but generosity and deep trust.

It was during *Camille* that Newton developed what he came to call "balcony acting," a way of giving shape to crowd scenes (such as the one in a balcony scene in *Camille*) by creating identities for each and every member of the crowd. "The idea is," he explained, "that every character in every scene has a life, a history, and an identity, even if the character never speaks a line." Thus, he argued, it was possible for crowd scenes "to take on a depth and texture that make every inch of the stage exciting to watch."

There was a "vigor and imagination" in *Camille* that Gina Mallet hadn't seen at the Festival before, but, really, *Camille* was all "trash" as far as she was concerned, "posh trash to be sure," but still "soft porn tarted up for the culture vultures." No one could be in any doubt now that Newton was set on changing the image of the Shaw Festival, but, argued Thor Eckert, "nudity and other gimmicks are not the stuff of inventive theater, but rather clichés demeaning to audience and player alike." That kind of "new image," does not belong at a "quality theater festival," Eckert told his *Christian Science Monitor* readers. Jamie Portman noted that "sexual decadence is now the order of the day at the Shaw Festival," but went on to praise Newton's "willingness to take unusually high risks, and a readiness to upset the tea-cup decorum of Niagara-on-the-Lake and the bland certainties of a predominantly middle-class audience." Newton couldn't have said it better himself, but "soft porn," "sexual decadence," a hostile local community – was this what the board expected when they appointed Newton?

Newton's second season was certainly ending with a bang rather than a whimper, but how many more explosions could the Festival tolerate? At the end of the season, Newton, fully aware by this stage that the board had serious doubts about the wisdom of having appointed him, was given an ultimatum – "We don't want you to put on the fluff that we had before," he was told by the board, "but don't go to the other extreme either. Either you bring some compromise to this or we're going to have to make some changes and re-assess very clearly your role, your future." Newton was furious, and vigorously fought back against board threats to fire him, but he knew that he had only one season left to work out how to hold on to his reformist principles while making the compromises that would keep him in his job.

MAKE OR BREAK

At the opening of the 1982 season Newton conceded to critic Jamie Portman that achieving a balance between a "tourist theatre" and "trying to excite an audience afresh" was proving "very hard." He nonetheless remained firmly committed to the view that the Festival, in the spirit of Bernard Shaw, had "an artistic obligation to be innovative, resourceful and provocative." So the kind of compromise required by the board would be difficult, and, on the face of it, Newton's 1982 season didn't show much sign of compromise. In a preview of the season in the *Sunday Sun*, McKenzie Porter noted that "Newton is ready to show off again his flair for experiment," but it was a flair, he advised his readers, that was "neither reckless nor pretentious."

The season opened in May with four shows, three at the Festival Theatre, one at the Royal George. One of the Festival Theatre shows was the controversial *Camille*. *Camille* had opened late in the 1981 season, and had run for only twenty-three performances. Now Newton scheduled a revival, with essentially the same cast (and still with an advisory of "some nudity and sexual explicitness") for a further thirty-four performances. On one level, Newton was thumbing his nose at the conservative elements on the board, among the critics, and in Festival audiences. On another level, he was making a sound business decision. Despite the controversy, and, no doubt, in part because of it, *Camille* had done well at the box office, and merited another run on purely financial grounds. But from Newton's point of view, the revival of *Camille* also sustained his reformist agenda, as well as attracting increasing – and positive – attention to the excellence of the ensemble work in the production.

PYGMALION, 1982   Newton's reformist agenda was also reflected, albeit it in a different way, in the season's Shaw opener, *Pygmalion*. Newton stirred the pot again by selecting a radical adaptation of an ostensibly safe choice (the Festival's third production of a perennial Shaw favourite). There was no need for warnings to Festival audiences about nudity or bad language in *Pygmalion* (Eliza's famous "Not bloody likely!" was as bad as it got), but there was another kind of caution in the 1982 season brochure to the effect that this *Pygmalion* was "an unconventional production entirely in Shaw's own words, freely adapted, edited and staged by Denise Coffey." That is, audience members who expected the familiar version of Shaw's story of the transformation of a Covent Garden flower girl into a duchess would be disappointed, perhaps even annoyed. Some were.

British director Denise Coffey's adaptation of *Pygmalion* was first produced at the Young Vic Theatre in London in January 1981. While maintaining the core text of the play, Coffey made a number of cuts to accommodate a new character – Shaw himself. Drawing from Shaw's preface to the play, his lengthy stage directions, his correspondence, and his essays, Coffey made Shaw (suitably bearded) an active participant in the play, both as a commentator on the action (and the post-play history of the major characters) and as an actor, taking some of the minor roles himself.

Coffey had taken care to get the full approval of the Shaw Estate for her adaptation, so there was no repeat with *Pygmalion* of the hullabaloo experienced at the Festival in 1981 over Newton's frustrated plans to cut the Epilogue from *Saint Joan*. To reassure those who might have worried about another such confrontation, the Festival brochure printed not only a letter from the Estate's Literary and Dramatic Advisor Dan H. Laurence granting approval for the Young Vic production, but also a statement from Denise Coffey thanking Laurence (now also Literary Advisor for the Festival) for his "knowledgeable, thoughtful and generous help and advice in the preparation of the text for this first Canadian production of the *Pygmalion* created for the Young Vic Theatre in 1981."

Newton hadn't seen the London production of Coffey's *Pygmalion*, and moving the production from the smaller, experimental theatre well outside West End geography and culture to the Festival Theatre in Niagara-on-the-Lake was a risk. As far as most critics were concerned, it wasn't a risk worth taking. The essence of the complaints was that the bare set (a black hexagon and four or five chairs on the Festival stage) robbed the play of social context; that the addition of GBS (played by Herb Foster, looking, said one critic, not like Shaw, but like Herb Foster in a wig) was tedious, awkward, and intrusive; and that the play was mis-cast, with a "boyish" Barry MacGregor as Higgins and a "sweet," but "rather elderly" Nicola Cavendish as Eliza – no chance of any Shavian life force sexual energy there. With virtually no set and cast of eleven actors (rather than the more usual twenty or so), was it all perhaps a Newtonian ploy to save the Festival money, wondered one critic?

There were complaints from audience members as well. Having read the reviews, one ticket buyer (who was "not interested in experimental theatre") wanted his money back. Don't trust the critics, Paul Reynolds responded, firmly rejecting the refund demand. "You were right," the complainant wrote to Reynolds after seeing the production. He and his friends "thoroughly enjoyed" the play. "The entire cast was superb," and "Denise Coffey's interpretation allowed the audience to focus attention on the play's most important attribute – its dialogue – so rich in social and political commentary." Here, perhaps, was the prototype of Newton's longed for Festival theatregoer, one receptive, if only given the opportunity, to fresh ideas, fresh approaches.

There were few complaints about the third play at the Festival Theatre, another farce, *See How They Run*, by Philip King (about an escaped German prisoner in the Second World War finding his way into an English vicarage), in which Nora McLellan shone as a cockney parlour maid. *See How They Run* was a predictable success; and even though Newton had to adapt the Sigmund Romberg 1926 operetta *The Desert Song* to fit the Royal George stage, it was a well-enough known show through Broadway success and film to attract audiences, and it did. This "brand new miniature version," as the Festival described Newton's adaptation (Newton also directed it), filled the Royal George for many of its 148 performances, its popularity persuading Newton to take it on a post-season tour throughout Ontario and into Quebec.

The jury, perhaps, was still out on Newton's future at the Festival after the opening four shows, but as the 1982 season progressed, with good box office and no fresh controversies, the odds turned in Newton's favour. There were three June openings: Shaw's *Too True to be Good* (Court House) and *The Music-Cure* (Royal George lunchtime show), as well as *The Singular Life of Albert Nobbs* (directed by Newton at the Court House), an adaptation by French playwright Simone Benmussa of a George Moore story about a young woman in Ireland in the 1860s who disguises herself as a man in a futile search for equality. *Too True*, described – not inappropriately – by one critic as a play that "runs out of plot at the end of the first act, out of characters by the end of the second, but not out of conversation until the conclusion of the third," was "briskly and intelligently" directed by Paul Bettis, but it couldn't match the surprise success of *The Music-Cure*. The story of a young man cured of a nervous breakdown by marriage to a concert pianist, this "piece of utter nonsense" (Shaw's description), directed by Paul Reynolds, was recognized as the "gem" that it is, and the art deco design by Mary Kerr

should, advised one critic, "be declared a national treasure." Praise for *Albert Nobbs* was, to be sure, more muted; but it was, for the most part respectfully received, and with just one show left to open, the 1982 season looked secure.

***CYRANO DE BERGERAC*, 1982, 1983**   Expectations for Edmond Rostand's 1897 French romance *Cyrano de Bergerac* (adapted and translated by Anthony Burgess) were modest – it was scheduled for only twenty-six performances in the Festival Theatre at the tail-end of the season – but the production became not only a defining moment for Newton's relationship with the Festival, but a defining moment for the Festival itself. It was also a personal triumph for Heath Lamberts.

Lamberts had first appeared at the Shaw Festival as long ago as 1967 (Paxton Whitehead's first season), when he performed the servant Nicola in Shaw's *Arms and the Man*. He appeared regularly through the early and mid-1970s, but was not in the company for 1978 or 1979, two years he spent with Newton at the Vancouver Playhouse. He came back to the Festival with Newton for the 1980 season as the eternal student Trofimov in *The Cherry Orchard* and for his one-man show *Gunga Heath*, and in 1981 as the Dauphin in *Saint Joan*. But it was his brilliantly madcap performances in *A Flea in Her Ear* in 1980 and *Tons of Money* in 1981 that endeared Lamberts to Festival audiences. Newton's inspired decision – "audacious," one critic called it – to challenge him with the role of Cyrano allowed Lamberts to draw on his physical skills (Cyrano is a master swordfighter), but also extend his emotional range deep into the psyche of a man whose physical appearance (a monstrously long nose) so circumscribes

his appeal as a lover that he is pathetically reduced to wooing the woman he loves through the poetry and letters he writes on behalf of a rival suitor.

Cyrano was directed by Derek Goldby, who had directed both of the farces Lambert had appeared in, and set and costume designs were by Cameron Porteous. Newton himself appeared in the play in minor roles in the biggest cast ever assembled for a Shaw Festival production.

Cyrano opened on August 14 (after four previews) to huge acclaim. Goldby's directing was praised as both sensitive and dashing – at the end of the first act he had the whole cast charge out through the auditorium to the sounds of Berlioz's *Roman Carnival* overture – while Porteous's costume designs flamboyantly and colourfully depicted the fops, courtesans, pickpockets, and soldiers of seventeenth-century Paris on five different sets (superbly lit by Robert Thomson). Rita Brown, then head of wardrobe, recalls the particular challenge of designing and building costumes from a century outside the usual historical range of Festival productions.

Porteous's costumes and sets were inspired by the work of several European painters, and, for the first time in a Festival production, rear-projections rather than painted flats were used for backgrounds. Scott McKowen has noted that it was also the first time at the Shaw Festival that pyrotechnics were used: "the battle scene at Arras was accompanied by all the sights, sounds and smells of musket and cannon fire."

Heath Lamberts was feted both by audiences and critics. It was a virtuoso performance, in which Lamberts – an actor of unheroic physical stature – made a hero of Cyrano by stoic acceptance of his misfortunes. And he made Rostand's poetry sing. "He can take the words," said Audrey Ashley in the *Ottawa Citizen*, "toss them in the air, give them life and colour and beauty, and so dazzle us with them that we forget his unromantic bearing." "The finest farceur in Canada, no, on the continent," wrote Gina Mallet in the *Toronto Star*, "Lamberts has always been unparalleled at suggesting that even beneath the silliest ass, a great soul may be lurking." In Lamberts' Cyrano Mallet saw that soul, a soul that "captures greatness irretrievably, bringing absurdity and heroism together with panache, an imperishable swagger of the spirit." This

was, concluded Mallet, the best production at the Shaw Festival since Tony van Bridge's 1977 *Man and Superman.*

Cyrano went on to further success and more accolades in the Festival's 1983 season ("You may never again have as grand a collection of acting, directing, and design talent in as great a play of romance and comedy on this stage," declared the Canadian Press), and, in the winter of 1984–85 at Toronto's Royal Alexander Theatre. Regrettably, a planned television production in 1983 never materialized. But of more immediate importance to Christopher Newton in the fall of 1982 was that the success of *Cyrano* (with a 99 percent box office) had capped a season that had, to a large extent, satisfied both the expectations of the board and Newton's own sense of objectives and priorities for the Festival.

From the board's point of view the 1982 season had garnered very positive press coverage, and it was especially pleasing to read that "for the first time, Shaw overshadowed the far bigger and richer Stratford Festival" (Gina Mallet), and that its programming was "far more exciting and innovative than that supplied by its big brother down the road" (Jamie Portman). In Portman's opinion, the Shaw Festival was now "the bold pacesetter on Canada's summer theatre scene." The bottom line was improving too. Newton had inherited an accumulated deficit in 1980 of over $700,000. Despite a small shortfall in revenue in 1982, a combination of effective fundraising and tight control over expenditures was bringing that number down rapidly, and the Canada Council, alert to the changes at the Festival, was increasing its support.

In a revealing interview with Gina Mallet in October 1982 Newton, described by Mallet as "a shy, enthusiastic, vulnerable idealist," conceded that he had had a tough three years, years marred by "misunderstanding and opposition" to what he was trying to achieve at the Festival. But now there was tangible evidence of progress in administrative reorganization to provide more accountability, in deficit reduction, in building a company ensemble, and in changing audience (and board) expectations of the Festival identity. He was beginning to think, he told Mallet, that "what I'm trying to do is finally being understood." For the first time in his three years at the Festival he was able to relax a little, sensing that he was "getting it going the way I want it to be."

The board's satisfaction with the way it was going was reflected in a two-year extension of Newton's original three-year agreement with the Festival, something that few would have predicted at the end of the 1981 season.

THE ROYAL GEORGE THEATRE

In his interview with Gina Mallet in October 1982 Newton didn't say anything about the Pavilion controversy, but he did refer to the problem of a shortage of seats for popular Shaw Festival shows. In September, for example, *Cyrano, Pygmalion,* and *The Desert Song* were all sold out. The aborted Pavilion project was Newton's hoped-for solution to this problem, but the problem could have been far worse had the Shaw Festival not acquired the Royal George Theatre in 1980.

The Royal George was built in 1915 (on the site of a blacksmith's shop) as a vaudeville house. It was used extensively throughout the First World War to entertain the several thousand troops based in Niagara-on-the-Lake. Seating capacity was 420 (main floor and balcony), and the theatre was equipped with a fly tower, dressing rooms, and two projectors (located above the balcony) to show silent movies. It was named the Kitchener after the British soldier and politician who had played dominant roles in the Boer War and other British conflicts and who went on to further military exploits in the First World War (when his face became famous on the recruitment poster, "Your Country Needs You").

Business slowed down after the end of the war, and in 1919 the American owner (a Mrs Norris from Bay City, Michigan) sold the theatre to a local businessman (George Reid) who owned another theatre, named the Royal George (after King George V – or, so unfriendly local gossip had it, after Reid himself), a few blocks east on Queen Street. Reid converted his theatre to a paint store (that subsequently burned down), and renamed the Kitchener the Royal George. Reid continued to operate the Royal George as a vaudeville and movie house, and also used it for stage productions by local amateur and visiting professional companies. Reid kept going through the 1920s, but the cost of converting the Royal George to accommodate the new "talkies" was too much for him, and the theatre fell into disuse in the 1930s.

BROCK CINEMA, C.1948.
PHOTO COURTESY OF JIM SMITH.

EXTERIOR PHOTO OF THE ROYAL
GEORGE THEATRE BY COSMO CONDINA.

INTERIOR PHOTOS OF THE ROYAL
GEORGE THEATRE BY DAVID COOPER.

THE BROCK   The Royal George was eventually purchased by another local businessman, John Allan, who invested in a major renovation that included new seats (435), a marquee, and new heating and projection systems. Renamed the Brock (after Canadian War of 1812 hero General Brock), it reopened as a comfortable and well-equipped movie theatre in February 1941, and again provided entertainment for another generation of war-destined troops based in Niagara-on-the-Lake. While changing management and ownership from time to time, the Brock stayed in business until 1972 when the then owner Marjorie McCourt sold it to the Canadian Mime Theatre. The building had again deteriorated, Ron Nipper, who came to the Shaw Festival as stage manager in 1971, recalling that there was a good chance of falling on the floor when you sat down in the Brock to watch a movie, so many seats were missing or broken.

THE CANADIAN MIME THEATRE   The Canadian Mime Theatre, the first professional mime company in Canada, was another Brian Doherty brainchild. He co-founded it in 1969 (and helped fund it by selling some of his art collection) with internationally renowned Canadian mime artist Adrian Pecknold as a sort of wordless counterpart to the "wordy" Bernard Shaw. The company ran summer seasons for four years in a dance hall converted to a 100-seat theatre (known as the Fire Hall Theatre) above the old fire hall adjacent to the Court House. The fifth season, however, 1973, was in the Brock cinema, now known again as the Royal George Theatre. Renovations designed by Niagara-on-the-Lake architect Peter John Stokes, not fully completed until 1975, reduced the seating to about 200, with the balcony now containing a control booth, offices, and a reception area. The biggest exterior change was the addition of a neoclassical palladian front, looking much as it does today (2011).

The Canadian Mime Theatre operated out of the Royal George Theatre – and mounted national and international tours from its Niagara-on-the-Lake base – until company disputes (Pecknold left in 1977) threatened the viability of the company only five years after the acquisition of the theatre. The Mime Theatre had proposed joint programming with the Festival in 1977, but the Festival had rejected the idea. The following summer – the final season of the Mime Theatre – the board began to explore ways of disposing of the Royal George, and approached the Shaw Festival about its possible interest in buying it. In August, Leslie Yeo (as artistic director for the 1979 season) and Christopher Newton (as artistic director-designate) joined members of the Festival's Community Affairs Committee to tour the Royal George. Both Yeo and Newton recommended that the Festival buy the theatre, though restoration of balcony seating, they argued, was essential. From Newton's point of view, the Royal George could not be seen as a replacement for the Court House, but it would give the Festival extra seats as well as allowing for more varied programming.

Discussions continued through the fall of 1978 with some sense of urgency from the Festival because of new uncertainties (eventually resolved) about access to the Court House beyond the 1979 season. On November 8, 1978, the executive committee of the board authorized a purchase offer, but it fell through, negotiations then dragging on through the whole of the following year. The theatre was eventually put on the open market, when the Festival (as the asking price dropped) again became interested. By April 1980 an agreement had been reached, one that cost the Festival about $185,000, including $12,000 for essential safety-related renovations.

RENOVATIONS   The Festival had only a matter of weeks to get ready for its first show in the Royal George, a selection of music and lyrics by Irving Berlin under the title of *Puttin' on the Ritz*, which, after one preview, opened on June 25, 1980. There was no time (or money) for major renovations, so seating was limited to the main floor, where about 240 patrons were squeezed in. In the absence of an orchestra pit, music was initially provided by a single piano – increased to two, one on each side of the stage, for *The Desert Song* in 1982 and subsequent musicals.

Renovations had to wait, but they occurred at regular intervals during the 1980s, as funds were raised. New seats were installed in 1982, using some of the 650 that had been purchased for the Pavilion project (the rest were used in the Court House). The first fundraising effort began in the summer of 1983, when an innovative "Let George Do It!" campaign was launched on Shaw's birthday (July 26). The campaign called on "all Georges" to buy a seat in the theatre. Anyone whose name was George (or a derivative, such as Georgina) "will qualify to contribute money." But those unfortunate enough not to be named George could still contribute by endowing a seat in the name of a "favourite or famous George." That George Bernard Shaw himself intensely disliked the name George – and never used it socially or professionally – was an irony not drawn to the attention of potential donors. The campaign (for $150,000) funded renovations for improved seating and for the reinstatement of the theatre balcony and structural repairs, all ready for the 1984 season.

Renovations in 1985 updated sound and lighting systems, and in 1988 a small orchestra pit and permanent proscenium arch (above which was mounted the Festival's newly acquired Coat of Arms) were installed. Following additional renovations to the interior of the theatre, designed by Cameron Porteous, the transition of the Royal George Theatre into a miniature Edwardian opera house was celebrated on May 26, 1990, at the opening performance of J.B. Priestley's *When We Are Married*, with special recognition to Walter Carsen, a prime supporter of the restoration and friend of Festival founder Brian Doherty. Carsen was also a lead donor for the installation of new seating in 1994.

MUSICALS   After using the Royal George in its first season (and his) for *Puttin' on the Ritz* and Heath Lamberts' one-man show *Gunga Heath*, Newton quickly established a pattern for programming the theatre. With some variations – though not many – the pattern consisted of a small musical from the mandate period (matinees and evenings), often adapted and directed by Newton, as well as a lunchtime show, with a heavy emphasis on Shaw. From 1985, with Agatha Christie's *Murder on the Nile*, Newton added a murder-mystery series to the mix – a genre that he thought nicely complemented the musicals. As Newton was wont to say in talks and in Festival publications, the Royal George was "where we do things for fun – old musicals and mysteries and the little plays by Shaw which seem like parlour tricks when set against masterpieces like *Saint Joan*."

Audiences had fun too, and, most of the time, so did the critics. There was some occasional grumpiness about the musicals – about dragging up "old turkeys" and "cornballs," and about campy and spoofy takes on the shows, and about "half-baked parodies" and "ham-fisted" attempts to "modernize" dated scripts – but for the most part critics and audiences alike joined in the spirit in which Newton offered these shows. Plaudits abounded: for the "enchanting" *Desert Song* (1982), for example, or the "light and lively" *Roberta* (1984), the "wonderful and wacky" *A Connecticut Yankee* (1991), the "lovely and loveable" *Lady, Be Good!* (1994), the "rare and enchanting" *She Loves Me* (2000), and the "endearing and entertaining" *Mystery of Edwin Drood* (at which audiences got to vote on how Dickens' unfinished novel should end). And while the intellectual qualities of such shows might have been mostly threadbare, the production qualities were high, constantly marked by outstanding ensemble work and, when a show needed it, eye-catching individual performances – by, for example, Nora McLellan, whose performance in Cole Porter's *Anything Goes* (1987) was so powerful that Ray Conlogue in the *Globe and Mail* said that *Anything Goes* should be renamed *The Nora McLellan Show*.

It was in the 1998 season that Festival music director Christopher Donison arranged and orchestrated *A Foggy Day*, a recreation of the unfinished Gershwin musical. This was the last assignment for Donison after a distinguished association with the Festival that began in 1980, and included ten years as music director. Donison was succeeded as music director by Paul Sportelli, whose first appearance was as musical director and conductor for a 1999 revival of Donison's *A Foggy Day*.

LUNCHTIME SHAW   The same could be said as well about lunchtime shows at the Festival. Introduced by Leslie Yeo, Newton's immediate predecessor, with a production of Shaw's *Village Wooing* at the Court House Theatre, lunchtime shows were maintained by Newton, and he also kept the Shaw focus. But he switched lunchtime performances from the Court House to the Royal George. Newton began with *The Man of Destiny*, which Andrew Allan had directed at the Court House in 1963. The Royal George production of *The Man of Destiny* marked the beginning of a remarkable fifteen seasons of lunchtime productions of Shaw plays (shared in 1994 with Granville Barker's *Rococo* and in 1995 with the Arthur Sullivan and Bolton Rowe musical, *The Zoo*). Nine of the plays were Festival premieres: *The Music-Cure* (1982), *The Fascinating Foundling* (1984), *The Inca of Perusalem* (1985), *Passion, Poison, and Petrifaction* (1986), *Augustus Does His Bit* (1987), *Shakes versus Shav* (1989), *The Glimpse of Reality*

(1989), *Annajanska, the Bolshevik Empress* (1994), and *The Six of Calais* (1995). There have been no subsequent productions at the Festival (up to 2011) of *The Music-Cure, The Fascinating Foundling, The Inca of Perusalem, Augustus Does His Bit, Shakes versus Shav, The Glimpse of Reality, Annajanska,* and *The Six of Calais*. Paul Reynolds, assistant to the artistic director from 1980 to 1982, and producer from 1983 until his death in 1992, directed all of the Shaw lunchtime plays for the first nine seasons.

There was a great deal of excitement (and gratitude) among Shaw scholars and Shaw enthusiasts at this unprecedented commitment to Shaw's minor plays – most of them rarely performed – but the challenge for Newton and, in particular, Reynolds was finding ways to make the plays connect with the general Festival audience. The last thing they wanted was a sense that these were museum pieces, done out of a sense of obligation to the Festival's mandate.

After a successful warm-up with *The Man of Destiny* in 1981, and a surprise hit with *The Music-Cure* in 1982, Reynolds went on to demonstrate beyond any doubt that there was still ample theatrical, intellectual, and emotional life in Shaw's one-acts (with a little directorial tweaking here and there) to engage and amuse the Festival's audiences. Like the musicals, they became an eagerly anticipated part of each season's Royal George offerings. Bob Pennington in the *Toronto Sun* marvelled at the "humour and scintillating wit" in *O'Flaherty, V.C.* with its withering attack on English militarism; Herman Trotter applauded "Shaw's incredible verbal, intellectual and theatrical gymnastics" in *The Fascinating Foundling* (Shaw's take on English adoption laws, among other things); Pennington declared *The Inca of Perusalem* and its exposure of the insanity of war "a treasure"; Stewart Brown of the *Hamilton Spectator* "chuckled until supper-time" over *Passion, Poison, and Petrification* with its large heavenly choir (virtually the whole of the acting ensemble) belting out "Won't You Come Home, Bill Bailey?"; Rod Currie of Canadian Press thought the mockery of the British ruling classes in *Augustus Does His Bit* showed Shaw "at his irreverent best"; and so on. Reynolds' final two Shaws, with puppeteer Ronnie Burkett, the puppet show *Shakes versus Shav* and *The Glimpse of Reality* (not written as a puppet show, but performed as one) disappointed, but couldn't diminish Reynolds' overall achievement.

A succession of directors took on the Shaw lunchtimes after Reynolds, by and large maintaining the standards he had set, culminating in a production, directed by David Oiye, of *The Six of Calais* in 1995 (a play inspired by Rodin's statue of the six medieval burghers of Calais and the story of their near-martyrdom at the hands of Edward III) that Stewart Brown described as "a perfect microcosm of the Shaw Festival itself: a brief, noon-hour taste of the Festival and the writer it celebrates that can move you to laughter, move you to tears, and send you out of the theatre uplifted by something considerably more affecting than you'd expected."

By the mid-1990s Newton was running out of Shaw plays suitable for lunchtime production. In 1996, for the first time, there wasn't a lunchtime Shaw at the Royal George. Nor in 1997. *Passion, Poison, and Petrifaction* was repeated in 1998, and *Village Wooing* in 1999. Jamie Portman had enjoyed the 1986 *Passion* because, he said in his review of the 1998 version (directed by Gyllian Raby), "the people involved trusted the material." This time it was played "frenetically over the top at every opportunity…there's not a single moment when somebody is not yelling or screaming or running about frantically." And a sound effects man "busily honks, tweets and bashes metal – all with the intent of forcing the audience into laughter."

Lunchtime Shaw, it seems, had run its course. It was time to try something new. But what? There was no single answer, and the last few seasons of lunchtime shows in the Royal George under Newton were something of a miscellany. Two shows, *The Zoo*, an operetta by Arthur Sullivan (in his pre-Gilbert days) and Bolton Rowe, and *Sorry, Wrong Number*, an American mystery play by Lucille Fletcher (1995 and 1997 seasons, respectively) crossed over from the other two categories of Royal George plays (musicals and mysteries). Others came from Shaw's major contemporaries (Granville Barker's *Rococo*, 1994; Barrie's *Shall We Join the Ladies?* and *The Old Lady Shows Her Medals*, 1996 and 2002; Coward's *Still Life* and *Shadow Play*, 2000 and 2001). There was Arthur Conan Doyle's *Waterloo* in 1998 and 1999, featuring Tony van Bridge, and a Canadian play (Merrill Denison's *Brothers in Arms*, 1998). And in 1996 there was the strange phenomenon of a magic show as a lunchtime offering. It starred magician David Ben, and arbitrarily qualified for the mandate by being set in a London theatre in 1909. To many people the show felt out of place at the Festival, but it sold so well that Newton brought it back (with some new magic content) for the 1997 season.

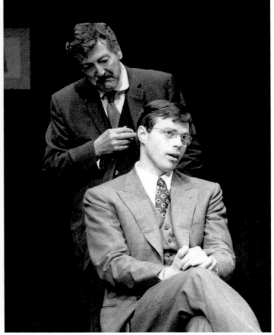

MURDER MYSTERIES   In the meantime, the murder-mystery series was going strong at matinee and evening performances at the Royal George in repertory with the musicals. The series was announced in a press release in January 1985 and began that summer with Agatha Christie's *Murder on the Nile*. In the Festival brochure Newton explained that he had been looking for a way to integrate the Royal George musical ensemble more fully into the company. "Eight times a week," he said, the musical ensemble play the same show, while "almost every other actor gets to be in at least two productions and they have the advantage of working with different material." So he had looked for another "popular form" that could both sustain revenue and provide a more varied Shaw Festival experience for the musical actors. "It dawned on me last year that there was a perfect answer: the Murder Mystery." Farce, musical theatre, and the murder mystery, Newton argued, had been popular forms throughout the Festival's mandate period, and for Festival audiences the three genres "present a nice complement to the 'art' theatre of Shaw and his academically respectable contemporaries." "With any luck," he concluded, "the mysteries will be as much fun for the acting ensemble as are the farces and musicals."

And, with any luck, they would be fun for audiences too. But only for those who bought into the spirit of the murder mysteries. If, as one refreshingly honest local critic admitted, they simply weren't your cup of tea then they were best avoided. John Law of the *Welland-Port Colborne Tribune* let his readers know that "I hate mysteries. Can't stand 'em. They are so hopelessly asinine in their set-ups, ridiculous in their characters, and indistinguishable in their plots that I truly can't believe that so many people get sucked in by them." This frank disclosure was a preamble to Law's review of Agatha Christie's *The Hollow*, directed by Paul Lampert in 1996. It was for Law another "clunker story" from Christie, "just another hokey date with a corpse." Not all critics were (or are) as open as Law in declaring their biases, but there were plenty around who sniped at the "dated mores" or "simplistic characters," or "mechanical and predictable plots" of the murder mysteries. On the other hand, there were devotees for whom the murder mysteries were the highlight of each season, as well as those who enjoyed – as Newton had predicted – the "refreshing" contrast between "classics and clever arguments in three acts" and the less demanding, but still engaging, murder mysteries.

Newton read widely to find murder mysteries that he thought worth reviving, and was praised by Jamie Portman, among others, for his "zest for theatrical archaeology," his "genuine knack for unearthing forgotten plays of the past and blowing off the dust, and proving that they are still eminently worth reviving." (Portman particularly had in mind Anthony Armstrong's *Ten Minute Alibi*, directed by Paul Lampert in 1992.) Newton's favoured authors

were Agatha Christie and J.B. Priestley, who between them accounted for eight of the murder mysteries produced between 1985 and 2002 (nine if Frank Vosper's *Love from a Stranger*, based on a Christie short story, is counted). Three of the Priestleys (*Dangerous Corner*, 1988; *An Inspector Calls*, 1989; and *When We Are Married*, 1990) were directed by Tony van Bridge, who also played the Inspector in *An Inspector Calls*. Neil Munro directed the fourth Priestley (*Time and the Conways*, 2000). Newton himself directed Dorothy Sayers' and Muriel St Clare Byrne's *Busman's Honeymoon* in 1994 and Daphne du Maurier's *Rebecca* in 1999.

It was frequently pointed out that the unintellectual nature of the murder mysteries was never used as a reason for skimping on production values. Experienced set, costume, and lighting designers such as Christina Poddubiuk, Peter Hartwell, Cameron Porteous, Leslie Frankish, Kevin Lamotte, and William Schmuck worked on many of the murder mysteries, and the company's leading actors regularly appeared in them. As Jamie Portman said (in his review of *Busman's Honeymoon*), "One of the great virtues of the Shaw Festival is that it approaches the lightweight works in its repertoire with the same care that it bestows on its more classic plays."

When Stewart Brown described Tony van Bridge's production of *An Inspector Calls* at the Royal George Theatre in May 1989 as "a tiny perfect play in a tiny perfect place," the theatre, though over seventy years old, was still in its infancy as a Shaw Festival venue. Many repertoire changes and physical improvements lay ahead, but Mrs Norris's vaudeville house had already proved its worth to Christopher Newton's artistic vision for the Festival, and had also in those few years endeared itself to Festival theatregoers.

NEWTON AND SHAW

In an overview of the 1982 season, the entertainment editor of the *St Catharines Standard*, Lorraine LePage, said that while she "wouldn't bother to cross the street" to see a production of *The Desert Song* staged in the traditional manner with a cast of two hundred, she thought the Shaw Festival production, with a cast of ten, was "a little jewel," which director Christopher Newton had "managed to polish to perfection." If Newton read the article, he might have wished he had stopped reading at that point. LePage's very next paragraph began "One is grateful that Newton decided this season not to direct any of GBS's plays." The positive outcome of that decision, in LePage's view, was that Festival audiences got to see Denise Coffey's adaptation of *Pygmalion*, "the most exciting *Pygmalion* ever presented at the Festival or anywhere else in this country." This was welcome praise, of course, but hardly a vote of confidence in Newton's ability to handle Shaw himself.

LePage was not alone. There had been calls for Newton to be fired after *Saint Joan* in 1981, and he was probably wise to take a break from Shaw in his third season. But it was hardly feasible for the artistic director of the Shaw Festival to avoid directing plays by Shaw indefinitely.

IN THE FESTIVAL THEATRE

CAESAR AND CLEOPATRA, 1983, 2002 Newton didn't long delay his return to Shaw. He opened the 1983 season with a lavish production of *Caesar and Cleopatra*, the Festival's second mounting of the play (the first was in 1975). Designed by Cameron Porteous, with Douglas Rain as Caesar (Rain's first appearance at the Festival since 1967) and Marti Maraden as Cleopatra, Newton's approach to the play benefited from what he had learned from directing *Misalliance* in 1980 and *Saint Joan* in 1981. He now knew, he said, that "there was more to Shaw than I had ever dreamed of: surreal, resonant, troubling." What he wanted to do with *Caesar and Cleopatra* – and with all the Shaw plays he subsequently directed – was to show the audience "the demons beneath the surface," that world of human and intellectual passions that should never be allowed to disappear beneath the surface weight of the language and action (and, sometimes, inaction) of a Shaw play.

Cameron Porteous's looming sphinx, exotically populated stage, eye-catching visual transformations, and sensuous costumes were deemed by some to be the stars of the production, but a more astute reading recognized the synthesis that Porteous and Newton had jointly created between the richness of the set and the political fireworks generated by Rain's Caesar and Maraden's Cleopatra. Looking in the wrong place for passion, some critics bemoaned the

lack of sexual tension between the middle-aged Caesar and the teenage Cleopatra, and others were still not convinced that *Caesar and Cleopatra* was much more than "five acts of Shavian preaching and moralizing" (as James Nelson of the Canadian Press put it). But Jamie Portman spoke for many when he saw no contradiction between witnessing at one and the same time "one of the most sumptuous" productions in the Festival's history and a play "that engages the mind with the wit and vigour of George Bernard Shaw's ideas about leadership."

Dan Laurence, now very forgiving of Newton's attempt to cut out the Epilogue from *Saint Joan* ("You can't deny him artistic experimentation"), was convinced that Newton had got things right with *Caesar and Cleopatra*. The production, he told Lorraine LePage, "will be held up as something against which to measure all other productions of this play."

Laurence didn't see the Festival's next production of *Caesar and Cleopatra*, directed by Newton – again at the Festival Theatre – in 2002, his last Shaw play as artistic director. So there is no way of knowing how he would have measured it against the 1983 production. Newton, however, was eager to take a new look at the play.

Designed by William Schmuck, the 2002 *Caesar and Cleopatra* featured Jim Mezon as Caesar and Caroline Cave (in her second season with the Festival) as Cleopatra. Schmuck's set and costumes, while just as sumptuous as Porteous's in 1983, correlated in a different way with the ideas of the play. The design challenged the audience to think about the politics of the play by mingling time periods, moving much of the action from ancient Egypt to Edwardian times. This created an unsettling time warp, but it successfully brought the concept of imperialist politics into the context of what Newton in his program note called the Edwardians' "terrifying finale," the First World War.

Whatever the differences between his 1983 and 2002 productions of *Caesar and Cleopatra*, they had one thing in common. Newton's *Misalliance* in 1980 had, by and large, left critics and audiences indifferent. His *Saint Joan* the following year had alienated many. In both productions of *Caesar*, however, he found a way – just as Shaw himself had – of cooperating with his audiences rather than confronting them.

That strategy was the hallmark of all of the Shaw that Newton directed after the 1983 *Caesar and Cleopatra*. Key to all of his productions was finding the passion in Shaw through intense work with the ensemble, collaborating closely with his designers to create visually engaging and appropriate settings and costumes, and then striving to bring the audience along with him in a mutually satisfying intellectual and emotional engagement with the play.

HEARTBREAK HOUSE, 1985 For Newton's *Heartbreak House* in 1985 (the Festival's "most impressive production since the triumphant *Cyrano de Bergerac*" in the view of Bob Pennington of the *Toronto Sun*), Michael Levine created a set that allowed Captain Shotover's (Douglas Rain) antiquarian mansion to grow or shrink, as in a kind of *Alice in Wonderland* dream. In this dreamlike house anything could happen, and Newton stripped characters down to the core to reveal their deep motivations – money, sex, power. And, in some cases, to reveal their emptiness as well. Robert Benson's Boss Mangan, for example, was transformed from powerful business tycoon to (as Crew saw it) "a blubbering wreck." On the other hand, the meek idealism of Ellie Dunn (Marti Maraden) strengthened into an intense blend of metaphysical insight and erotic power. And then at the end, as the bombs begin to fall, the dream turned into the nightmare of a world bent on destroying itself. Full realization of what Shaw says in his preface to the play became blazingly clear: Shotover has in his house not just a self-indulgent group of British eccentrics, but the whole of "cultured, leisured Europe before the [first world] war." Mark Czarnecki (*Maclean's*) described the production as "an unforgettable apocalyptic vision of a world irrevocably in love with death." Box office figures of 85 percent (the best yet achieved by Newton for a Shaw play) suggested that audiences found it memorable as well.

It was this production of *Heartbreak House* that convinced Bob Pennington that "no more gifted an ensemble is to be found in London or New York than the one artistic director Christopher Newton has assembled here with great affection and supreme professionalism."

MAJOR BARBARA, 1987   Newton's next Shaw play in the Festival Theatre, *Major Barbara* in 1987, fared even better than *Heartbreak House* at the box office, averaging 87 percent in a seventy-three performance run, though Newton wasn't entirely satisfied with the production. Cameron Porteous's sets – a marbled library, smoky and oppressive London back alleys, a spotless and futuristic munitions factory – gave Newton the environments that reflect the contrasting moral and social milieux in the play: the privileged upper-classes, the Salvation Army domains, and industrial nirvana. These are the environments in which Barbara must struggle with her conscience (and her father) about how best to meet the needs of the poor. But Newton also wanted something of the raw emotions he had successfully uncovered in *Heartbreak House*. Plenty of intellectual tension between the capitalist Undershaft and the scholarly Cusins was generated by Douglas Rain and Jim Mezon, but the erotic tension Newton sought to establish between Cusins and Barbara (Martha Burns) fizzled. In his program note, Newton spoke of Cusins's urgent desire to be physically close to Barbara, "to touch her, to smell her." The sexual energy, though, that Newton believed brought the couple together was kept well in check by Mezon and Burns.

OPPOSITE: *YOU NEVER CAN TELL* BY BERNARD SHAW, 1988. DIRECTED BY CHRISTOPHER NEWTON, DESIGNED BY CAMERON PORTEOUS, LIGHTING DESIGNED BY ROBERT THOMSON, ORIGINAL MUSIC COMPOSED BY CHRISTOPHER DONISON. PHOTO BY DAVID COOPER.

THIS PAGE: LUNCHEON AT THE MARINE HOTEL; ANDREW GILLIES AND SANDY WEBSTER IN *YOU NEVER CAN TELL* BY BERNARD SHAW, 1995. DIRECTED BY CHRISTOPHER NEWTON, DESIGNED BY WILLIAM SCHMUCK, LIGHTING DESIGNED BY KEVIN LAMOTTE. PHOTOS BY DAVID COOPER.

YOU NEVER CAN TELL, 1988, 1995 Newton's production of *You Never Can Tell* in 1988 was the Festival's fourth of one of Shaw's most popular plays. It was selected by Newton for inclusion in the Olympic Arts Festival in Calgary (host city for the 1988 Winter Olympics). He gave the play a short run (five performances) in Niagara-on-the-Lake in January 1988, and then took it to the Manitoba Theatre Centre in Winnipeg for twenty-nine performances before a seven-performance run at the Olympics. The production stayed on in Calgary for twenty-four further performances at Theatre Calgary before returning to Niagara-on-the-Lake to open the Festival season on April 14. Douglas Rain (The Waiter) and Frances Hyland (Mrs Clandon) were in the company for the tour, and Newton wanted "something that would show them at their best." For the Festival run, however, Hyland was replaced by Barbara Gordon, and, among other cast changes, Craig Davidson replaced Jim Mezon as Bohun. Rain remained as The Waiter.

Cameron Porteous's light, summery, harlequinade setting served its purpose splendidly for the surface mood of the play, but Newton was equally interested – again – in digging beneath that surface, to find what he called in his program note the "inner truth" of the characters. Shaw's characters, he said, "have these public faces that glitter, but underneath, in the strange water where life exists, are complex creations that strive to break out of the structures – whether these structures be superficial characteristics or the convoluted plot of a well-made play." There is pain (represented by the dentist's chair in the opening scene) as well as joy in this play about a society grappling with post-Victorian values and attitudes (especially as regards the place and role of women). Keith Garebian was convinced that Newton's production captured Shaw's "extraordinary balancing of levity and gravity, intellectual argument and emotional tremors," but most critics, nonetheless, paid more attention to the "witty, eyefilling delight" (Jamie Portman) that they saw on the Festival stage, than to the "rich characterization" that Robert Crew, for one, appreciated. Audience appreciation, whether derived from setting, characterization, or both, was again high. *You Never Can Tell* had an 87.5 percent box office, only marginally higher than for *Major Barbara*, but it ran for six more performances.

When Newton returned to *You Never Can Tell* in 1995 he wanted to maintain a carnival-like feel to the play (with set and costumes designed by William Schmuck), while still showing characters struggling to define and protect what he called their "boundaries of behaviour." His approach reflected Max Beerbohm's observation that *You Never Can Tell* is a play in which "realism and sheer fantasy are inextricably entangled." Stewart Brown's praise, then, of this "treat for the eyes and the ears" caught something of what Newton was seeking, and this time around Jamie Portman also saw that the play "is firmly rooted in character and in the social tensions that were starting to rend the fabric of late Victorian society." Kate Taylor in the *Globe and Mail* also made the case that while *You Never Can Tell* "is a light piece," it's not "a simple one." Newton, she argued, had opted to include "some subtlety of character, where it would have been easy to settle for farce." That subtlety was captured in many ways in the production, but perhaps as tellingly as anywhere in Michael Ball's Clandon, played at times like "a raging old walrus," but forced in the end to acknowledge his isolation and loneliness in a world that has passed him by.

MICHAEL BALL, WILLIAM HUTT, AND
KATE TROTTER; THE *DON JUAN IN HELL*
SCENE IN *MAN AND SUPERMAN* BY
BERNARD SHAW, 1989. DIRECTED BY
CHRISTOPHER NEWTON, DESIGNED
BY EDUARD KOCHERGIN, MUSIC COM-
POSED BY CHRISTOPHER DONISON,
LIGHTING DESIGNED BY ROBERT
THOMSON, SOUND DESIGNED BY
WALTER LAWRENCE.

OPPOSITE: MICHAEL BALL AND KATE
TROTTER IN *MAN AND SUPERMAN*,
1989. PHOTOS BY DAVID COOPER.

MAN AND SUPERMAN, 1989   In stark contrast to the exuberant naturalistic designs of his early Shaw productions, the minimalist set of Russian designer Eduard Kochergin for Newton's 1989 *Man and Superman* signalled a radical new direction for Shaw at the Shaw Festival. Each act was framed simply in squares and rectangles, with slide projections indicating a change of scene. Furniture and props were also minimal. The "revolution in the way that the Festival presents Shaw's work" was warmly welcomed by *Maclean's* critic John Bemrose, among others. "Freed of its usual realistic Victorian or Edwardian settings," Bemrose argued, "the Shavian vision seems much more up-to-date and exciting." Newton clearly thought so too, but he was aware of potential pitfalls of using what he called "a serious set...for real actors." "This space could easily intimidate the beginner," he said, "because everything points to the actor, and the actor is expected to act." And by now, in his tenth season as artistic director, Newton knew who could act and who couldn't.

He did, however, bring in a significant new company member for *Man and Superman* – William Hutt, one of Canada's leading actors, who moved from the Stratford Festival to the Shaw for the 1989 and 1990 seasons. (Newton described working with Hutt as "like having champagne in bed.") Newton also brought back Kate Trotter, another highly experienced actor who had been a Festival ensemble member in 1986. Hutt played Roebuck Ramsden in *Man and Superman*, Trotter played Ann Whitefield. Festival regulars such as Michael Ball (John Tanner), Peter Krantz (Octavius Robinson), Jennifer Phipps (Mrs Whitefield), William Vickers (Henry Straker), Al Kozlik (Mr Malone), Barry MacGregor (Mendoza), and Tom Wood (Duval) were also in the cast, all of whom, to say the least, knew how to act.

The result was one of Newton's most impressive Shaw productions. The *Don Juan in Hell* scene was added to thirteen of the seventy-nine performances of *Man and Superman*; the abridged version, by comparison, was "like listening to a major symphony minus the slow movement," said critic Robert Crew. But whether in the full or abbreviated version, the performance itself was anything but slow. The political and sexual energies of Ball's Tanner and Trotter's Whitefield pointed firmly to a new world order, the revolutionary nature of the new order emphasized by Robert Thomson's striking red lighting design. The production, John Bem-rose noted, "pared down Shaw's work to its passionate essentials, creating a palpable tension between the play's portrait of conventional social surfaces and the repressed sexuality seething beneath." "The sensual, almost tortured, exuberance of Newton's *Man and Superman* will be remembered," Bemrose concluded, "as one of the landmarks of the Festival's history."

MISALLIANCE, 1990   Kochergin came back to the Shaw Festival in 1994 to design *Arms and the Man*, directed by Jim Mezon, but in the meantime Newton again chose to work with a new designer for his next Shaw play in the Festival Theatre, *Misalliance*, the Festival's fourth production of the play. The designer was Leslie Frankish, who had designed the Royal George musical (*Good News*) in 1989, and was to spend the next ten seasons designing plays at the Festival.

Like Kochergin, Frankish came up with an extraordinarily innovative design, but one conceptually quite the opposite of Kochergin's. While the set for *Man and Superman* could be described as lean and sparse, Frankish's for *Misalliance* was dense and busy. She furnished the conservatory of underwear magnate John Tarleton (Barry MacGregor) with long trailing ferns, hanging vines, and a profusion of plants that looked to one critic like "a luxuriantly overgrown indoor jungle." Which is exactly the effect that Newton wanted. In his program note Newton spoke of "an Amazonian growth that suggests the proliferation of theories, discoveries, constructions and behaviour patterns of the nineteenth century." These "thousands of ideas," he said "create a dense canopy blotting out the sun." The jungle-like set, then, was a powerful symbol of the stifling and inhibiting restrictions of the nineteenth century, restrictions about to be smashed by the imposing entrance (by way of a plane crashing into the conservatory) of Polish aviatrix Lina Szczepanowska (Sharry Flett), symbol of sexual and political revolution.

The challenge for the actors on this set was exactly opposite to the challenge facing the cast of *Man and Superman*. There they were exposed in sparseness; here they were in danger of being buried by profusion. Some coped better than others in establishing their space and identity. Barry MacGregor revelled in the profusion as the Yorkshire business man blessed (or cursed) with "superabundant vitality," while some of the less experienced members of the cast (there are a number of young characters in *Misalliance*) struggled.

PYGMALION, 1992   Among the other major Shaw plays directed by Newton at the Festival Theatre was *Pygmalion* in 1992. If not quite as radical as the Denise Coffey version ten years earlier, Newton's *Pygmalion* still dug deep below the surface, complemented again by a compelling set by Leslie Frankish into which she built stylized carvings of words, many of them spelled phonetically. As with any set whose ingenuity calls attention to itself, there is always a danger

that it ends up as a distraction rather than a complement to the play. In this case – as, indeed, with Frankish's *Misalliance* set – the set was more enriching than distracting. David Richards in *The New York Times* put it well: "It's an imaginative conceit and thoroughly appropriate." "After all," he said, "hasn't Eliza ventured into a labyrinth of words? Wherever she turns, there's a perverse conjunction or pesky adjective waiting to trip her up. You could say that *Pygmalion* is the story of how she makes her way out of the diabolical maze to safety."

In this labyrinth of words Higgins, played by a boyish Andrew Gillies, cared only for instructing Eliza (Seana McKenna) how to master the words. Any humanity he might have possessed was concealed behind this facade of words, and Eliza's humanity was far less important to him than the success of his experiment. Doolittle, too (Barry MacGregor), had a dark, slightly menacing aspect to his character, adding to the sense of Eliza as a victim of men, a situation she triumphantly escapes from at the end (as Shaw intended). Newton, then, removed much of the romantic *My Fair Lady*-like veneer from the play, looking instead, as *Globe and Mail* critic Liam Lacy expressed it, for "the harder questions about just what it means to apply ideas to people, to be a reformer and to 'improve' people who are different from yourself."

While respecting Shaw's text, Newton did, however, add one nuance to the play that diverged from Shaw's intentions. There were several moments, particularly in the last act, when subtle pauses, glances, and gestures pointed at least to the *potential* for emotional engagement between Higgins and Eliza. Such moments led to an ending in which Higgins's boisterous and mocking laughter at Eliza's impending marriage to the hapless Freddy subsided into pensive silence, a silence indicating not indifference to life without Eliza, but an awakening sense of loss, of missed opportunity.

***THE DOCTOR'S DILEMMA*, 2000** Newton's penultimate Shaw play in the Festival Theatre as artistic director, *The Doctor's Dilemma*, provoked some interesting criticism. While the production was "as thought-provoking as it is entertaining," Newton's take on the play was, thought John Coulbourn (*Toronto Sun*), "a trifle short on subtext." And a similar accusation, but more specific, was made by Kate Taylor in the *Globe and Mail* over Blair Williams' portrayal of bachelor, but now love-smitten, doctor Sir Colenso Ridgeon. "The script," Taylor argued (interestingly enough), "hints at lifelong solitude and sexual repression" in Ridgeon, but Newton and Williams had not found a way "to make the hidden visible." Whatever Newton thought of such criticism, the very fact that it was made was evidence of his success in leading audiences and critics to expect more – much more – than meets the eye in a Shaw play.

Nor did the criticism diminish the overall success of the production, the Festival's third of Shaw's pointed attack on private medicine. Design, this time by Sue LePage, was again a striking feature. There was, Robert Cushman approvingly noted, an absence of "stodgy realism." The scene changes, increasingly an innovative feature of Festival productions, were a delight in themselves – but a relevant delight. As furniture was shifted around, a nightmarish group of frock-coated, skull-masked actors cavorted, bellies protruding, to the music of Mexican composer Arturo Márquez. The inspiration came from the Mexican celebrations for the Day of the Dead, but with or without this knowledge (Newton did explain it in his program note), it was clear to audiences that these self-satisfied doctors were in fact merchants of death.

116

IN THE COURT HOUSE THEATRE

ON THE ROCKS, 1986 For the most part, Newton chose to put his Shaw productions in the Festival Theatre. Some Shaw plays, though, by virtue of the shape and size of the play itself, or because it wasn't likely to attract audiences large enough to justify using the Festival Theatre, he put in the Court House.

Newton's first Shaw play in the Court House was *On the Rocks*, which Shaw wrote in 1933 and subtitled "A Political Comedy." A Festival premiere, *On the Rocks* began previews on July 3, 1986, and opened on July 10 for a run of forty-nine performances, garnering a creditable 73 percent box office. A political sequel to *Heartbreak House*, *On the Rocks* is about various types of leaders, all of whom are guided by self-interest rather than the public good. The play reflects Shaw's grave doubts – broadly hinted at in *Heartbreak House*, now overtly expressed – that parliamentary democracy was capable of solving the economic and social problems of the Depression years. Ray Conlogue dismissed the play as "an impenetrable compendium of British Depression-era politics, with unusually copious jaw-wagging," but strong performances by Michael Ball, Norman Browning, George Dawson, and the rest of the seventeen-member cast led Jamie Portman to encourage Newton to follow this "sizzling" production with "that skeleton in GBS's dramatic cupboard" – *Geneva*. Which is exactly what Newton did two seasons later.

GENEVA, 1988 Shaw wrote *Geneva* in 1938, and revised it several times to reflect rapidly changing circumstances in Europe in the late 1930s. Featuring Hitler, Mussolini, and Franco under only thinly disguised names (Battler, Bombardone, and Flanco de Fortinbras), *Geneva* is based on the premise that the three dictators are called before the International Court at The Hague to answer charges against them (including, in Battler's case, attempts to exterminate the Jews). Previews of *Geneva* (the Festival's first, and, so far, only production) began at the Court House on June 30, 1988, for a July 7 opening and a run of fifty-eight performances. Shaw was treading a fine line in what he called his "political extravaganza" between rejection of democracy and support of dictatorial leadership, but Robert Crew for one felt that Newton and the cast negotiated their way through the politics "with confidence and energy." "As with the best of the Festival's work," Crew said, "there's clarity, accuracy, and clever pacing, combined with tight ensemble work." Bob Pennington added that "despite all dire omens and warnings, *Geneva* proves to be one of the offbeat pleasures of the Shaw Festival season" – with a "delicious and unexpected bonus" of Wendy Thatcher's (Begonia Brown in the play) impersonation of her namesake (but unrelated) British Prime Minister Margaret Thatcher.

While not everyone was enamoured of Shaw's political explorations – even generally supportive Jamie Portman couldn't get his head around the "distinctly dishevelled specimen of a play" that he found *Geneva* to be – it was remarkable that the Festival had the confidence and audience support to mount significant runs of plays as demanding as *Geneva* and *On the Rocks*. No other major theatre in the world would have – or has – attempted it.

THE MILLIONAIRESS, 1991 When Andrew Allan directed the first Festival production of *The Millionairess* in 1965 he had no option but to put it in the Court House Theatre. Paxton Whitehead chose the Festival Theatre for his 1977 production, and then in 1991 Newton took it back to the Court House. It's a play that can easily fill the Festival Theatre stage, but Newton preferred the intimacy of the Court House. It could, he felt, better accommodate the framework of the musical-hall review that he chose to give the play. There are no songs in Shaw's text, but Newton inserted several of them as a way of getting inside the characters or the mood of the play. Sometimes they were character-related, sometimes more mood or theme-related. A full-cast ironic rendition of "Happy Days Are Here Again" ended the show. The intimacy of the Court House also brought the audience much closer to the intensity of Nicola Cavendish's Epifania, the pain that the sweat-shop owners (Tony van Bridge and Irene Hogan) endure, and, by way of contrast, closer as well to the play's physical comedy and farce – which Newton highlighted rather than subdued. Nor did he attempt to impose a reconciliation on these disparate moods and emotions, leaving it up to the audience (as Lisbie Rae has put it) "to wriggle with the discomfort of their juxtaposition." For another critic, however, this merely amounted to "a hodgepodge of styles that never finds a coherent purpose."

CANDIDA, 1993 Until Jackie Maxwell's 2002 production in the Festival Theatre tested assumptions that the Court House was the most appropriate space for *Candida* (see below, page 238), all the Festival productions of this small-scale play (by Shaw's standards), including Newton's in 1993, had been in the Court House. By 1993 Newton had thoroughly discombobulated audience expectations of familiar Shaw plays – an *Alice in Wonderland* approach to *Heartbreak House*, a minimalist *Man and Superman*, a metaphorical *Misalliance*, a word-mazed *Pygmalion*, a vaudevillian *Millionairess*. What, they must have wondered, would he come up with for *Candida*? The answer was surprising. In collaboration with set designer Yvonne Sauriol (with whom Newton had worked the previous season on Coward's *Point Valaine*) and costume designer Cameron Porteous, Newton created what looked like a very conventional environment for the play – recognizable living and working spaces occupied by people dressed as one might expect middle-class late Victorians to dress. Where in such conventional surroundings could those Shavian "demons beneath the surface" be lurking? Well, they were there, it's just that Newton had unearthed a different way of finding them.

Newton's *Candida* looked conservative, but he was convinced that he could still probe deeply into characters' emotions and motivations in such a setting. The key to unlocking relationships in the play, Newton determined – paradoxical though this sounded for a Shaw play – was silence. John Coulbourn in the *Toronto Sun* was at it again (in another unintended backhanded compliment), in accusing Newton of "ignoring" the play's subtext, of not discovering "enough sexual tension." But Coulbourn wasn't watching carefully enough – at the way, for example, that Candida (Seana McKenna) erotically fondled a poker – or listening carefully enough, not just to the dialogue, but also to the silences. Not quite like a Pinter play, but certainly moving in that direction, Newton's *Candida* searched for the subtext through pauses in the dialogue. The best example was the initial meeting between Candida and her father, Burgess (Sandy Webster). After a curt greeting, Candida took a long pause, causing her father, not knowing how to react, to turn away before Candida spoke again. As Lisbie Rae saw it, "a straightforward meeting between father and daughter was given depth and complexity by this pause, which opened up latent possibilities in the relationship." Perhaps Candida was simply angry at Burgess's three years of ignoring her and her family. Or, as Rae suggests, was she remembering an unhappy childhood? Perhaps even abuse? Shaw is often wrongly accused of failing to give his characters emotional depth. Throughout *Candida*, Newton helped Shaw to give the lie to this charge, as he had in his previous Shaw productions. This time, though, Newton did it more subtly, using pauses and silences in the dialogue to put the audience on notice that troubling questions about the relationships among any and all of the characters in the play might arise at any time.

OTHER SHAW UNDER NEWTON

Much as Newton's enthusiasm for Shaw grew in the years following his appointment as artistic director, he couldn't direct all of the Shaw plays himself. Nor, of course, did he want to. Both as actor and director he had a keen interest in exploring other plays from the mandate period, and regularly did so. During his tenure as artistic director Newton directed sixteen productions of Shaw plays, but there were eight seasons in which he didn't direct any Shaw at all (including four consecutive seasons from 1996 to 1999). He confidently assigned many of the Shaw one-act plays to Paul Reynolds in the Royal George Theatre (see above, page 94), but finding other suitable directors for the Shaw plays in the Festival and Court House Theatres wasn't easy. On principle, and perhaps also mindful of the problems his predecessor Paxton Whitehead had encountered with his perceived over-reliance on foreign artists, Newton looked exclusively to Canada for company members. He brought some of the country's leading directors to the Festival to do Shaw, both from major regional theatres and from smaller "alternative" theatres; but in the absence of a strong tradition of Shaw productions by other Canadian theatres it was difficult to find directors with much Shavian experience at all, let alone directors who could bring to Shaw's plays the kind of intellectual and emotional frisson that Newton wanted.

CANADIAN DIRECTORS

Among the Canadian directors who came and quickly went without leaving much of a mark were, for example, Bill Glassco, co-founder of Toronto's Tarragon Theatre (*Candida*, 1983),

Larry Lillo, co-founder of Vancouver's Tamahnous Theatre and subsequently artistic director of the Vancouver Playhouse (*The Devil's Disciple*, 1984), Leon Major, co-founder of Halifax's Neptune Theatre (*Arms and the Man*, 1986), and actor, director, and playwright Richard Greenblatt (*The Apple Cart*, 2000).

British-born Paul Bettis, who became a leading figure in Toronto experimental theatre in the 1970s, made a slightly bigger impact, directing *In Good King Charles's Golden Days* in 1981 and *Too True to be Good* in 1982 (both at the Court House), but he didn't return to the Festival in subsequent seasons. Duncan McIntosh, who also first came to the Festival in 1981 (as an actor – he was a Page in Newton's *Saint Joan* and also had a small part in *Camille*) stayed much longer, both as an actor and director. McIntosh became one of Newton's principal directors in the 1980s, responsible for some of the biggest productions in the Festival's history – notably Noel Coward's *Cavalcade*, which he co-directed in 1985–86 with Newton (see below, page 172). But McIntosh's contribution as a director of Shaw was limited to a 1987 production of *Fanny's First Play*, remembered mainly for its updating of Shaw's lampooning of theatre critics, McIntosh replacing Shaw's contemporaries with their 1980s' equivalents from Toronto – the *Globe and Mail*'s Ray Conlogue ("Raymond Trickowood"), the *Toronto Star*'s Gina Mallet ("Eugena Hammer"), and Southam News' Jamie Portman ("Jamie Winebibber"). Some critics complained about the in-jokes, but they tended to be those critics overlooked by McIntosh.

Marti Maraden (born in California, but she came to Canada in 1968) was another director who spent several seasons at the Festival but was used sparingly by Newton to direct Shaw. While Maraden shone at the Festival as an actor throughout the 1980s in Shaw (Cleopatra in 1983, Ellie Dunn in 1985) and other major productions (Roxanne in *Cyrano de Bergerac*, 1982–83, and Wendy in *Peter Pan*, 1987–88), her only involvement with Shaw as a director was a solid but unexceptional *Getting Married* in 1989.

National Theatre School graduate Paul Lampert had been Associate Director of Persephone Theatre in Saskatoon before coming to the Shaw Festival in 1990 to direct *Village Wooing* at the Royal George Theatre. He returned the following year to direct *The Doctor's Dilemma* at the Festival Theatre, and again in 1994 to direct *Too True to be Good* (Court House). Both productions were well received, although when *The Doctor's Dilemma* went to Ottawa's National Arts Centre in October 1991 audiences and critics – less accustomed to Shaw than those who were Festival regulars – had a hard time appreciating it. It opened on October 17 to a 60 percent house, and was roundly dismissed by the doctor-friendly *Ottawa Citizen* critic as "hollow, pompous verbosity."

ALLEN MACINNIS Another Western Canadian director, Allen MacInnis, who trained at the Vancouver Playhouse Acting School (founded by Newton), directed mainly musicals when he began at the Festival (*Hit the Deck*, 1988; *Good News*, 1989; *Nymph Errant*, 1990), but Newton later (1997) invited him to direct *In Good King Charles's Golden Days*, which hadn't been done at the Festival since Paul Bettis's production in 1981. It astonished London's *Times Literary Supplement* critic Robert Tanitch that this play of "all talk and no action" was playing to full houses, for which he gave credit not so much to Shaw as to "Allen MacInnis's vigorous production," "the fine ensemble playing of the cast" (led by Peter Hutt as Charles), and the "intimacy of a studio space" (the Court House Theatre). So impressed was he by the Shaw Festival production that Tanitch urged England's Chichester Festival to do the play "with an all-star cast" – good advice that was, however, ignored. MacInnis was back at the Festival in 2001 to direct *The Millionairess*, this time with less critical success; however, an outstanding performance from Sarah Orenstein in the title role, and some worthwhile efforts by MacInnis helped the audience through one of Shaw's wordiest plays (new music by Paul Sportelli and Jay Turvey; Shaw quotations about economic inequality projected onto the curtain between acts; framed tableaux of actors) and kept the box office humming (to the tune of an 84 percent attendance).

GLYNIS LEYSHON A Canadian who met some of Newton's aspirations for Shaw productions was Glynis Leyshon, a British Columbia actor and director who, like MacInnis, was a graduate of the Vancouver Playhouse Acting School, and whose subsequent work Newton had known in Vancouver. By the time Newton invited her to the Shaw Festival in 1990 Leyshon had become artistic director of the Belfry Theatre in Victoria. She directed just one play in 1990 – *Mrs*

Warren's Profession – but her contribution to the Festival continued over several seasons, and included plays by the Gershwins (*Lady, Be Good!*, 1994), Arthur Sullivan and Bolton Rowe (*The Zoo*, 1995), and Lillian Hellman (*The Children's Hour*, 1997) as well as more Shaw.

Leyshon's *Mrs Warren's Profession* tested preconceptions of Mrs Warren – and perhaps also preconceptions of female sexuality held by some male critics – by having a decidedly older madame than usual. Joan Orenstein was sixty when she played Mrs Warren – probably the oldest actress ever to take the part (Shaw gives Mrs Warren's age as between forty and fifty). Leyshon made no effort to disguise Mrs Warren's age; if anything Orenstein looked older than she was, more like "a dowager duchess" than the "brassy, domineering madame" that *Star* critic Robert Crew had in mind. To Doug Bale of the *London Free Press* Orenstein's Mrs Warren was simply "an old woman." Her daughter Vivie (Tracey Ferencz), on the other hand, looked the age that Shaw intended her to be (twenty-two), the age disparity between mother and daughter making the mystery of the identity (and age) of Vivie's father even more intriguing. The most unsettling moment of the production, however, was at the beginning of Act Two when Mrs Warren kisses the twenty-year-old Frank (who may be Vivie's half-brother). Immediately after kissing him, Mrs Warren regrets her sexual impulsiveness, dismissing it as "only a motherly kiss." But what looked to audiences more like a *grandmotherly* kiss – and a sexual one at that – was greeted with nervous, uncertain laughter.

After a lunchtime production of *Press Cuttings* at the Royal George in 1991, Leyshon returned to Shaw with *The Devil's Disciple* at the Festival Theatre in 1996. A well-received but generally run-of-the-mill production, this might have been her last Shaw for Newton; but when Polish director Tadeusz Bradecki (see below, page 132) became ill and had to withdraw from directing *The Simpleton of the Unexpected Isles* at the Court House Theatre in the same season that Leyshon was in Niagara-on-the-Lake for *The Devil's Disciple*, Newton turned to Leyshon to take over Bradecki's show. Those who remembered Denise Coffey's 1983 rousing production of *Simpleton* (see below, page 129) must have wondered what Leyshon could come up with to make sense of what Newton himself described as "the oddest of all Shaw's plays," full of surprise and wonder. One surprise that Leyshon conceived was to take a leaf out of Coffey's book – not *Simpleton*, but *Pygmalion* – in introducing Shaw himself into the play. As audiences entered the Court House Theatre they saw a bearded Al Kozlik on stage reading a newspaper. He remained on stage for the whole play, not saying much (Coffey's GBS in *Pygmalion* said quite a lot), but often mouthing the lines as the actors spoke them, and sometimes scribbling them down ahead of when they were spoken. For Kate Taylor this made sense in reminding the audience that – in an almost Brechtian way – they weren't watching a naturalistic play, but one in which Shaw's eclectic and sometimes shambolic mind was the human and intellectual protagonist at one and the same time, now satirizing the British empire, now contrasting Eastern spiritualism with Western rationalism, now arguing for cultural relativism. And to make the whole thing more pleasing to the eye, Leslie Frankish provided a set covered in a carpet of colourful flowers, Shaw's Garden of Eden on his exotic unexpected island.

JIM MEZON   Also prominent among Canadian directors of Shaw under Newton was Jim Mezon, another Vancouver Playhouse Acting School graduate, who had come to the Shaw Festival with Newton from the Playhouse as an actor in 1980. In his first season, Mezon wasn't cast in a Shaw play (he was in *The Cherry Orchard* and *A Flea in Her Ear*), but after a gap in 1981 and 1982 he returned to the Festival in 1983 as Lexy in *Candida*, followed throughout the 1980s by a series of major Shaw roles – Dudgeon in *The Devil's Disciple* (1984), Doyle in *John Bull's Other Island* (1985), Sergius in *Arms and the Man* (1986), and Cusins in *Major Barbara* (1987), for example. After another hiatus in his Shaw Festival career in the late 1980s and early 1990s, Mezon returned in 1992 as George Simon in Elmer Rice's *Counsellor-at-Law* and to direct Shaw's *Widowers' Houses*, his first play (about slum landlords), not done at the Festival since Paxton Whitehead's 1977 production.

While neither *Widowers' Houses* nor Mezon's second Shaw play, *Arms and the Man* in 1994, set many pulses running, Mezon's 1995 production of another early Shaw play, *The Philanderer*, created a good deal of interest. There were two reasons. The first was the decision to include the North American premiere (in a limited number of performances of the play), an act that Shaw wrote for *The Philanderer*, but discarded before the play was ever produced or

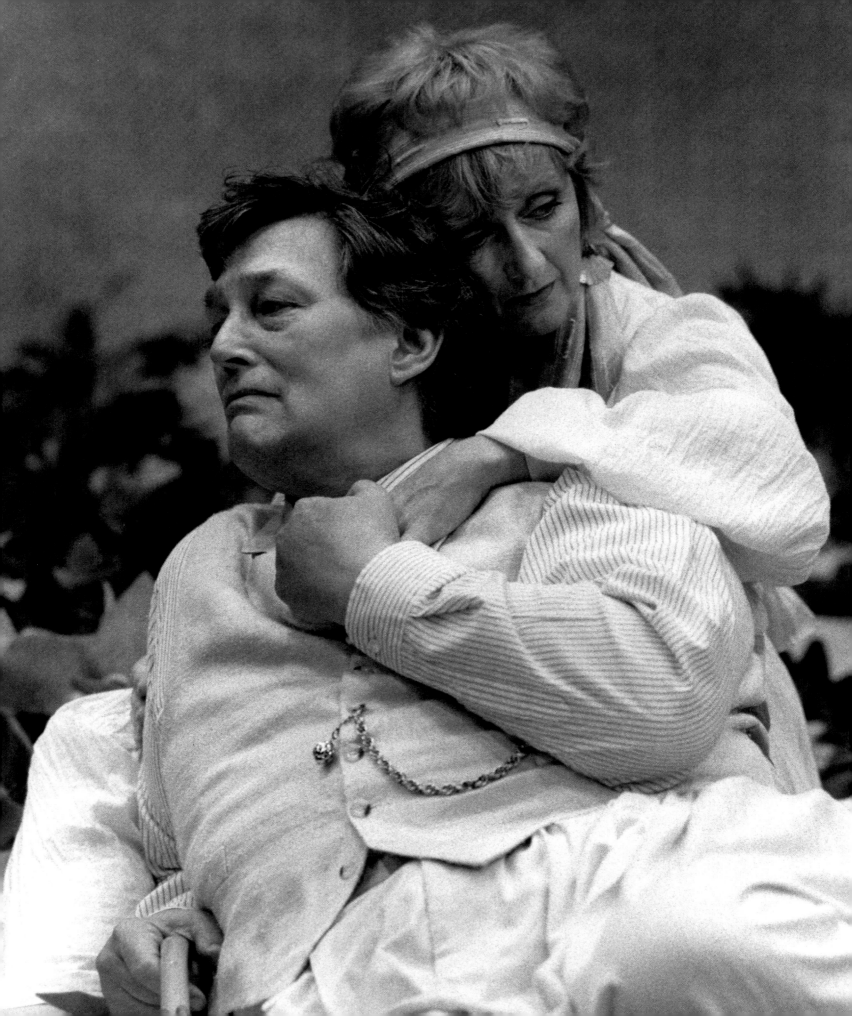

published. The second was the quality of the production, which was widely acknowledged to be Mezon's most successful Shaw to date.

The restored act of *The Philanderer* takes the story of the main characters four years into the future after the end of the action of the three-act play, and allows Shaw to explore and expose the iniquities of British divorce laws. Added to what was already a full-length play, the extra act made it a long evening – too long for some critics and audience members, some of whom beat a hasty retreat to the exit during the curtain call. They were, though, a minority. Eight performances of the four-act version of *The Philanderer* were scheduled, but such was the demand for tickets that four extra performances were added. But whether in the three-act or four-act version, Mezon's *Philanderer* sizzled, encompassing both a tough-minded depiction of the sexual tensions caused by Leonard Charteris's (Simon Bradbury) philandering and the rich comedy of dialogue and situation that runs throughout the play.

Mezon's fourth Shaw play under Newton was *John Bull's Other Island* in 1998 (the first since Denise Coffey's 1985 production), a time when even more attention than usual was being paid to the political and military situation in Northern Ireland, as glimmers of hope emerged that the conflicts there could be resolved without further bloodshed. As in Coffey's 1985 production, Mezon, while not dampening the comedy of the play, made sure that the darker aspects of Anglo-Irish relations were not obscured by humour. Not one given easily to praising Shaw – or Shaw directors – the *Globe and Mail*'s Kate Taylor noted how well, under Mezon's "tidy and intelligent" direction, David Schurmann had captured Broadbent's "blind activism" as a developer, riding roughshod over Irish sensitivities and Irish land. Taylor praised as well George Dawson's "truly nasty" Father Dempsey, a "conniving, power-hungry, and ultimately worldly man." Against these two, Peter Hutt's defrocked priest Peter Keegan, "with burning eyes and lilting accent," revealed charm and humility, but also "an unforgiving soul and dark vision." The tensions and conflicting values among these three – as well as others in the play – are not easily resolved. As Taylor recognized, Shaw does not take sides, nor did Mezon, making the play and its debates, for Taylor, "deeply engaging."

Buffalo News critic Terry Doran was also full of praise for Mezon, who according to Doran had "made his reputation at the Shaw Festival as an actor," but was now also "a first-rate director." That reputation was solidified by the last Shaw play that Mezon directed under Newton, *Getting Married* in 1999. The kind of play that, according to Kate Taylor, "gives Bernard Shaw a bad name" (all talk and no action), *Getting Married*, in Mezon's hands (helped by the strong ensemble), made sure that the extended discussions in the play about marriage maintained sufficient focus and energy to win over the doubters. Even Robert Cushman, who, despite being "a fan of Bernard Shaw," drew the line at *Getting Married*, declared himself "just about converted" to the play by Mezon's production – the discussions were never tedious, wrote Cushman, and in fact at times were "downright scintillating."

NEIL MUNRO The enormous contribution made by Neil Munro to the Shaw Festival is such that it merits special attention (see below, page 148), but the one Shaw play that he directed while Christopher Newton was artistic director should be recognized here. It was *Saint Joan* in 1993. Given the furore over Newton's 1981 production of *Saint Joan* (see above, page 77), there was bound to be enhanced interest in Munro's, only the Festival's second production of the play. If not quite as controversial as Newton's version, Munro's approach to the play was hardly conservative. As Newton conceded in an interview in *Maclean's* in June 1993, he knew very well that Munro's *Saint Joan* "would raise eyebrows." Munro, Newton said, was not afraid of "pushing towards the edge," or, some would add, over the edge.

Munro's approach to *Saint Joan* was to "get rid of the pageantry," to "take away the comfort of distance," to "let the play fly right in your face." In rehearsal Munro showed the cast gruesome film footage of the Bosnian war, then at its height, and he began the play with a tableau depicting the kind of massacre everyone was reading about in their newspapers. Cameron Porteous's set was replete with airplanes (a crashed jet), jeeps, computers, modern battle dress, helicopter search lights, body bags, and, in Joan's trial, television monitors.

For many people, the trial scene represented the Shaw Festival at its very best, a near-perfect blend of directing, design, and acting excellence. Joan (Mary Haney), downstage with her back to the audience, faced her interrogators, upstage, seated at a table with microphones. As she responded to their questions and accusations, a television camera captured close-ups

THE TRIAL SCENE; GEORGE DAWSON
AND MICHAEL BALL IN *SAINT JOAN*
BY BERNARD SHAW, 1993. DIRECTED
BY NEIL MUNRO, DESIGNED BY
CAMERON PORTEOUS, LIGHTING
DESIGNED BY ROBERT THOMSON.

OPPOSITE: MARY HANEY IN *SAINT
JOAN*, 1993. PHOTOS BY DAVID
COOPER.

of her face, which were transmitted to the audience through a bank of television monitors on either side of the stage. Haney's performance – anguish, fear, stubbornness, pride, courage, naivety – "reaches the sublime," said John Bemrose in *Maclean's*. "Rarely," he wrote, "has the struggle between individual conscience and the collective will been so powerfully presented." Notwithstanding Robert Cushman's complaint that "the last thing I want to do in a theatre is look at a TV screen," many found the scene among the most compelling they had ever seen at the Shaw Festival. For John Coulbourn it was "absolutely riveting," and for Jamie Portman the scene on the large Festival Theatre stage somehow achieved "a degree of intimacy and intensity unrivalled in this reviewer's memory."

Munro's *Saint Joan*, concluded *Village Voice* critic Michael Morrison, was "as exciting a Shavian production as one could hope to see." It included Shaw's Epilogue, though Munro, like Newton, would have preferred to leave it out. He made sure, though, that it didn't become tedious by making numerous cuts and having some speeches spoken simultaneously. Even so, for Robert Cushman (having recovered from the television monitors) the Epilogue "made the play's final point, that the world will always reject its saints, more powerfully than any other I have seen."

For Carolyn Mackenzie, who spent twenty-five seasons at the Shaw Festival in a variety of positions, including stage manager, Munro's *Saint Joan* was the most challenging show she worked on. There were frequent problems, for example, with the television monitors, even after thorough checking before the beginning of each performance of the trial scene. Mackenzie's solution was to create a role in the scene for one of the stage technicians, sending him on (she had headset connection) as needed during the scene as a kind of studio staff member for the interrogators. On the first occasion the actors weren't aware of what was happening. Barry MacGregor, the Inquisitor, paused, had a brief word with the technician, and then carried on as normal.

INTERNATIONAL DIRECTORS

DENISE COFFEY Although Newton was determined to give priority at the Festival to Canadian actors, directors, and designers, he never wanted to abandon international connections and influences. Thus, from England, he brought Denise Coffey, whose 1982 *Pygmalion* successfully reflected Newton's wish to revitalize Shaw (see above, page 82). Coffey was rewarded by

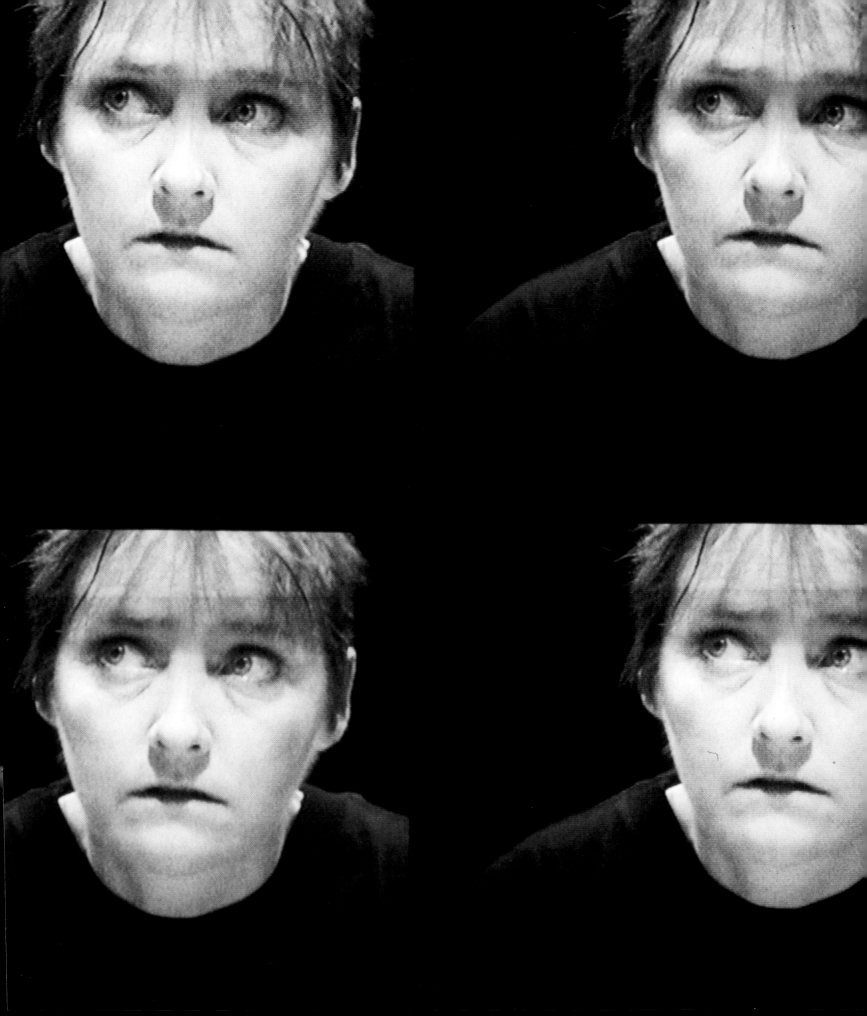

offers from Newton for the next five seasons. During that time she directed a further four plays by Shaw: *The Simpleton of the Unexpected Isles* in 1983, *Androcles and the Lion* in 1984, *John Bull's Other Island* in 1985, and *Back to Methuselah* in 1986. All of these productions were shaped by Coffey's aversion to the ordinary and conventional as well as her offbeat sense of humour. Like Newton, Coffey was always searching for new ways of understanding and presenting Shaw: respectful, but not reverential, in her approach to Shaw's text, and always in search of ways of engaging her audience. Thus the almost impossibly loosely structured *Simpleton* – set on a small island outpost of the British Empire (shades of the 1982 Falklands War) where the fantastic trumps the realistic – made a virtue of what has been called Shaw's "cheerful mess" of a play by celebrating rather than suppressing its eclecticism, throwing in vaudeville routines, Beatles music, and a dipsomaniac angel in the shape of Douglas Rain. Never before attempted by the Festival, *Simpleton* was pulled from the dust-heap of Shaw plays (most reviewers thought the 1935 premiere in New York showed signs of Shavian senility) and turned into a resounding hit by a director who, Jamie Portman said, had "sufficient guts to take risks and sufficient brilliance to bring them off."

(It was prior to the opening of *The Simpleton of the Unexpected Isles* on June 30, 1983, that the Festival announced the naming of part of an island in Ungava Bay, Quebec, as "Pointe Bernard Shaw." The resemblance between the southern tip of the island and Shaw's left profile was first noticed, from an aerial photograph, by Trent University geography professor A.G. Brunger. Brunger brought the resemblance to the attention of general manager Christopher Banks whose discussions with Canadian and Quebec government officials led to the designation.)

For *Androcles and the Lion* Coffey again collaborated (as she had on *Pygmalion*) with Dan Laurence, this time to create an additional scene for *Androcles* set in the trenches of the Second World War. This allowed her to present *Androcles* as a play-within-a-play, linking the anti-military theme of the play firmly within a modern context. Coffey's inventiveness with *Androcles* prompted McKenzie Porter to praise her – and Newton – for giving "new life" to Shaw, who had, he said, "been placed in danger of impending obscurity by a slavish directorial cleaving to theatrical techniques of the 1890s." Coffey's *John Bull's Other Island* did not contain (or need) new material since she kept virtually the whole of the original text, making for a long (and some said, tedious) evening. The production showed a more restrained, even introspective, side of Coffey's directorial skills, compassion as well as humour, even melancholy for both the past and the future of Shaw's Ireland as seen through the eyes of Irish romantic imaginations and British political and commercial ruthlessness.

But Coffey's biggest triumph with Shaw at the Shaw Festival was her 1986 *Back to Methuselah*, one of the great moments in the history of the Shaw Festival. The main problem with *Back to Methuselah*, in Shaw's view, was "finding a lunatic who is fool enough to produce it." Consisting of five related plays, with a cast of about twenty-five actors, *Methuselah* takes some seven-and-a-half hours to perform. The Festival's single-day performance, never before attempted in North America, began at 2pm with the first two plays of the cycle, *In the Beginning* and *The Gospel of the Brothers Barnabas*. With two intermissions, the afternoon session ended at 6pm. There was a two-and-a-half hour dinner break, and then the evening performance of *The Thing Happens*, *The Tragedy of an Elderly Gentleman*, and *As Far as Thought Can Reach*, which lasted until nearly midnight. Twelve performances were given between August 5 and September 12. Shaw had found his lunatic, or in this case his lunatics – Christopher Newton and Denise Coffey.

The Festival had produced the first part of *Back to Methuselah* in 1969, but 1986 was the twenty-fifth anniversary season, and Newton felt it was the appropriate time to tackle this "Everest" of a play. The text runs to about 90,000 words, and although Coffey at first thought she could cut it significantly, she discovered – as many directors do with Shaw's plays – that "it's so knitted together" that "it's madness" to try to chop it up. So "we're doing the complete text, near as dammit," she told Robert Crew. She also told Crew that during rehearsals all kinds of arguments and discussions were breaking out among the cast about the ideas in the play, the time span of which runs from the Garden of Eden to the year 31,920. By then Shaw envisaged a Utopian society governed by three-hundred-year-old "Ancients" – the earliest age at which, Shaw believed, there might be sufficient wisdom to govern a world heading for self-destruction (*Methuselah* was written just after the First World War). Coffey was hoping that the play would

prove as provocative for audiences as it was for her cast: "fierce arguments, people knocking each other out, people bumping tables and pointing vituperatively at each other, so excited they can't sleep, walking around the town with their heads bursting with excitement."

Well, it perhaps wasn't quite like that, given the lateness of the hour at which audiences left the Festival Theatre. There were, inevitably, some grumps among audiences and critics, for whom the *Hamilton Spectator*'s Stewart Brown was a spokesman. For Brown, "Shaw's windiness" made the play "an endless haul," a "back-breaking, bum-numbing bore." But it spoke volumes for the quality of Coffey's production and the astuteness (and, no doubt, physical stamina) of Festival audiences and most critics that Brown's view was in the minority. McKenzie Porter was perhaps a touch over-enthusiastic in describing *Back to Methuselah* as "the greatest play written since the death of Shakespeare," but there was no doubting his genuine admiration for what Coffey, designers Cameron Porteous (set and costumes) and Jeffrey Dallas (lighting), and the large cast had achieved. The experience, Porter said, had exhausted him, "mentally and physically," but he deeply appreciated the "once-in-a-lifetime chance to soak in deep and beautiful monotheistic profundities expressed with superb clarity and seasoned with pungent comedy." Unfortunately, the audiences that shared the experience with Porter were not large. While the three other plays in the Festival Theatre in 1986 averaged 88 percent attendance, *Back to Methuselah* drew just 56 percent.

Coffey had successfully brought a British sensibility to the Shaw Festival – not of the Paxton Whitehead (or even Christopher Newton) kind to be sure; closer, perhaps, to a quirky Python-esque view of the world. But Newton's next foray into England wasn't so successful.

Polish-born and trained Helena Kaut-Howson had established an international reputation, mainly through her work as artistic director of Theatre Clwyd in Wales, where, for example, she had mounted (directed by Gale Edwards) a brilliant *Saint Joan* in 1994, starring Imogen Stubbs. But things didn't go nearly so well with Kaut-Howson's unfocussed and heavy-handed *Major Barbara* in 1998 – almost, but not quite, rescued by Kelli Fox's intelligent and intense Barbara, and Jim Mezon's powerful Undershaft. Mezon's Undershaft was, at that point, the greatest Shaw performance Christopher Newton had ever seen, and it remains very high in his esteem.

TADEUSZ BRADECKI   Newton had long been interested in Polish and Eastern European theatre before he invited Polish director Tadeusz Bradecki to the Shaw Festival in 1994 on the recommendation of the Ministry of Culture in Warsaw (following contacts made in Poland by Cameron Porteous). A graduate of the Krakow Academy of Dramatic Arts, Bradecki rose to become artistic director of Krakow's famed Stary Theatre, which is the position he held when Newton invited him to the Festival to direct a black comedy called *Ivona, Princess of Burgundia*, by Polish playwright Witold Gombrowicz. Bradecki returned in 1997 to direct Shaw's *Mrs Warren's Profession* and again in 1999 to direct *Heartbreak House*. Newton brought him back once more in 2002 to direct Federico García Lorca's *The House of Bernarda Alba*, and when Jackie Maxwell became Shaw Festival artistic director in 2003 she cemented the Festival's relationship with Bradecki, inviting him to direct plays in 2003 (Brecht's *Happy End*), 2005 (a revival of *Happy End*), 2006 (Arthur Miller's *The Crucible*), 2007 (Ivan Turgenev's *A Month in the Country*), and 2009 (Shaw's *The Devil's Disciple*). Maxwell also invited Bradecki to the Festival in 2008, but commitments to his new position as artistic director of the Slaski Theatre in Katowice kept him in Poland. In 2011 he directed *Candida*, replacing the original director Gina Wilkinson after her untimely death in December 2010.

Bradecki provocatively gave *Mrs Warren's Profession* a startlingly Brechtian treatment. Each act was introduced by a music-hall routine and an actor reminding the audience that they were watching a "scandalous" play. Actors came out of character to speak directly to the audience, and at the end of the play designer Leslie Frankish's painted backdrop was removed in an illusion-crushing moment to reveal the Festival Theatre's bare walls and the rigging that had supported the backdrop. For some, there was more gimmick than substance in Bradecki's approach, but for many it was an exhilarating experience, generating intense discussions about

the play, its ideas, its emotions, its presentation, as audiences left the theatre. And nor did the Brechtian style deny characters their individuality, particularly Nora McLellan's Mrs Warren, "wonderfully earthy, sometimes coarse, with a lower-class accent, braying laugh and bold manners," as Kate Taylor described her. For the theatre critic of London's august *Financial Times*, this was a production "that I can scarcely imagine improved upon."

There was a general consensus as well that Bradecki got things right with his *Heartbreak House* that opened the 1999 season. Newton, who had directed *Heartbreak House* himself in 1985, set the bar high for Bradecki by declaring (in the season brochure) *Heartbreak House* to be Shaw's "masterpiece," in which Shaw was "at the height of his powers." Bradecki and the company rose to the challenge with a production that Kate Taylor – with an uncharacteristically rhetorical flourish – praised as "a glowering symphony of turn-of-the-century anxiety and nihilism that thundered powerfully on a dark spring evening at the end of the millenium." The musical metaphor was apt in that Bradecki used Mahler and Stravinsky for mood and context, complementing the discordant geometric angularity of Peter Hartwell's set (more Japanese than the traditional nautical atmosphere), full of wood and canvas frames suggesting early, yet threatening, airplane wings, or, more ominously, Zeppelins. Kevin Lamotte's lighting and Christina Poddubiuk's costumes emphasized the singularity of the house's inhabitants and visitors, all – save Douglas Rain's prescient Shotover – heedlessly lurching their way to oblivion. And jerky projections from silent movies increased the sense of clumsiness and lack of communication on this ship of vainglorious fools.

THE "RISK" SERIES

A Shaw Festival press release on August 17, 1983, announced "the new and exciting RISK series," a series that "offers an opportunity for members of the Shaw Festival company to embark on an exploration of interesting, yet rarely performed, plays written during the period of Bernard Shaw's lifetime." In a subsequent interview, Newton elaborated on his aims for the series, explaining that he was looking for plays "that deserve an airing but that may not appeal to a large enough cross section of the public to justify a full-scale mounting." Resources for the Risk productions would be limited – "something less than a full-scale production, but more than a workshop." Sets and costumes came from stock: "You may think you recognize a desk from *Candida* or a dress from *Camille* – you will be right," Newton wrote in a program note to *Tropical Madness No. 2* in 1985. Rehearsal time would also be limited, though casting was from the full company ensemble, and the productions were brought to audiences "with all the love, taste, and knowledge that we have."

The germ of the idea for the Risk series came from Newton's experience with the obscure Canadian play *Canuck* in 1980, which failed, from Newton's point of view, not because it is a bad play or because the production was inadequate, but because audiences and critics "had no structure" in which to place an unknown play. The Risk series, Newton explained in the *Tropical Madness* program note, signals to audiences that while the Festival may find a play "intriguing," it "may not be to everyone's taste." "We are testing the water of audience reaction." And when that audience reaction was enthusiastic, as it very much was with two of the plays from the series, those plays could be held over for a full-scale production and longer run in the following season. The series, then, was good for the company and audiences alike in that it presented opportunities for expanding theatrical horizons within the Festival's mandate, and it made financial sense for the Festival in that initial production costs were low, but potential for significant box office returns in re-mounts was high. All Risk productions were in the Court House Theatre, renovated by Cameron Porteous in 1981 to create the thrust stage that provided the kind of flexibility that many of the Risk plays needed.

The first Risk play was Noel Coward's *The Vortex*, which ran for five performances in late August and early September. It was followed by Romanian playwright Ion Caragiale's *The Lost Letter* (adapted by Newton and Sky Gilbert, six performances, 1984); *1984*, a company adaptation of George Orwell's novel (one performance, 1984); Polish playwright Stanisław Witkiewicz's *Tropical Madness No. 2: Metaphysics of a Two-Headed Calf* (six performances, 1985); Luigi Pirandello's *Tonight We Improvise* (six performances, 1986); Strindberg's *Playing with Fire* and Wilde's *Salomé* (on the same bill, as "Hot House Plays from the 1890s," eight performances, 1987); Russian playwright Leonid Andreyev's *He Who Gets Slapped* (seven performances, 1988); Cole Porter's *Nymph Errant* (nine performances, 1989); and – the last in the series – French playwright Alfred Jarry's *Ubu Rex* (seven performances, 1990). *The Vortex* and *Nymph Errant* were both held over to the following season for further performances – fifty for *The Vortex* in 1984, and seventy for *Nymph Errant* in 1990.

The plays selected by Newton had an extensive international scope – English, Romanian, Polish, Italian, Swedish, Irish, Russian, American, and French – and the style and content of the plays were equally diverse. *The Vortex* shows a darker side of Coward – drug abuse, adultery, repressed sexuality; *The Lost Letter* pokes fun at nineteenth-century Romanian politics; *Tropical Madness* is a 1921 expressionist play set in exotic locales that delves into deep psychological problems of the protagonist; *Tonight We Improvise* is a play about theatre and the blurred lines between the reality of theatre and the reality of life (at one performance the town fire alarm on the Court House roof went off, and the audience had no idea whether this was part of the play or not); *Playing with Fire* is – for Strindberg – a surprisingly funny play about sexual tensions and obsessions in a middle-class family; *Salomé* (the Festival's first play by Oscar Wilde, in an adaptation by director Sky Gilbert) is about a different kind of sexual obsession, that of the biblical Salomé for the head of John the Baptist; *He Who Gets Slapped* is about a Russian intellectual who changes careers to become a circus clown (and gets slapped a lot for his trouble); *Nymph Errant* (the first and only musical "risk" of the series) traces the racy adventures of a young woman around Europe; and *Ubu Rex* is an 1896 play about violent political usurpation, the form of the play itself reflecting in its absurdist, anarchic form a usurpation of nineteenth-century theatrical conventions.

In his review of *Nymph Errant*, *Globe and Mail* critic Ray Conlogue noted that during a song about sexual permissiveness the singer (Bernadette Taylor) handed out condoms to audience members in the first row (of the Court House Theatre). It was an intriguing idea, but Conlogue quickly had to publish a clarification. Audience members had actually been given Girl Guide cookies. Conlogue blamed "the seriousness of Cole Porter's lyrics for inspiring this error," and he assured readers that the Shaw Festival "would never do such a thing." "Ever."

The Risk series was a cornucopia of theatrical treats, a feast of plays that, as one critic bluntly but admiringly put it, "wouldn't be touched with a barge pole" by other theatres in North America. But there was one play in the Risk series that was so extraordinary that it defied all expectations of even a series mandated by risk.

1984 Neither the Shaw Festival nor Niagara-on-the-Lake had seen anything quite like it before. On the evening of September 18, 1984, the town centre was transformed by the Festival into Oceania, the society presided over by Big Brother in George Orwell's novel, *1984*. A dramatization of Orwell's famous work was announced by Newton early in November 1983 as part of the 1984 season, a season that already included several large-cast productions, including Shaw's *Androcles and the Lion* and Thornton Wilder's *The Skin of Our Teeth*. But when in January 1984 Johanna Mercer accepted Newton's offer to take on the production she little knew what challenges lay ahead. She was about to direct one of the largest – perhaps *the* largest – piece of environmental theatre ever attempted.

It was Mercer's role to script the production and coordinate its staging in the Festival's three theatres, its warehouse, and in the streets and parks of Niagara-on-the-Lake. All for just one daunting six-hour performance. The entire Festival company was involved, not just actors, designers, directors, and technicians, but administrators, box office staff, ushers, communications staff – some 300 in all. Tickets – which very quickly sold out – were limited to 600, and all audience members were checked in by computer as they arrived at the warehouse for the first scene, and issued with Oceania overalls and passports. Some audience members would later be "arrested" and transported to prison in the Ministry of Love.

Mercer built major scenes from Orwell's novel into the production – a Hate Rally, an Anti-Shakespeare Lecture, Room 101 (the torture room, set up on the Festival Theatre stage), a Victory Parade (held down Queen Street, accompanied by low flying planes in formation), a musical Propaganda Play (in the Royal George), all accompanied by propaganda music blasting from loudspeakers and posters of Big Brother, who also dominated Simcoe Park from a giant movie screen. (Big Brother was played by Murray Morrison, head of set construction.) Audience members were served a canteen meal of spam and peas on tin plates, washed down with a tin cup of gin.

Eighty press members participated as well, joining the twenty-four audience groups who moved around the twelve performance locations. With minimal rehearsal time and huge technical and logistical demands, it was, Mercer said, a "terrifying" experience, but it was also an experience that "caught the imagination of the company, the town, the audience, businesses, and the press."

***MARATHON '33*, 1987** The designated Risk series was discontinued after the 1990 season, Newton judging that audiences were now ready for challenging and provocative theatre as an integral part of the Festival repertoire. Indeed, he had never in any case limited risk to a few performances in the Court House towards the end of each season – a kind of danger zone off-limits to all but the theatrical cognoscenti or curious. What, for example, was *Marathon '33*, one of the opening plays at the Festival Theatre in May 1987, if not a huge risk? A Depression-era play about men and women participating in degrading marathon dance sessions for the promise of food – dancing until they dropped, sometimes for over 3,000 hours with short breaks for sleep – *Marathon '33* was written by a marathon participant (June Havoc) as a grim metaphor for a broken America. With a cast of over thirty (and a small orchestra), *Marathon '33* was a huge artistic and financial gamble (especially in the Festival Theatre), and it provoked complaints from some patrons, one of whom was told by Festival Literary Adviser Dan Laurence (who had recommended the play to Newton) that there are times – such as this – when "the audience is a failure" and the company's "artistic triumphs go unappreciated." One measure of the unappreciated triumph was, unfortunately, a low 51.5 percent box office return on the play.

    Marathon '33 was directed by Duncan McIntosh, who also took on the challenge of another large-cast risk in the Festival Theatre in 1988 – German playwright Erwin Piscator's 1922 adaptation of Tolstoy's *War and Peace*, an epic novel compressed by Piscator into a two-and-a-half-hour play. The production boasted a sumptuous set designed by John Ferguson, but all the vigorous and praiseworthy efforts by Ferguson, McIntosh, and the cast didn't convince critics or audiences (another low box office, 54 percent) that Piscator's script was worth the trouble.

LULU, **1991** Undeterred, Newton continued to take risks in the Festival Theatre. In the first season when there was no official "risk" play, 1991, he scheduled (and directed) another play by a German contemporary of Shaw, Frank Wedekind's *Lulu*, in an adaptation by British playwright Peter Barnes. As the Festival's own press release about the play stressed, Lulu is "a woman of extremes" whose "obsession is sexual." Or, as *Globe and Mail* critic Ray Conlogue put it, Lulu (played by Helen Taylor) "is free of social conditioning, and possesses the untrammelled sexuality of an animal." It made for an interesting evening of theatre. Unlike in his *Camille* in 1981, Newton didn't include any nudity in *Lulu*, but lust and raw sexuality pervaded the production, reinforced by Leslie Frankish's set (lots of mirrors) and costumes ("everything from great gowns to garter belts," noted one critic), Robert Thomson's lighting (scarlet colouring and dancing laser beams), and the suggestive music and choreography of Christopher Donison and Caroline Smith. There was some very positive reaction from the critics. A Festival advertisement for *Lulu* showing an embrace between two women – one naked (but seen only from the rear) – included a string of quotes from reviews: "Brilliant...arresting...ravishing," "Stunning...theatrical magic," "One of the most exciting and mesmerizing evenings of theatre southern Ontario has seen in a very long time," "Sensational theatre." But for some audience members it was all a bit much. Conlogue reported that the "crème de la crème" opening night audience "were in a mild state of shock," and subsequent performances witnessed some audience walk-outs and empty seats after the intermission, with many patrons "disgusted" with such a "terrible" show demanding (but not receiving) their money back. Box office came in at only 52 percent.

***RASHOMON*, 1996**   Although one person's risk is another person's sure-fire certainty (if there is such a thing in theatre), there's good reason to argue that Newton took other calculated risks in the Festival Theatre, even if the play or its content could be said to be reasonably familiar. Akira Kurosawa's 1950 film *Rashomon* (the Golden Lion winner at the 1951 Venice Film Festival), for example, was familiar to many. But the 1959 stage version by American writers Fay and Michael Kanin of this story of an encounter in a forest between a samurai and his wife and a bandit, chosen by Newton as one of the opening plays of the 1996 season, was, despite a short run on Broadway, less well-known. It was to be directed by Neil Munro, which made it, according to one critic, "the most eagerly awaited show" of the 1996 season. But it was still, countered another critic, "a gamble," "the riskiest venture of the Festival's opening week." As things turned out, the risk didn't pay off. If far from the "dramatic dud" that Jamie Portman judged it, *Rashomon* was a critical disappointment and a box office disaster (under 40 percent in the Festival Theatre).

***LORD OF THE FLIES*, 2000**   William Golding's 1954 novel *Lord of the Flies* was far better known than *Rashomon*, and British writer Nigel Williams' stage adaptation had received a major production by the Royal Shakespeare Company in 1995. Again, though, it was hard to know how Festival audiences in the 2000 season would receive this story of the descent into savagery of a group of English schoolboys stranded after an air crash on a South Pacific island. When Mike Shara, who played Jack, first read the script he thought "Oh, God, this is impossible. It's just so huge. The stakes are enormous." And so they were. An account of Neil Munro in an early

rehearsal with his cast describes him ("with blazing eyes and grizzly beard") asking for the cast's patience with this "very unusual play in an unusual theatre [the Festival Theatre] for such a play." Newton knew that the play's depiction of raw violence would be upsetting, but that, as he saw it, was part of the point: "We live in a world where we have to deal with many kinds of violence," he said, "and as a theatre company we must reflect that." And to remain vital and relevant the Shaw Festival must be "a place where you're stimulated to take away ideas."

Jamie Portman thought that it was "a gutsy decision" to stage *Lord of the Flies*, and also gutsy of Newton to choose Neil Munro as director. Munro could be trusted, Portman said, to depict the violence in the play "to a stomach-churning degree." And he did. Kate Taylor thought Munro left the audience "nowhere to look except into the face of violence, sadism, and tyranny that Golding depicted as man's natural state" (there are no females in the novel or the play). Not for the first time (or the last) at the Festival, there were audience walkouts – and houses barely half-full – but also bravos for Munro's direction, for the mesmerizing acting of adults playing boys, and for the stunning designs by Cameron Porteous (set and costumes) and Kevin Lamotte (lighting).

MARSH HAY, 1996   The international emphasis of the Risk series itself was continued right up to the end of Newton's term as artistic director, and plays (all in the Court House) such as *The Unmentionables* (Carl Sternheim, German, 1993 season), *Ivona, Princess of Burgundia* (Witold Gombrowicz, Polish, 1994), *S.S. Tenacity* (Charles Vildrac, French, 1999), and *The House of Bernarda Alba* (García Lorca, Spanish, 2002) could all have fitted comfortably into the Risk series. One exception to the European panorama was *Marsh Hay*, a 1923 Canadian play by Merrill Denison that Newton included in the 1996 season, with Munro again directing. If not quite as obscure as *Canuck*, *Marsh Hay* – despite a Toronto (amateur) production in 1974 – was unfamiliar territory for all but a small minority of Festival audiences. But Newton's assessment of the play as a "fine and moving" depiction of the tribulations of family life in the

Ottawa Valley in the 1920s – poverty, domestic abuse, teenage pregnancy – struck a chord with audiences and critics alike. Canadian plays, *Toronto Star* critic Geoff Chapman said, "haven't been given much of a run at Shaw, but if *Marsh Hay* is an example of what's hiding out there, let's have more." Newton obliged with another Denison play in 1998, *Brothers in Arms*, which had a short run as a lunchtime offering in the 1998 season. The "Reading" series – initiated by Newton in 1996 as single (sometimes two) rehearsed readings in the Royal George Theatre of short unfamiliar plays from the mandate period – also included work by Canadian writers such as Herman Voaden, Gwen Pharis Ringwood, and Stephen Leacock.

The importance of the Risk series and the numerous risky productions that Newton continued to mount after the series nominally closed was well captured by Dan Laurence in the letter he wrote on Newton's behalf to the disgruntled patron who walked out of *Marathon '33* in 1987. "No company," Laurence said, "can produce quality work without experimentation and constant challenge. It *must* take risks – it must *break through* – or it will grow complacent, dull, and die." Yes, there were failures among the risks, but "every major theatrical company has its artistic failures" – "it is the price that must be paid for its ultimate successes."

NEWTON OUTREACH

OUTREACH FOUNDATIONS   Like all great theatre companies, the Shaw Festival was never about simply putting on plays and waiting for audiences to come and see them. From the beginning Brian Doherty and Calvin Rand saw the Festival as not "just a theatre," but a hive of artistic activity encompassing music, dance, literature, and film. And the Festival should also, in their view, reach out to and engage local, regional, national, and even international communities in the Festival's programming.

One of Doherty's earliest outreach initiatives, in cooperation with Brock University, was the establishment of a seminar series in 1965 that gave Festival patrons an opportunity to see plays, hear lectures, participate in discussions, meet company members, and attend social events, all in a four-day package. Speakers in the first seminar included leading Shavian scholar Stanley Weintraub from the Pennsylvania State University and Claude Bissell, President of the University of Toronto. Subsequent seminars boasted speakers of the calibre of Robertson Davies, Northrop Frye, Eric Bentley, Jacques Barzun, and Dan Laurence. The seminars remain the longest-running feature of Festival outreach programs, continuing into 2011 (and, no doubt, beyond) in essentially the same format adopted from the beginning in 1965.

Brock University sponsored the first six seminars, followed by McMaster University and York University, and although the seminars have been administered by the Festival itself since 1989, links with colleges and universities have remained important to the Festival. Another early link, for example, was with nearby Niagara College in Welland, Ontario, which joined with the Festival in 1968 to offer a theatre training course in management, design, acting, and directing, the first joint College-professional theatre program of its kind in Canada.

When the Festival Theatre opened in 1973 then general manager Tom Burrows stressed the importance of using the facility year-round through a variety of activities. Thus, a School of Dance was opened at the end of the 1973 season, and dance and musical events were held in the Festival Theatre throughout Paxton Whitehead's term as artistic director. In 1974, for example, the Shaw Festival International Concert Series hosted the Royal Winnipeg Ballet in March, and then, in the fall, the Vienna Boys Choir, the Moscow Chamber Orchestra, the Canadian Opera Company (with *La Bohème*), and pianist Anton Kuerti. A Summer School of Music, with Camerata, a Toronto chamber group, in a two-month residency, further enriched the 1974 season. As if that wasn't enough, 1974 also saw visits to Niagara-on-the-Lake by the Manitoba Theatre Centre with a production in October of John Hirsch's adaptation of the Jewish folktale *The Dybbuk*, and in November by Toronto Workshop Productions with its dramatization of Barry Broadfoot's 1973 oral history of the Great Depression in Canada, *Ten Lost Years*.

The Festival was also busy in 1974 with tours of *The Devil's Disciple* (pre-season) and *Too True to be Good* and *Charley's Aunt* (post-season), touring being another significant means of reaching out to wider audiences (see page 43 for an account of Paxton Whitehead's tours).

The range, frequency, and quality of outreach activities under Whitehead did not consis-

CHRISTOPHER NEWTON AND FIONA
REID IN *BREAKING THE SILENCE*,
BY STEPHEN POLIAKOFF, 1985–86.
DIRECTED BY MARTI MARADEN,
DESIGNED BY CAMERON PORTEOUS,
LIGHTING DESIGNED BY PATSY LANG,
SOUND DESIGNED BY WALTER
LAWRENCE. PHOTO BY DAVID
COOPER.

GERAINT WYN DAVIES AND MATTHEW
WALKER IN *GOODNIGHT DISGRACE*,
BY MICHAEL MERCER, 1985. DIRECTED
BY LEON POWNALL, DESIGNED BY
DIZ MARSH, LIGHTING DESIGNED BY
DONALD FINLAYSON, ARTWORK AND
SLIDES BY PAUL KUZMA. PHOTO BY
DAVID COOPER.

tently match those achieved in 1974, but important outreach precedents and standards were set under his leadership. Both of Whitehead's successors – Christopher Newton and Jackie Maxwell – remained committed to outreach activities, but each set their own priorities and directions.

TOURING   For Newton, touring was not a major priority. "I'm not a great one in promoting us touring," he said in Calgary during a tour of *You Never Can Tell* in 1988; "I think people should come to us and see us in our setting." Nonetheless, Newton toured some twenty productions during his twenty-three seasons as artistic director (Whitehead toured twelve in his ten seasons), covering much of Canada (Toronto, Ottawa, Montreal, Calgary, Victoria) and some major American cities (Seattle, Philadelphia, Rochester, Ann Arbor). There were many successes – artistic and financial – but also some disappointments, such as the cancellation of a 1986 tour of *One for the Pot* when host theatres in Detroit and Los Angeles pulled out, and sparse attendance for *Arms and the Man* and *The Front Page* at a University of Michigan residency in November 1994. (For a full list of tours under Newton, see Appendix C, page 302.)

THE TORONTO PROJECT   Newton was much more enthusiastic about another outreach project, one that took the company to Toronto for off-season productions throughout the 1980s. Newton firmly believed that the company could not reach the highest levels of quality without active involvement in performing new work. "I deeply believe," Newton told one interviewer, "that you can't do the best work on old plays unless you do some new ones as well." (When he was pitching the concept to board members in 1983 Newton told them that "a theatre without new plays is like life without sex.") And he thought the best place to do new work was in a large urban environment such as Toronto where, he believed, audiences could be challenged, "pushed further," he said, than was possible in a tourist destination such as Niagara-on-the-Lake. He often cited the model of Britain's Royal Shakespeare Company, with bases both in Stratford-upon-Avon and in central London. Creating a Toronto base for the Festival would also allow the company to engage more fully (though not exclusively) with Canadian playwrights, countering criticism from organizations such as Playwrights Canada that the Festival was ignoring them.

Newton's first Toronto production took place before the Toronto Project was officially approved and launched. In February 1982 he directed Vancouver playwright John Lazarus's *Dreaming and Duelling* (about two teenagers duelling over a girl) in a Festival co-production with Young People's Theatre. That went well enough to help persuade the board to endorse Newton's proposal for an ongoing Toronto presence, which was announced in a Festival press release on November 23, 1983, in which Newton described the initiative as "a new and exciting venture for the Shaw Festival which will allow us to explore new works by interesting playwrights in an urban setting." The first play was the North American English-language premiere of *Delicatessen* by French playwright François-Louis Tilly, adapted and co-directed by Derek Goldby and David Hemblen, and featuring members of the Festival acting ensemble (Joyce Campion, Al Kozlik, Dan Lett, and Marion Gilsenan). *Delicatessen* was co-produced with Toronto Free Theatre, where it ran for fifty-one performances in January and February 1984.

Further co-productions followed: Canadian Michael Mercer's *Goodnight Disgrace* at Toronto Free Theatre in March 1985; Canadian Sheldon Rosen's *Souvenirs* at Factory Theatre in December–January 1985–86; American William M. Hoffman's *As Is* at Toronto Free Theatre in January–February 1986. For the 1986–87 winter season the Festival assumed full responsibility for two productions: the North American premiere of *Breaking the Silence* by British playwright Stephen Poliakoff (in which Newton took the lead role) and *B-Movie*, a play by acting ensemble member Tom Wood that had originally been workshopped at the Festival. But while these were Festival productions, there was no Festival space in Toronto in which to present them. In both instances the theatre of Toronto Workshop Productions was used.

It had been Newton's ideal from the beginning that the Festival would have its own five- to six-hundred-seat theatre in Toronto, and he elaborated on his Toronto vision in an article (headed "Vivat! Vivat Toronto!") in the 1987 Festival brochure. A permanent Toronto presence had recently been confirmed as board policy, and now the search was on for space for the development and performance of new work. These activities would be complemented by transfers to large Toronto theatres of box office successes in Niagara-on-the-Lake – such as had happened with *Cyrano de Bergerac* at the Royal Alexandra Theatre in the winter of 1984–85.

It was a bold vision that, if successful, would guide the Festival "triumphantly into the new century," said Newton. No buildings materialized during the regular 1987 season, and the only Toronto production in the winter season was a large-scale co-production with the Canadian Opera Company of Murray Schafer's opera *Patria I: The Characteristics Man*, directed by Newton in the Tannenbaum Opera Centre (six performances). And then, in 1988, came the final production of the Toronto Project. It was another Canadian play, a musical called *Fire*, by Paul Ledoux and David Young, directed by Brian Richmond at Theatre Passe Muraille. It ran for forty-six performances, but closing night on December 4, 1988, marked not only the end of the run of *Fire* but the end also of the Toronto Project.

Ultimately, the Toronto Project fell victim to difficult financial conditions. Although the Festival's 1987 season ended with a $100,000 surplus, the 1986–87 Toronto season lost money. And then both the 1988 and 1989 regular seasons ran deficits, leading to an accumulated operating deficit of over $1 million. Producer Paul Reynolds advised the board in the middle of the 1989 season that it would be necessary to cut "ALL extra activities which do not have a very strong likelihood of turning a profit." The situation was such, he said, that "it will demand a COMPLETE hold on any new initiatives to ensure that there are no risks." In such circumstances the major financial implications of buying property in Toronto and running a regular winter season there were no longer tenable.

THE ACADEMY   The demise of the Toronto Project affected another of Newton's outreach initiatives. In his one season as artistic director (1979) Leslie Yeo had created an Actors Studio at the Shaw Festival. This was strictly an in-house arrangement that provided training opportunities in voice and movement for members of the acting company. The Actors Studio didn't survive Yeo's departure, and Newton had other priorities in his early seasons at the Festival. But arising from initiatives taken by company members themselves – Marti Maraden and Goldie Semple, for example – in 1985 Newton announced the creation of the Academy, which encompassed, he explained in the 1985 season brochure, "new play workshops...voice and movement classes... [a] training programme...[a] video workshop...production classes...and [an] actors' research centre." The research function was supported by the Festival's library, which Brian Doherty had started from his own personal collection in the Festival office on Queen Street. When the Festival Theatre opened in 1973, a space off the lobby housed the library, which under the direction of volunteer librarians – most notably Nancy Butler – expanded to a collection of over 4000 volumes, selected to assist Festival directors, designers, and actors in play selection and research. Under the direction of Duncan McIntosh, the Academy expanded into many other areas – including even courses on "Acting Shakespeare" – and was open to all Shaw Festival employees. Newton saw the Academy as a key component of his Toronto Project, with a Toronto location, but when that ambition was thwarted the Academy stayed in its first home in a boathouse beside the Niagara River. That remained its home until fire destroyed the building on May 7, 1991 (together with props, a turntable stage, lighting and sound equipment, and the set for the 1990 production of *Present Laughter* – losses to the building and contents amounted to some $2 million). The Academy relocated temporarily to the rectory of St Mark's Church before moving into new space in the Festival Theatre – "Christopher's Loft" – in 1995.

Two years after the founding of the Academy, an outreach component was added with the opening up of a select number of classes to the general public, and the Academy continued throughout the 1980s and 1990s to provide programs internally and externally. A Directors Project was launched in 1988 (and is still running) that brings young directors to the Festival as interns to give them experience of working with directors of Festival productions, and also to provide them with the opportunity of directing one-act plays cast from the acting ensemble, with an audience of company members and invited professionals. Education programs for the general public and for high schools, colleges, and universities were created, and in some cases partnerships were established – with the University of Guelph, for example, which in 1983 became the repository for the Shaw Festival archives, and (for the second time) with Niagara College's Theatre Arts Program in 1988. Further afield, the Festival formed a partnership in 1991 with the Bolshoi Drama Theatre in Leningrad (Saint Petersburg), a relationship that began with the visit of the theatre's chief designer Eduard Kochergin to the Festival in 1989 to design Newton's *Man and Superman*. Other international partnerships were formed with the Stary Theatre in Krakow and the Melbourne Stage Company in Melbourne.

ACADEMY HEAD OF VOICE AND
DIALECT EDDA SHARPE WORKS
WITH ACTOR KELLI FOX. PHOTOS
BY DAVID COOPER.

Newton and his colleagues continued the practice of their predecessors in bringing leading dance and music artists to the Festival, including, for example, Les Ballets Jazz de Montréal (1982), Peter Appleyard and the All-Star Swing Band (1987), George Shearing (1989), and the National Youth Orchestra (1990). New musical series were started – Musical Mondays (1983 onwards), for example, in the Court House Theatre, and in 2000 a Musical Reading Series (ongoing) in the Royal George Theatre, in which Newton himself was prominent as actor and arranger.

FUNDRAISING   Outreach activities sometimes served a parallel and important function as fundraisers. Natalee Roseberg Benstock, the first special projects coordinator at the Festival (as well as the first audience development officer and first public relations director), set one precedent in the 1970s with the Shaw Festival Show Train. This consisted of two sleeping compartments, a lounge, a dining car, and a caboose. The caboose was turned into a cabaret space, in which actor Tom Kneebone and singer Dinah Christie performed at stops as the train travelled from Toronto to Vancouver. Some forty Festival supporters paid to travel with the cabaret, and publicized the Festival at the various stages of the journey, while cabaret ticket revenue added to the bottom line. A more adventurous train ride was planned for Egypt, Israel, and Jordan in 1979, but was vetoed by the Canadian and American governments who said that they could not guarantee the safety of the travellers.

Newton didn't come up with anything quite as exotic as a Festival train trek through the Middle East, but his idea for a "Gentlemen's Boxing Evening," which he first suggested to the board in November 1984, struck some people as almost as bizarre. How, they wondered, could a boxing event at which meat and alcohol and tobacco would be consumed in profuse quantities honour a pacifist non-smoking vegetarian teetotaller? The meat, alcohol, and tobacco component was, Newton had to concede, decidedly un-Shavian, but the boxing was another matter. As a young man Shaw took boxing lessons, and in 1883 he both completed a novel (*Cashel Byron's Profession*) about boxing and entered a boxing competition (though never actually made it into the ring). And in later life Shaw developed a close friendship with undefeated world heavyweight boxing champion Gene Tunney, whose pugilistic skills (and intelligence) he much admired.

So the boxing evening went ahead. The first was held (at a Toronto hotel) in 1986, and (in 2011) it is still going strong. One newspaper reported on the 1991 event: "More than 450 gentlemen in black tie dined on terrine of Atlantic salmon and snow crab claw, potage Parisienne, pepper crusted lamb rack, and triple cream chocolate pâté followed by a snifter of Cognac Marnier V.S.O.P. and a Havana Tueros cigar. Then they watched men try to beat each other senseless." Among the guests over the years have been Canadian boxer George Chuvalo and former world heavyweight champion Joe Frazier. It is doubtful that these gentlemen – or many of the non-pugilist guests at the boxing evenings – have ever read or seen a Shaw play, but no matter. Newton's 1984 brainchild, widely recognized as one of the most innovative fundraising initiatives in Canadian theatrical history, has raised the profile of the Shaw Festival among Toronto's financial elite and – more importantly – has generated over $7 million for the Shaw Festival.

THE COMMUNITY   The Shaw Festival Guild was another important outreach program that came into its own during the Newton years. Initially, in the early 1960s, dozens of volunteers, most of them women, helped the Festival with all kinds of administrative and social activities, such as selling and taking tickets and catering the opening night receptions. Margherita Howe, for example, recalls working with another Guild member, Audrey Wooll, bringing "tablecloths and silverware and the candelabra and silver dishes and trays" from their homes to the Court House. As more volunteers got involved, however, it became obvious that some kind of structure was needed. It was all "pretty slapdash…not the least organized in any structured way," Howe recalled in a 1986 interview. So a meeting was called at Audrey Wooll's home, a meeting that led to the formation of the Women's Guild in 1964. The Guild soon began operating a soft-drink stand at the Court House, and making and serving sandwiches at Festival functions. Ten years later men were admitted as Guild members and the name changed to the Shaw Festival Guild. When Newton arrived, he quickly became, according to Elfie Northey (Guild President in 1988), a strong backer, and membership increased to around 250. In 2011 Guild membership

stood at over 350, members volunteering their time as docents, gardeners, and hosts who greet patrons as they arrive at the theatre. In 2006 the Shaw Guild Endowment Fund was set up to support areas of Festival activity in which Guild members are active.

The Guild, most of whose members were (and are) residents of Niagara-on-the-Lake, was also an important link between the town and the Shaw Festival. Even when major town-Festival disputes had been resolved – the location of the Festival Theatre while Paxton Whitehead was artistic director, the controversy around Christopher Newton's proposal for a tent theatre on the Commons in 1981 – the potential for conflict was ever-present. The Guild's assistance in organizing events such as the annual Village Fair and Fête, which began in 1988 to support local charities, was invaluable, but Newton nonetheless had to face regular *contretemps* with townspeople who could never quite accept that the Shaw Festival was a permanent feature of the town's physical and economic landscape. The opening of the 1985 season, for example, was greeted by a letter to the *Niagara Advance* with the accusation that the Festival had "once again" opened its "gaping jaw" and was about to "swallow this once lovely town." Residents of Victoria Street complained about "Shaw Party Time" in a neighbouring house at 2:39 (precisely) one morning in June 1985. A visitor from New York, "here for a few days of quiet relaxation," wondered "what kind of neighbours" were "making such a racket at this hour." And so the police were called. In the spring of 1987 there was a flurry of letters about traffic problems in Niagara-on-the-Lake. As tour buses drove through town, some residents, it was reported, were seen "to shake their fists, fling gravel, and tell the driver to get lost." Property taxes kept going up, and the "nonrenewable resource" of the old town was being destroyed for "short-sighted tourism reasons." One of the strongest complaints about commercial intrusion came, ironically, from Shaw-enthusiast, Niagara-on-the-Lake resident, and *Toronto Sun* critic and columnist McKenzie Porter, who had no problem with the "middlebrows and intellectuals who come to see the plays" at the Shaw Festival, but who resented, in regrettably elitist and racist terms, the "lowbrows and clods," "masticating masses," and "scruffy day trippers," who were making the town resemble "the back streets of Cairo, Bombay, or Mombassa." And, moreover, "Asian cheapjacks are moving in" to replace "quality shops" with "souvenir schlock and kitsch."

Resentment of the Festival's impact on Niagara-on-the-Lake may not have represented a majority view in the town, and there was no shortage of letters to the press that stressed the economic "vibrancy" that the Festival had brought, but opposition was relentless. When the Festival proposed an affordable housing project (thirty townhouses and apartment units on Lakeshore Road) for Festival employees in 1989 there was vigorous opposition from nearby residents and the town council – overriding the recommendation of its planning committee – rejected the proposal. And even something as innocuous as a statue of Bernard Shaw on Queen Street raised hackles because, as another resident put it, "this man has done nothing for the town to merit a public monument." The statue, by distinguished Ontario sculptor Elizabeth Holbrook, was nonetheless installed at Queen and Victoria streets on April 1, 1996.

What was often overlooked in discussions – rational and otherwise – of the Festival's impact on Niagara-on-the-Lake was that only a small proportion of the tourists who came to the town each summer were (and are) theatregoers. In 1995, administrative director Colleen Blake explained in a letter to the *Niagara Advance* that the Festival sold approximately 300,000 tickets a season "many to repeat customers who see several plays during their visits." "We also welcome," Blake added, "many of our local residents and their guests." Blake's calculation – a disappointing one from the Festival's point of view – was that of the "millions" of tourists who visited Niagara-on-the-Lake each year only about 50,000 were Festival patrons.

NEIL MUNRO

While outreach and fundraising activities made ever-increasing demands on Newton's time, he still had an artistic program to run. In his first few seasons Newton worked steadfastly to build both an acting ensemble and an artistic team he could depend on – set designer Cameron Porteous, lighting designer Jeffrey Dallas, directors Paul Reynolds, Duncan McIntosh, and Denise Coffey, among others. Then in 1988 Newton invited another director to the Festival. His name was Neil Munro.

Born in Scotland in 1947, Neil Munro came to Canada at the age of nine. After graduating from the National Theatre School in Montreal, he acted at several major theatres across the country, including Theatre Calgary in 1968 in Christopher Newton's inaugural season there as founding artistic director. After the end of that first season, in what Newton described as "an otherwise unremarkable production," Newton played Hamlet to Munro's "quicksilver" Laertes in Victoria, British Columbia. In a busy career, Munro also squeezed in one season at the Shaw Festival in 1977, Paxton Whitehead's final year as artistic director. Munro played Harry Trench in Shaw's *Widowers' Houses*, directed by Whitehead. Munro didn't return to the Festival until Newton invited him in 1988, by which time (after a serious attack of stage fright in 1986) he had switched his theatrical interests from acting to writing and directing. In the first season at the Festival with Christopher Newton, Munro directed just one play, Harley Granville Barker's *The Voysey Inheritance*. But that proved to be the beginning of an extraordinary relationship between Munro and the Festival, one that lasted until his retirement shortly before his untimely death in July 2009.

HARLEY GRANVILLE BARKER   Not having encountered Newton for ten years or so, the phone call offering him a job at the Festival surprised Munro – the Christopher on the phone "was as likely to be Christopher Reeves as Christopher Newton," he said. Nor was Munro enamoured of the Shaw Festival, which he linked with the Stratford Festival as "British colonial bookends that had little to say about the modern world, or the world that I lived in at any rate." Still, he agreed to read the play that Newton offered him, even though he had never heard of Granville Barker or *The Voysey Inheritance*. When he had finished it, in one sitting, he "just sat there," feeling, he said, "as if I had stumbled across something stuffed with treasure." Much to his surprise and delight, *The Voysey Inheritance* wasn't "some creaky old piece dragged from the dungeons of the mandate. It was a work of art – tough, difficult, uncompromising." Munro was hooked. Not only did he agree to direct *The Voysey Inheritance*, he directed six more plays by Granville Barker at the Shaw Festival over the next several seasons, successfully bringing Barker's work into the mainstream of theatrical culture and practice.

Instrumental in establishing Shaw's reputation in London by producing several of his plays at the Royal Court Theatre between 1904 and 1907, Barker was an accomplished playwright himself. His own plays, however, were largely undervalued during and after his lifetime. Convinced that the neglect was unjustified, Newton put his faith in Munro to prove him right.

The Voysey Inheritance – a 1905 play about financial embezzlement and deceit by a respected solicitor whose family "inherit" the consequences of his behaviour – began previews at the Court House Theatre on July 1, 1988. It ran for sixty-three performances, was well received – with particular praise for Douglas Rain as the family patriarch and Joseph Ziegler as his son – and did well at the box office (80 percent). Newton was impressed enough with Munro to bring him back the next season to direct John L. Balderston's *Berkeley Square*, and although there was then a two-year hiatus for Munro at the Festival he was back in 1992 to direct another American play, Elmer Rice's *Counsellor-at-Law*. That was the beginning of sixteen straight seasons for Munro at the Shaw Festival, during which he directed some thirty plays.

In the second of those seasons, 1993, Munro took on his second Granville Barker play, *The Marrying of Ann Leete*, written in 1899 and first performed in 1902. Written, as Munro himself described it, "in a deliberately oblique, obfuscatory, even expressionistic style," this play about a young woman in late eighteenth-century England defying her wealthy family's expectations by marrying a gardener, demanded – and got – from Munro's direction not the bold theatricality of *Saint Joan*, which he was also directing at the Festival in 1993 (see page 124), but something altogether more restrained. The opening of the play was startling – the young woman's scream in the blackness of a summer's night – but the subdued elliptical talk, punctuated by Pinter-like silences, led insistently to the image-driven ending of a candle in the darkness, a small and fragile symbol of hope and new beginnings for the young woman. No slamming doors here, but as equally a courageous journey into a new world as Nora's at the end of Ibsen's *Doll's House*.

Another facet of Barker was seen next season (1994) in *Rococo*, a short farce about a family squabble after the reading of a will about who gets a valuable rococo vase. Audiences didn't much care for *Rococo* (box office for the lunchtime production in the Royal George was under 50 percent), and next season's Barker play, *Waste*, didn't fare much better.

***WASTE*, 1995** While both Shaw's *The Philanderer* and Wilde's *An Ideal Husband* were draw-ing close to capacity audiences in the Court House, *Waste* was managing only 53 percent in a much shorter run in the same theatre (twenty-four performances against fifty-nine for Shaw and forty-two for Wilde). But few who saw *Waste* doubted either the quality of the play or of Munro's directing. Like Shaw's *Mrs Warren's Profession*, *Waste* had been banned from the public stage in England in the early twentieth century for delving into sexual matters – prostitu-tion and incest in *Mrs Warren's Profession*, abortion in *Waste* – but for Munro *Waste* went far beyond the abortion issue itself. On the surface a play about political and sexual scandal, *Waste*, he suggested, was on a deeper level about "multi-dimensional worlds" in which the "secret life" of individuals "swims in pools of sexual tension and existential angst." The dispar-ity between the secret self and the "outer political life," Munro said, "is the essential ingredient of *Waste*, as it is of any Barker play."

Munro's ability to recognize and communicate that disparity made all of his Barker pro-ductions memorable, but *Waste* was the triumph. For Christopher Newton, *Waste* was "the greatest production done while I was Artistic Director. It represented all the things that I dreamed of for the Festival. It was a great play that no one had ever seen. It had a superb cast. It had a magical set [designed by Peter Hartwell] and it had Neil to guide it." Newton saw the production many times. "I cried. I admired. I was so proud that we had achieved this master-piece." Newton was not alone in his acclaim of *Waste*. Rochester critic Michael Lasser wrote that he had seen "a great play" in "a superb ensemble performance" (that included Ben Carlson in his Festival debut season, as well as such talented and experienced actors as Irene Hogan, Wendy Thatcher, Mary Haney, Fiona Reid, Andrew Gillies, Peter Hutt, David Schurmann, and Robert Benson). "This," Lasser concluded, "is as good as the Festival gets." And while *Globe and Mail* critic Kate Taylor wasn't bowled over by the production, she paid both Newton and Munro the compliment of seeing what Newton meant when he said that the Festival was in the business of doing plays "that show us the beginning of the modern world." In *Waste*, she wrote, "there are regularly moments when one feels the veil that separates us from our great-grandparents is finally being lifted."

Munro did three more plays by Barker, none quite hitting the heights of *Waste*. *The Secret Life*, the title of which spoke to what Munro saw as the core of Barker's plays – in this case reflected, as one critic usefully put it, in the lives of characters "mired in the ashes of what they regard as their under-achieving lives" – did far better at the box office than *Waste*, achieving 87 percent in a twenty-one performance run at the Court House in 1997. Ironically, though,

critical reaction to *The Secret Life* was far more muted, despite widespread praise again for the ensemble (including Newton himself as a retired and unfulfilled politician).

The Madras House, which Munro directed in 1999, also did well at the box office (83 percent in a forty-three performance run at the Court House), though some of Munro's directorial decisions – not for the first (or last) time – divided the critics. For example, he framed the action by taped recordings of himself reading some of Barker's stage directions. Robert Cushman thought the conceit intrusive, but he still praised the production as "a sophisticated essay in verbal and visual cross-reference." Many of the visual elements were provided by Peter Hartwell's diverse sets and Christina Poddubiuk's dazzling array of costumes, including those of the models in the London fashion house (named after the family that owns it) that gives the play its title. It's this environment that allows Barker to expose deep levels of sexism in Edwardian society. As Munro put it in his program note, the women in this society – and not just the models – "spend their lives trying to accommodate a patriarchal system that desires and rejects them at the same time."

The final play of the Barker series was *His Majesty*, never performed in Barker's lifetime, and only once (at the Edinburgh Festival in 1992) before the Shaw Festival production in 2002. Both a "political thriller and a story of personal adventure" (Munro's description), *His Majesty* is a play about the political chaos in Europe after the First World War, centred on attempts to persuade a reluctant monarch to return from exile to his throne. Newton gave it a longish run in the Court House (thirty-eight performances), but it didn't catch on with audiences (54 percent box office). The critics weren't enthusiastic either, with the exception of one of the astutest of them, Robert Cushman. Cushman thought *His Majesty* made "a great capstone" to the Barker cycle, judging it "as fine and dense a political play as the twentieth century has to offer" – notwithstanding Shaw's *The Apple Cart*, which, as Cushman recognized, bears many similarities to *His Majesty*.

In his review of *His Majesty*, Cushman praised the Shaw Festival's Barker series as "one of their finest achievements," and if Neil Munro had done nothing else for the Festival than direct the Barker plays his mark would still have been indelible. In fact, he did more, much more.

Following Munro's radical *Saint Joan* (discussed above, page 124) and second successful Granville Barker production (*The Marrying of Ann Leete*) in 1993, Newton offered Munro the newly created permanent position of Resident Director. Munro's acceptance of the offer was both a reflection of his personality and his approach to theatre. "I'm delighted," he said in a press release, "with the invitation to become Resident Director, if for no other reason than to find out what it is." There was a whimsicality, a quirkiness, about Neil Munro and, often, about his productions. These characteristics, while sometimes unsettling for audiences and critics alike, grew from a deep-seated commitment to serious exploration of drama and theatre, always from a starting point of rejecting easy questions and comfortable answers. His theatrical, social, and personal interests were wide-ranging, informed by extensive and eclectic reading and an insatiable intellectual curiosity. Munro's attention to contextual detail is legendary among actors; one actor who worked with him recalled the "small plastic box" that Munro carried around, "filled with cue-cards packed with information about every last detail of the world he was directing." Another actor remembers the Munro binders, "overflowing with notes, pictures, and magazine clippings." Munro used this kind of research to help create lives for even the most minor of characters, and he never failed to push all actors not just to their perceived limits, but beyond. All Munro's colleagues remember his determination to challenge norms, wherever he encountered them. As James Bradshaw wrote in his obituary in the *Globe and Mail* in 2009, Munro "fought constantly and tirelessly against complacency and stasis, both on and off the stage." That fight against complacency shaped in one way or another virtually everything he directed for the Shaw Festival, and – both under Christopher Newton and Jackie Maxwell – impinged upon all areas of the Festival mandate during the eighteen seasons he spent at the Shaw.

MUNRO AND SHAW Under Christopher Newton Munro directed only one Shaw play, *Saint Joan*. Under Newton's successor, Jackie Maxwell, he did another two, *Misalliance* in 2003 and *Man and Superman* in 2004. As with *Saint Joan*, both *Misalliance* and *Man and Superman* were done with daring panache.

MISALLIANCE, 2003 Munro's *Misalliance* (the Festival's fifth production) opened Maxwell's first season as artistic director of the Shaw Festival (as it had Newton's first season in 1980), and it gave notice that Munro's directorial inventiveness would continue unabated under new leadership. Containing a line that is often turned against Shaw – Hypatia's complaint about too much "talk, talk, talk, talk" – *Misalliance*, in Munro's hands, was cause for celebration of, rather than apology for, the talk. Peter Hartwell's set design was papered in Shaw's own phrases, and from time to time Munro had his actors move to lecterns on either side of the stage to emphasize, not disguise, the debating elements of the play. At the same time, Munro was determined to strip his production of any solemn reverence for Shaw, bringing on Shaw himself in a comic cameo appearance in old film footage, and using a bust of Shaw when a stage direction calls for the smashing of an ugly punchbowl.

Munro's production didn't set any box office records, but it was still the bestseller of the 2003 season (over 60,000 tickets) and it delighted most critics. *The Times* had likened *Misalliance* at its 1910 London premiere to "the debating society of a lunatic asylum." Jamie Portman chose a homelier simile for the 2003 Shaw Festival production. Munro, he said, "plunges us into the theatrical equivalent of a ping-pong match – verbal, intellectual, sexual, philosophical." The result? A "transport of delight," said Portman.

MAN AND SUPERMAN, 2004 Keeping audiences on edge, never quite knowing what might come next, was a favourite Munro strategy, one he used to telling effect in his production of *Man and Superman* in 2004. The play opened on an unadorned stage on which black-clad stagehands moved some chairs and stools around on a skeletal set (designed by Peter Hartwell, lit by Kevin Lamotte). It looked more like a rehearsal room than a set for one of Shaw's major plays. But here and throughout the production Munro shunned naturalistic period detail to force attention – as in his *Misalliance*, though in a different way – on language and ideas. In the *Don Juan* scene, Hell was simply chairs and stools again, the stools covered by a huge red cloth that made it difficult for the actors to navigate their way around the stage. This, Munro knew, made some audience members nervous on behalf of the actors (would they stumble?), which is exactly the tension-creating atmosphere that Munro wanted for one of the most intellectually exciting and finely balanced discussions in the dramatic canon about Heaven and Hell, good and evil, and the future of the human race. The audience needn't have worried, this wasn't a stumbling production. It was, by almost universal agreement, an outstanding ensemble achievement, as well as a personal triumph for Ben Carlson as John Tanner/Don Juan. *Hamilton Spectator* critic Gary Smith described it as "an evening of thirst-quenching, mind-stirring theatre," proving, "once again," that the Shaw Festival "can create theatre of monumental consequence." And few who were present at the opening of the full-length production will forget the ovation at the end of the play, described by Robert Cushman – veteran of many opening nights – as "an ovation of a fervour I have never encountered before at this Festival and rarely anywhere else." Standing ovations, he said, have become "standard politeness" in Canadian theatre, but "it's still unusual" for an audience "to refuse to shut up and leave when the lights are raised so that the actors have to take their calls all over again." As for Carlson, New York critic John Simon extolled his ability to deal with Shaw's "long and convoluted speeches" in *Man and Superman*. Carlson, Simon said, "tossed [them] off with machine-gun speed and bull's eye precision, with unparalleled elocution and infectious humor." Carlson won applause not just *after* his performance but *during* his performance. "I have never in the non-musical theatre," Cushman said, "felt an audience to be so completely *with* an actor; and never can the solidarity have been more deserved."

In 1977 (Tony van Bridge's production) there had been fourteen performances of the full *Man and Superman* (with the *Don Juan in Hell* scene). In 1989 (Christopher Newton's production) there had been thirteen. In 2004 there were eleven, a disappointingly low number in Robert Cushman's view, so he urged Festival patrons to "beat the doors down" in the hope of "perhaps shaming the management into bringing the whole thing back next year." It didn't happen, but Cushman's criticism was, of course, really a handsome compliment to the quality of the full-length production.

And, to add to the compliments, *Man and Superman* was one of the shows that prompted John Simon to express the belief that the Shaw Festival "is the best repertory theater on the entire continent, with standards that consistently aim high and generally generously deliver."

GRAEME SOMERVILLE AND JANE PERRY IN *MISALLIANCE* BY BERNARD SHAW, 2003. DIRECTED BY NEIL MUNRO, DESIGNED BY PETER HARTWELL, LIGHTING DESIGNED BY ROBERT THOMSON. PHOTO BY MICHAEL COOPER.

No other British or Irish playwrights of the mandate period appealed to Munro quite as much as Granville Barker and Shaw, but under Newton he did also direct plays by John Galsworthy (*Joy*, 1998) and J.B. Priestley (*Time and the Conways*, 2000); and under Jackie Maxwell by Sean O'Casey (*The Plough and the Stars*, 2003), Terence Rattigan (*Harlequinade*, 2004), and Somerset Maugham (*The Constant Wife*, 2005, and *The Circle*, 2007). He was also scheduled to direct Priestley's *An Inspector Calls* and Rattigan's *After the Dance* in 2008, but illness forced him to withdraw from both assignments.

Joy and *Harlequinade* were, respectively, the first Galsworthy and Rattigan plays to be seen at the Festival. Only one O'Casey (*The Shadow of a Gunman* in 1965) and one Maugham (*The Circle* in 1967) had been done before.

AMERICAN PLAYWRIGHTS Neil Munro's interests spread as well to American plays of the mandate period, particularly plays from the period between the two world wars. "I'm drawn to these plays," he said, "because they represent such a fertile period in American literature and also because they tend to be neglected." His first foray into this world was a 1929 work by John L. Balderston called *Berkeley Square*, which ran to decent houses (67 percent) at the Festival Theatre for eighty-one performances in 1989. There is a strange time shift in the play from the late eighteenth century to the 1920s that allowed Munro to work with set designer Cameron Porteous and lighting designer Sholem Dolgoy on some unsettling effects – explosions in the

fireplace, blackouts, spooky noises – while a cast headed by Peter Hutt effectively explored conflicting cultural and moral values between two societies.

Berkeley Square was followed by Elmer Rice's Counsellor-at-Law in 1992, Ben Hecht's and Charles MacArthur's The Front Page (1994), Robert Sherwood's The Petrified Forest (1995), George S. Kaufman's and Moss Hart's You Can't Take It With You (1998, revived 1999), Arthur Miller's All My Sons (1999), Kaufman's and Hart's The Man Who Came to Dinner (2001), Sidney Kingsley's Detective Story (2002), and (Munro's last American play for the Festival) Tennessee Williams' Summer and Smoke (2007). All these productions were marked by distinctive Munro characteristics, but three large-cast shows particularly stood out.

COUNSELLOR-AT-LAW, 1992   Rice's Counsellor-at-Law, for example, had a cast of twenty-eight. Munro got them firing on all cylinders; each character, however minuscule the role, acquired a specific identity, from Jim Mezon's Jewish lawyer George Simon throughout the whole array of lawyers, clients, and sundry hangers-on who crowd into a bustling Depression-era Manhattan law office. The production also contained some unmistakable Munro directorial trademarks. In one scene a conversation between George Simon – his mouth full of cream-filled chocolates – and a local political boss chewing on a cigar was completely muffled; but even if the audience couldn't make out what was being said the scene cleverly suggested, as critic Liam Lacey pointed out, that "there's an old language these two boys from the street understand that's deeper than words."

JIM MEZON; MICHAEL BALL; MARY HANEY IN *COUNSELLOR-AT-LAW* BY ELMER RICE, 1992. DIRECTED BY NEIL MUNRO, DESIGNED BY CAMERON PORTEOUS, LIGHTING DESIGNED BY KEVIN LAMOTTE. PHOTOS BY DAVID COOPER.

THE FRONT PAGE, **1994** With a large cast (two dozen actors), *The Front Page* was another major ensemble piece. Munro kept the pace at breakneck speed, often giving his actors overlapping lines. But individual performances still shone through. Michael Ball had been acting at the Festival, with just a few seasonal gaps, since 1976, and his performance in *The Front Page* led Jamie Portman to open his review with the declaration that "It's time something special was done on behalf of Michael Ball – such as declaring him a national treasure." His work, Portman said, has been so consistently fine "that it's easy to take his contribution to Canadian theatre for granted."

Not one to shy away from controversy, Munro resisted using an expurgated text for *The Front Page*, a decision that caused discomfort for many audience members. Set in the press room (designed with appropriate grunginess by Cameron Porteous) of the Chicago Criminal Courts Building in the late 1920s, the language of the reporters reflects prevailing prejudices, and Jamie Portman wasn't the only critic present on opening night who heard collective gasps and murmurs as one reporter says that a story isn't worth pursuing because it only involves "niggers." The discomfort was increased by a description of a "pickaninny" being born in a cab. Munro said he had "played around" with changing the text ("coloured" for "negro"), but in the end had decided that he "wanted to be true to the original text and expose the moral corruption of the times." By and large, the press were on his side. "It's to the credit of director Neil Munro," wrote Portman, "that he hasn't done a cop-out." The world of the play, Portman argued, is "racist, sexist, misogynist, profane. A less courageous production might have tried to deal with this problem by taking scissors to the script."

DETECTIVE STORY, 2002 Munro's skill at handling a large cast was shown to even better effect in *Detective Story*, in which thirty-three ensemble members appeared. For *The Front Page* Cameron Porteous had designed a grungy Chicago press room. For *Detective Story* Munro needed from Porteous a similar grunginess in a Manhattan police station: grim, grey, littered with cigarette butts. On that set (on the Festival Theatre stage), crammed with cops and crooks, Munro did again what he had done with *Counsellor-at-Law* and *The Front Page*. He kept the ensemble working seamlessly together, while again fashioning individual characters out of them all, from Peter Krantz's brutally self-righteous detective, to Lorne Kennedy's silky abortionist, to Jennifer Phipps's deranged complainant, and so on through another thirty characters down to the smallest walk-on part. It was, said Robert Cushman, "a superbly orchestrated production...the Shaw Festival at its very best...a stageful of actors with skill and humanity pouring out of their ears." For Jamie Portman *Detective Story* was simply "as rich a display of ensemble acting as you will encounter on any of the world's great stages...a resounding triumph for director Neil Munro."

Detective Story was the last show designed by Cameron Porteous at the Shaw Festival under Christopher Newton's artistic directorship. Porteous had left his position as Head of Design at the end of the 1996 season, but had continued to work at the Festival on a freelance basis (and has continued to do so since Jackie Maxwell became artistic director in 2003). In an appreciation of Porteous in the catalogue of a 2009 exhibit honouring Porteous's contributions to Canadian theatre, Newton recognized his singular contribution to the Shaw Festival. "I am proud to say that he is my friend," Newton wrote, "and that without him neither the Vancouver Playhouse in the heady seventies nor the Shaw Festival would have touched that great mystery, which is both a completion and a search, which is, indeed, great theatre."

YOU CAN'T TAKE IT WITH YOU, 1998, 1999 Inevitably, Munro's probing for unsettling effects and his wont for flouting expectations were sometimes aggravating to audiences and critics. The two Kaufman and Hart plays he directed – *You Can't Take It With You* in 1998 (revived in 1999), and *The Man Who Came to Dinner* in 2001 – are both comedies, but how far can the comic elements be pushed? Munro thought quite far – too far for some tastes. He argued in his program notes for *You Can't Take It With You* that the energy in this Depression-era satire on material possessiveness "threatens to explode into farce, but the inner warmth of the characters

holds it back." It wasn't clear to everyone, however, that he succeeded in holding back the farce. Why, complained Jamie Portman, "does Munro repeatedly sabotage [his own] viewpoint by coarsening the play with labored, increasingly unfunny bits of over-the-top comic business?" Other critics intensified the criticism: "in a directorial emulation of a kid in a candy store, [Munro] piles on pratfalls and double-takes to such an absurd degree that the production stumbles under the sheer weight of his excess baggage and has to drag itself home," was John Coulbourn's reaction in the *Toronto Sun*. At least one critic disagreed – Robert Cushman praised Munro for refusing "to get frenetic" – but it hardly mattered to Munro. He laughed all the way to the box office as *You Can't Take It With You* pulled in a whopping 93 percent attendance over 101 performances in the Festival Theatre and was held over for a further fifty-seven performances in 1999 with an 87 percent attendance.

THE MAN WHO CAME TO DINNER, 2001 *The Man Who Came to Dinner* provided Munro with a golden opportunity to upset expectations, and he gleefully took it. In the course of the story of a guest who outstays his welcome, a crate of penguins is famously delivered to the hosts' home. The penguins escape – offstage – and the audience only hears about, never sees, the mayhem they create. In Munro's production the unseen became the seen. First the penguins were visible through frosted glass, then – children delightfully costumed by Christina Poddubiuk – they came into full view on stage. This time it was Cushman's turn to grumble about Munro's "extravagantly misguided" direction as the penguins began to steal the show. Misguided or inspired? For the most part, audiences thought the latter, filling 75 percent of Festival Theatre seats in a seventy-nine performance run.

Munro was criticized as well for finding what Gary Smith in the *Hamilton Spectator* described as "specious, overt comedy" in Tennessee Williams' *Summer and Smoke* (the first Williams play at the Festival). But, again, audiences didn't seem overly concerned. If *Summer and Smoke* didn't match the box office success of *You Can't Take It With You*, it did respectable business at close to 72 percent in sixty performances in the Royal George Theatre.

Heavily involved in the American and British aspects of the Festival mandate, Munro spent less time on its European components. He directed Chekhov's *The Seagull* in 1997 in the Festival Theatre in an adaptation by Canadian playwright David French, and he directed Ibsen's *Rosmersholm* in his own adaptation in the Court House Theatre in 2006. He also adapted and directed a Feydeau farce, *Something on the Side*, in the Royal George Theatre in 2005. The Feydeau was a box office hit (89 percent), but neither *The Seagull* (52 percent) nor *Rosmersholm* (46 percent) met much support from patrons or critics.

Christopher Newton said that he simply "didn't connect" with some of Neil Munro's productions. But Munro was, for Newton, "the conscience of the Festival." It was Munro's unwavering commitment to rejecting the commonplace, to pushing artistic boundaries, to challenging audiences, to championing creative irreverence that earned him this praise. Munro was the Festival's risk-taker *par excellence*, and it was, therefore, both right and appropriate that a prize established by the Shaw Festival in his memory should be "for the risk-takers in the performing arts."

WANETA STORMS AND PATRICK GALLIGAN IN *ROSMERSHOLM*
BY HENRIK IBSEN, ADAPTED BY NEIL MUNRO, 2006. DIRECTED
BY NEIL MUNRO, DESIGNED BY PETER HARTWELL, LIGHTING
DESIGNED BY KEVIN LAMOTTE, VIDEO DESIGNED BY SIMON
CLEMO. PHOTO BY DAVID COOPER.

OPPOSITE: FIONA REID IN *THE SEAGULL* BY
ANTON CHEKHOV, 1997. DIRECTED BY NEIL MUNRO,
DESIGNED BY PETER HARTWELL, LIGHTING DESIGNED
BY KEVIN LAMOTTE, MUSIC COMPOSED BY CHRISTOPHER
DONISON. PHOTO BY DAVID COOPER.

SHAW'S CONTEMPORARIES

NOEL COWARD The plays of Harley Granville Barker were seen in seven of Christopher Newton's twenty-three seasons at the Shaw Festival. Next to Shaw, however, the most frequently produced playwright under Newton was not Barker, but – by far – Noel Coward. Coward plays were part of fourteen Newton seasons. Before Newton took over the Festival there were Coward plays in the 1971 and 1979 seasons, and under Jackie Maxwell Coward plays have been produced in two seasons, 2006 and 2009. That is, Noel Coward has been present in eighteen of the Shaw Festival's first fifty seasons.

London (Ontario) critic Doug Bale thought he had figured out what it was about Coward that appealed to Newton. "Newton and Coward," he wrote, "have much in common both on and off the stage. Like the Master, as Coward was known, Newton is a showman through and through; not only an astute impresario of other artists' talents but a consummate performer himself." Like Coward, Bale continued, Newton "has a passion for hard work and the gift of making it seem effortless. Like him too, he presents an Olympian persona to the outside world while reserving a franker one for co-workers – and placing ultimate reliance on an inner circle of tried friends." Be all that as it may, Newton had a more prosaic, but also more persuasive, explanation for Coward's frequent presence in the Festival repertoire. Coward, he said, "is not only central, but may well be the period's second most important playwright in English."

Newton's enthusiasm for Coward was reflected not only in the wide range of Coward plays he chose for the repertoire, but also in his decision to direct (and, in one case, co-direct) some of those plays himself and to act in others. It was a Coward play (*The Vortex*) that Newton selected for his first "Risk" play (see page 137) in 1983, and in the same season he asked Denise Coffey to direct *Private Lives* (following her unconventional *Pygmalion* in 1982). Newton played Elyot Chase in *Private Lives*, opposite Fiona Reid (in her Festival debut) as Amanda Prynne, with Nicola Cavendish (Sybil Chase) and Jim Mezon (Victor Prynne) in the strong cast. After playing to over 98 percent capacity in the Festival Theatre in a thirty-five performance

run, *Private Lives* was brought back by Newton for the 1984 season (with one cast change – Camille Mitchell replacing Nicola Cavendish), when in a longer run (fifty-five performances) in the Festival Theatre it still achieved an 84.5 percent box office. Newton's other acting appearance in Coward was as Gary Essendine in *Present Laughter* in 1990, directed by Bob Baker for a forty-seven performance run in the Festival Theatre (80 percent box office), a production that longtime Festival patron John Panabaker remembers as "polished, hilarious, and beautifully staged."

In addition to *Private Lives* in 1983, Denise Coffey also directed *Hay Fever* in 1987, a production that went on to the National Arts Centre in Ottawa later that year. The other directors selected by Newton for Coward were Susan Cox for *This Happy Breed* in 1991 – a scaled-down *Cavalcade* told from a middle-class point of view – and *Blithe Spirit* in 1993; Dennis Garnhum for *Still Life* in 2000; and David Savoy for *Shadow Play* in 2001. *Still Life* and *Shadow Play*, both part of Coward's *Tonight at 8:30* cycle, were given as lunchtime performances at the Royal George Theatre. (*Tonight at 8:30* was performed in its entirety at the Festival in 2009; see page 264.)

Newton himself directed three Coward plays: the little-known *Point Valaine* in 1992, *Easy Virtue* in 1999 (revived in 2000), and *Hay Fever* in 2002 (his last season as artistic director).

POINT VALAINE, 1992 Set in a tumbledown resort on a Caribbean island in the 1930s, *Point Valaine* was decried by Coward as "scarcely one of my major triumphs," but he declared that he nonetheless cherished "an irritable affection for it." In Newton's hands, and with a powerful performance by Fiona Reid in the lead role of the widowed, lonely, and sexually charged proprietor, it came across, in the words of one critic, as a "rare gem." As much Tennessee Williams as Noel Coward, *Point Valaine*'s raw emotional power perhaps did not surprise those who had seen *The Vortex* in 1983, but it showed a side of Coward that was not familiar to many theatregoers.

THIS PAGE: SARAH ORENSTEIN IN *BLITHE SPIRIT* BY NOEL COWARD, 1993. DIRECTED BY SUSAN COX, DESIGNED BY LESLIE FRANKISH, LIGHTING DESIGNED BY ROBERT THOMSON.

ROBERT PERSICHINI AND FIONA REID IN *POINT VALAINE* BY NOEL COWARD, 1992. DIRECTED BY CHRISTOPHER NEWTON, DESIGNED BY YVONNE SAURIOL, LIGHTING DESIGNED BY ROBERT THOMSON.

PATRICK R. BROWN AND PATTY JAMIESON IN *SHADOW PLAY* BY NOEL COWARD, 2001. DIRECTED BY DAVID SAVOY, MUSICAL DIRECTION BY PAUL SPORTELLI, CHOREOGRAPHY BY WILLIAM ORLOWSKI; DESIGNED BY JUDITH BOWDEN, LIGHTING DESIGNED BY JEFF LOGUE.

OPPOSITE: HELEN TAYLOR, JENNIFER PHIPPS AND RICHARD BINSLEY IN *HAY FEVER* BY NOEL COWARD, 1987. DIRECTED BY DENISE COFFEY, DESIGNED BY JOHN PENNOYER, LIGHTING DESIGNED BY SHOLEM DOLGOY, SOUND DESIGNED BY WALTER LAWRENCE.

PHOTOS BY DAVID COOPER.

EASY VIRTUE, 1999, 2000   *Easy Virtue* was not much better known than *Point Valaine*. The Festival's 1999 production was the Canadian professional premiere of the play (it marked the centenary of Coward's birth). Its theme – a woman with a past – was familiar enough, but Coward's treatment of the subject (witty and satiric rather than melodramatic) and Newton's directing (unobtrusively trusting the text and the actors) combined to create (to quote Jamie Portman) "a triumph of the memorable over the mundane." As with *Point Valaine*, Coward and Newton were immeasurably helped by the lead actor, in this case Goldie Semple, whose performance as the divorcee who has married into a prim, hypocritical English family was one of the most riveting of her distinguished career at the Shaw and Stratford Festivals and other Canadian theatres.

HAY FEVER, 2002   For *Hay Fever* it was Fiona Reid's turn to shine again, this time as retired actress Judith Bliss opposite Michael Ball as her popular novelist husband David Bliss. Together with their children Sorel (Severn Thompson) and Simon (Mike Shara), this family of monsters makes a weekend of hell for their unsuspecting house guests, and an evening of hilarity for audiences. But not hilarity at the expense of credibility. Yes, the production was frequently "screamingly funny" (Robert Cushman) and "full of wildly inventive physical humour" (Richard Ouzounian), but the effectiveness of the humour was firmly grounded in strongly defined and intelligently considered characterizations – a consistent mark of Newton's approach to Coward.

CAVALCADE, 1985, 1986, 1995   And then there was *Cavalcade*. The Festival announced its decision to mount the North American professional premiere of Noel Coward's epic patriotic play in a press release on July 22, 1985. First produced in London in October 1931, *Cavalcade* follows the lives of two families (one "upstairs," one "downstairs") through thirty years of British his-

CLOCKWISE FROM TOP LEFT: THE RAIL-
WAY STATION SCENE; THE NIGHT CLUB
SCENE; FIONA REID; THE KENSINGTON
GARDENS SCENE IN *CAVALCADE* BY
NOEL COWARD, 1985–86, 1995.
DIRECTED BY CHRISTOPHER NEWTON
AND DUNCAN MCINTOSH, DESIGNED
BY CAMERON PORTEOUS, LIGHTING
DESIGNED BY JEFFREY DALLAS (BY
ROBERT THOMPSON, 1995), MUSICAL
DIRECTION BY CHRISTOPHER DONISON.
PHOTOS BY DAVID COOPER.

tory from 1900 to 1930, years that encompassed such events as the death of Queen Victoria, the sinking of the *Titanic*, and the First World War. *Cavalcade* was described in the press release as "a spectacular marvel of theatrical brilliance, incorporating 22 glorious scenes, with over 300 historical costumes." There was to be a cast of forty-three actors, "the largest acting company ever assembled at the Shaw Festival" (with the exception of the outdoor production of *1984* in 1984, described on page 138), co-directed by Duncan McIntosh and Christopher Newton, and designed by Cameron Porteous (set and costumes) and Jeffrey Dallas (lighting), with musical direction by Christopher Donison. *Cavalcade* opened at the Festival Theatre on August 16, 1985, after previews on August 11, 13, and 15.

Interviewed by Jamie Portman shortly before the opening, Newton said he was regularly waking up in the middle of the night "wondering why we're doing this." Cameron Porteous likened his role as set and costume designer to that of a marathon runner, "wondering at the start, not whether he will win, but whether or not he will finish." In addition to the technical challenges of multiple and rapid scene and costume changes, there was the problem of rehearsing the large cast in over two hundred different roles. Newton had no doubt, though, that the Festival, with its experienced ensemble and a track record of large-scale productions, was up to the job. And he was absolutely right.

Few Shaw Festival productions have matched the virtually unanimous critical acclaim received by *Cavalcade* – *Cyrano de Bergerac* in 1982–83, *Man and Superman* in both 1977 and 2004, and *Peter Pan* in 1986–87 perhaps come the closest. The audience reaction on opening night of *Cavalcade* – and every subsequent night – was jubilant. Robert Crew in the *Toronto Star* reported spontaneous cheering and applauding; the audience was "still standing and clapping long after the house lights went up," wrote Barbara Crook in the *Ottawa Citizen*; McKenzie Porter (*Toronto Sun*) was amazed to hear "shouts and whistles of praise from one of the most sophisticated audiences in North America"; the sustained standing ovation "was one of the most enthusiastic I have heard in a theatre," declared Bob Pennington, also in the *Toronto Sun*; no one at the Festival, according to Alide LePage in the *St Catharines Standard*, could "recall seeing an audience there rise for an ovation before the final curtain had started to come down"; and Jamie Portman noted for Southam News that even opening night guest and former Prime Minister Pierre Trudeau, "a man not normally given to public expressions of this nature," was "standing and applauding" (though in the circumstances it would have been difficult for him to have done otherwise).

Critical judgment was equally fervent: "a rare, unforgettable evening of theatrical magic" (Crew); "the most memorable production in the history of Canadian theatre" (Porter); "a five star award for an Everest of excellence" (Pennington – only the second time he had given five stars for a Festival show; the other was for *Cyrano*).

Pennington was not alone in worrying before he saw *Cavalcade* that Coward's unabashed patriotism would come across as outrageous British snobbery and jingoism. What he actually experienced, however, was a rich blend of compassion, courage, tears, and laughter. Like everyone else who saw *Cavalcade*, Pennington had his most memorable scenes – the silent vigil for a dying Queen Victoria; the bantering of honeymooners on the doomed *Titanic*; Nora McLellan singing "Roses Are Blooming in Picardy" against a backdrop of a First World War bloodbath; and Goldie Semple, Jennifer Phipps, and others in numerous "marvellous cameos by a company of distinguished actors."

Put more generally, the success of *Cavalcade* came from the ability of Newton and McIntosh to create what Robert Crew described as "a profusion of vivid, poignant images that remain etched on the memory," to transform dialogue and situations that look trite and melodramatic in print into scenes charged with truth and integrity. And central to this success were the designs of Cameron Porteous and the lighting of them by Jeffrey Dallas. The "visual and technical marvel" admired by Barbara Crook (*Ottawa Citizen*) would have been even more difficult to achieve without the Festival Theatre's stage turntable. The turntable was specially created by Porteous for *Cavalcade*, and had to be built in such a way that it could be removed for other Festival Theatre shows. As far as the audience was concerned, mood and location changed effortlessly from one scene to the next, all coming together for the memorable closing scene as the whole company revolved to the spine-tingling strains of Beethoven's "Ode to Joy" (sensibly changed by Newton from Coward's original ending with "God Save the King").

It was quickly apparent after opening night that the short thirty-seven performance run of *Cavalcade* in 1985 would not be sufficient to meet audience demand. Almost all performances sold out, final box office figures showing 99 percent paid attendance. With a few cast changes *Cavalcade* was remounted for the 1986 season. Previews began on May 14, and the formal opening was on May 29. It ran until October 12 for a total of eighty-six performances. It was a hit with audiences again (92 percent box office), and the critics remained exhilarated. Critics from the British press came for the revival, and compared the Shaw Festival version favourably with the "dreary" 1985 revival at the Chichester Festival. Perhaps, Irving Wardle reflected in *The Times*, the virtues of *Cavalcade* "are more visible to a class-free Canadian director."

There was one more revival of *Cavalcade* at the Shaw Festival, in 1995, again directed by Newton and McIntosh, with reprises from many members of the original cast. This time the run was for ninety-one performances, and box office was again over 90 percent. For Stewart Brown in the *Hamilton Spectator*, as for other critics, it was still a "moving, magnificent, and memorable" show. In all, *Cavalcade* played 214 times in its three seasons, selling 171,669 tickets, the biggest-selling play in the Festival's history. And indisputably one of its greatest artistic achievements as well.

OSCAR WILDE Noel Coward was born in 1899, a year before the death of another famous (and infamous) contemporary of Shaw, Oscar Wilde. Wilde's dramatic output was slight compared to Shaw and Coward, his reputation resting on just five plays: *Salomé*, *Lady Windermere's Fan*, *A Woman of No Importance*, *An Ideal Husband*, and *The Importance of Being Earnest*. None of Newton's predecessors as the Festival's artistic director attempted a Wilde play, and it wasn't until his eighth season (1987) that Newton chose one, the least familiar of the group – *Salomé*, adapted and directed by Sky Gilbert (see page 137). This was followed by *An Ideal Husband* in 1995 (revived in 1996), *Lady Windermere's Fan* in 1998, and *A Woman of No Importance* in 2000. Surprisingly, Newton never selected Wilde's most famous play, *The Importance of Being Earnest*, though he did direct it for the Festival in 2004, Jackie Maxwell's second season as artistic director. Maxwell also included *An Ideal Husband* in her 2010 season.

Newton selected Duncan McIntosh to direct *An Ideal Husband*, a production not greatly admired by the critics (he directed the play "in a manner ranging from the haphazard to the wrong-headed," according to Jamie Portman), but certainly admired by audiences. It sold so well in 1995 (the bestselling play of the season at 97 percent box office at the Court House Theatre) that Newton brought it back in 1996, when it again outsold everything else (99 percent). McIntosh stressed the darker side of this play about moral dilemmas facing a politician with a promising future and dishonourable past, at the expense, some said, of the witty, epigrammatic Wilde. Newton himself faced a similar balancing act with *Lady Windermere's Fan*, which he directed (in the Festival Theatre) in 1998. Again, as always in Wilde – even in *Earnest* – there are secrets and misunderstandings from the past that impact profoundly on people's lives in the present. Serious moral issues are raised in *Lady Windermere's Fan*, especially about the place of women in Victorian society, but Wilde's wit is there in abundance too. In a thoughtful review in the *Globe and Mail* Kate Taylor pinpointed the problem: "You have to strike a fine balance: polishing up the flippant wit, smoothing over the extravagant plot, and letting the deeper emotions shine through." She thought Newton had got it just about right, "toning down and pumping up as needed." William Schmuck's design was integral to this balance. His use of the Festival stage's two turntables, rotating in different directions, not only created fluidity in the action but also integrated past and present, public and private, surface and reality. The ballroom scene in *Lady Windermere's Fan* (costumes designed by Christina Poddubiuk), described by Taylor as "one of the most lushly beautiful things to grace the stage of the Shaw's Festival Theatre," was just one of the many images that served to disguise the hypocrisy beneath the elegance.

It wasn't so clear that director Susan Ferley (from London Ontario's Grand Theatre) got the balance right with her 2000 production of the last Wilde play under Newton's artistic directorship, *A Woman of No Importance*. Kate Taylor thought she had "dampened the fun to make plausible the melodrama," but Tony Brown in the Cleveland *Plain Dealer* was less ambivalent. In Ferley's hands, he complained, *A Woman of No Importance* had become simply "a gloomy melodrama" in which "the life goes out of the party." Once more, however, audience reaction diverged from the critics. There was enough life in the party to attract a 97 percent box office at the Court House Theatre. Wilde was again the season's bestseller.

CLOCKWISE FROM LEFT: TOM MCCAMUS;
MARTI MARADEN WITH THE LOST BOYS;
CHRISTOPHER NEWTON IN *PETER PAN*
BY J.M. BARRIE, 1987–88. DIRECTED
BY IAN JUDGE, DESIGNED BY CAMERON
PORTEOUS, LIGHTING DESIGNED BY
ROBERT THOMSON, SOUND DESIGNED
BY WALTER LAWRENCE, ORIGINAL MUSIC
COMPOSED BY CHRISTOPHER DONISON.
PHOTOS BY DAVID COOPER.

J.M. BARRIE AND *PETER PAN*, 1987, 1988, 2001 Other bestsellers were J.B. Priestley, whose plays were popular in Newton's murder-mystery series at the Royal George (see page 97) and J.M Barrie. The first Barrie play at the Festival was *The Admirable Crichton*, directed by Barry Morse in 1976 (and revived in 2011 in a production directed by Morris Panych). Newton scheduled two other plays by Barrie, *Shall We Join the Ladies?* and *The Old Lady Shows Her Medals* as lunchtime performances at the Royal George in 1996 and 2002 respectively. They were popular productions. *Shall We Join the Ladies?* drew 80 percent houses, and *The Old Lady Shows Her Medals* did 10 percent better than that. One regular Festival patron (C.A. Hutton) recalls leaving the Royal George after a moving performance of *The Old Lady Shows Her Medals* (directed by Todd Hammond). As the audience exited "into a blinding noonday summer sun," "every single person was either in tears or had wet eyes, and we all had to pull ourselves together before we were ready to let this beautiful production go." But the biggest Barrie hit at the Festival under Newton was *Peter Pan*.

Directed by British director Ian Judge, the 1987 Shaw Festival production broke convention by casting adults in the children's parts: Tom McCamus as Peter, Marti Maraden as Wendy, and a formidable array of Festival acting talent as the Lost Boys – Michael Ball, Jim Mezon, Guy Bannerman, George Dawson, Rod Campbell, and William Vickers. Even baby Michael was played by an adult – Ted Dykstra, whose "rubbery, mobile features and buzzsaw voice," said one reviewer, "somehow coalesce into an enormous and improbable infancy." Judge also wanted to undermine memories of cartoon and sentimental musical versions of *Peter Pan* by reminding audiences of the disturbing sides of the play, such as the psychological complexities of Peter's character (more easily achieved by an adult than child actor). Judge included, for example, a scene often omitted from productions, one in which Peter is wounded by Captain Hook.

Alone on a rock in the middle of the lagoon, Peter declares that "to die will be an awfully big adventure."

But that approach didn't dampen the overall joy and exuberance of the production. Christopher Newton did his part in a "hilarious romp" as Captain Hook (as well as a more subdued Mr Darling), and the full technical capacities of the Festival Theatre stage were exploited by Cameron Porteous and his stage crews with a daunting array of scene changes – the Darlings' nursery, the Lost Boys' underground home, the pirate ship, the mermaids' lagoon – as well, of course, as the giant crocodile (Dean DeGruijter and Gabrielle Jones), the fly-pasts of Peter, Wendy, and her brothers, and Tinker Bell (Gail Hakala). The stage crew justifiably joined in the curtain call for *Peter Pan* (as they had for *Cavalcade*).

As with *Cyrano de Bergerac* and *Cavalcade*, it was obvious from early on in the run of *Peter Pan* that the scheduled thirty-nine performances would not meet audience demand. Very few performances were not sold out, and final box office figures showed a 98 percent paid attendance. It was frequently Newton's strategy to use August openings (*Peter Pan* opened on August 14) as try-outs that, if successful, could return the following season. And so he had *Peter Pan* back on the Festival stage as one of the opening shows of the 1988 season, this time for an eighty-four performance run. Ian Judge did not return for the re-mount. He was credited with directing the original production, while Newton and Duncan McIntosh (the *Cavalcade* directorial team) were credited with "restaging" it. There were a few cast changes for 1988, some tightening up of technical manoeuvres, and a more detailed shading of minor characters (something that Newton and McIntosh had paid careful attention to in *Cavalcade*). Audiences responded to the play just as enthusiastically, box office for the much longer run still coming in at an impressive 92 percent.

Newton continued to think about *Peter Pan*, and by 2001 he was asking if it wasn't "the most significant play in English from the twentieth century." Even if he wouldn't go further in response to his own question than "there are people who think so," he was putting the play in exalted company (including most of Shaw's major plays). One of the things that appealed to Newton about *Peter Pan* was that "there are always new meanings, new revelations" in it. He set out to explore them in his own production of the play in 2001.

He explained his thoughts about the play in a *Globe and Mail* interview in April 2001. On reflection, he thought that despite Ian Judge's attempts to capture some of the more disturbing aspects of *Peter Pan*, the 1987–88 productions had the feel of a "charming dream" about them rather than the more nightmarish element he now wanted to uncover. He didn't think, for example, that his own Captain Hook in the Judge reading was dangerous enough. And he also felt there was the sense that the children could at any time wake up from their dream and escape from Hook and other dangers. In his new production Newton wanted rather to give the sense that the children might not be able to escape, that they "may be trapped" in the dream forever. "Only debased forms of the *Peter Pan* legend," he argued, "dilute the danger and the menace."

Newton's designer for *Peter Pan* was Sue LePage. LePage had first designed for the Shaw Festival in 1985, a lunchtime show at the Royal George called *Mrs Bach*, featuring singer Mary Lou Fallis. She then designed for theatres across Canada before returning to the Festival in 1998 to design Neil Munro's production of *You Can't Take It With You*. That show was remounted in 1999, the season in which LePage also designed *Uncle Vanya*. In 2000 Christopher Newton invited her to design his *Doctor's Dilemma*, and then *Peter Pan* in 2001. One of the Shaw Festival's (and Canada's) most consistently successful designers, LePage has designed at least one show in every season since 1998. For *Peter Pan*, LePage drew inspiration from the work of post-impressionist French painter Henri Rousseau, whose skewed sense of reality and symbols of omnipresent threat and danger reflected Newton's ideas for the play.

Like Judge, Newton used adult actors for the children's parts. Dylan Trowbridge played Peter; Fiona Byrne, Wendy. Jim Mezon replaced Newton as Mr Darling and Captain Hook, and the new Mrs Darling was Goldie Semple. Newton also gave an expanded role to Liza, the Darlings' maid (Sherry Smith), who narrated Barrie's stage directions, giving an almost Brechtian distancing feel to the play. As Captain Hook, Mezon, said Richard Ouzounian in the *Toronto Star*, became "an insinuatingly dark and evil presence" (albeit at times still "terribly funny"), and the crocodile (mechanical, not human) was gargantuan, "a veritable Moby Dick to Hook's Ahab," said Robert Cushman in the *National Post*.

For Cushman, Newton's *Peter Pan* was "the best all-round production" of the play of the

many he had seen, "the first straight *Peter Pan* that didn't make me secretly wish I were watching the musical." Other critics, while recognizing that Newton had succeeded admirably in revealing the play's darker elements, wondered if he hadn't gone too far. While applauding Newton for "refusing to turn *Peter Pan* into a Disneyesque romp," Jamie Portman found the production an "unusually sombre, even joyless reading of the play." And audiences? Over 58,000 tickets were sold for the 108-performance run, but the 63 percent box office was far below the levels achieved in 1987–88.

HAROLD BRIGHOUSE, ST JOHN HANKIN, AND CHRISTOPHER FRY Newton introduced several other British contemporaries of Shaw to Festival audiences: Arthur Wing Pinero (*The Magistrate*, 1981, and *Trelawny of the 'Wells'*, 1989–90), Henry Arthur Jones (*The Silver King*, 1993), Harold Brighouse (*Hobson's Choice*, 1996–97), Christopher Fry (*The Lady's Not for Burning*, 1998), John Galsworthy (*Joy*, 1998), and St John Hankin (*The Return of the Prodigal*, 2001–2). Of these, the most successful were *Hobson's Choice*, *The Lady's Not for Burning*, and *The Return of the Prodigal*.

HOBSON'S CHOICE, 1996, 1997 *Hobson's Choice* was described by Robert Cushman in the *Globe and Mail* as "one of the few genuinely infallible pieces in the English-speaking repertoire." Perhaps so. But no director worth his or her salt will take anything for granted, and Newton had no expectations of automatic success with the play. The phrase (from a seventeenth-century

saying denoting no choice) that gives the play its title was probably better known to audiences than the play itself. The storyline of the relationship between an oppressive father and his three daughters, who seem to have no choice in life other than to work – unpaid – for their father in his Lancashire shoe shop, is, however, straightforward enough. The story develops into a Shaw-like condemnation of Victorian patriarchal society as the women struggle to create an identity for themselves, but it's a condemnation that comes without "a canned Shavian lecture about women's rights," *Detroit News* critic Lawrence Devine was relieved to discover. Regardless of Devine's understanding (or mis-understanding) of Shaw, Newton had no problem in finding the human element in the discordant family, particularly in the relationship between the father (Michael Ball) and his eldest daughter Maggie (Corrine Koslo), between whom the power relationship drastically alters at the end of the play as Maggie triumphs over her father in business and he sinks into alcohol driven ill-health.

In addition to powerful performances from Ball and Koslo, *Hobson's Choice* was memorable for William Schmuck's design. In his first season as head of design at the Festival (succeeding Cameron Porteous), Schmuck created stunningly detailed sets and costumes, complemented by an industrial landscape backdrop that matched the dreariness of the women's lives.

All in all, concluded another Detroit critic, Kenneth Jones, *Hobson's Choice* was an example "of everything the Shaw Festival does right." The production "overflows with warm period detail, rich character acting, and subject matter that articulates the Festival mandate to explore plays about the beginning of the modern world" (a phrase to define the mandate that Newton had coined during a dinner conversation with Larry Lillo in 1984, and subsequently used to promote the Festival). The box office for the 1996 run of eighty-six performances in the Festival Theatre was a healthy 82 percent, though it dropped off to 71 percent for a shorter forty-one performance run the following season. Among the audience members in 1996 were former U.S. President Jimmy Carter and his wife, celebrating their fiftieth wedding anniversary

THE LADY'S NOT FOR BURNING, 1998 Fry's *The Lady's Not for Burning* just about squeezed into the mandate period by virtue of its date (1948), but its style and setting (a verse romance set in medieval times) was, on the surface at least, very un-Shavian. But this story about a soldier who wants to be hanged for murders he says he has committed, and a suspected witch who doesn't want to be burned, actually has very Shavian ingredients – an "undisciplined abundance" of ideas, a "talkfest structure," and "a fascinating argument about the meaning of existence," as different critics have put it. Here, Newton said, "is scintillating talk and ideas that tease the imagination." It's a play, *Toronto Star* critic Geoff Chapman advised his readers, that "will engage your imagination, but not your emotions." Newton's direction, however, once more convinced critics and audiences that he had found a neglected work that deserved a better fate than theatre history had assigned it. Its seventy-four performance run at the Court House sold over 20,000 tickets for an 84 percent box office. *The Lady's Not for Burning* remains, however, the only Christopher Fry play produced by the Shaw Festival.

THE RETURN OF THE PRODIGAL, 2001, 2002 St John Hankin's *The Return of the Prodigal* had been on Newton's "list of plays to do" for some years before he included it in the 2001 season. Hankin's plays had never enjoyed commercial success during his lifetime, but John Gielgud had felt strongly enough about *The Return of the Prodigal* to revive it in London in 1948, with a cast that included Sybil Thorndike. Newton, with himself as director, initially gave it a short run (twenty-one performances in the Court House) towards the end of the 2001 season, but it was another case where demand exceeded supply, and he remounted it for a longer run (seventy performances) the next season.

Based on the biblical story, the plot of *The Return of the Prodigal* revolves around the disruptive return of spendthrift son Eustace Jackson (Ben Carlson) to his prosperous family home after an absence of five wasted years in Australia. Newton saw a blend of Coward-like wit and Chekhovian clarity of characterization in *The Return of the Prodigal*, and there was a consensus of critical reaction that he achieved a perfect balance to capture this dichotomy. The strong ensemble – Carlson, Patricia Hamilton, Kelli Fox, Sharry Flett, Bernard Behrens, Blair Williams, and others – and William Schmuck's economical but elegant design of the Jackson family's Gloucestershire house helped Newton demonstrate again his remarkable ability (as Richard Ouzounian put it) "at discovering a forgotten play of merit, staging it with care, and

leading some of his best actors to help us discover its riches." Robert Cushman went further in praising Newton for introducing "a brilliant and almost-forgotten playwright in a performance that shimmers, provokes and finally hits greatness." "Yet another play and playwright," Robert Crew said of the 2002 remount, "have been rescued from the shadows."

Not all of Newton's choices of Shaw's British contemporaries, however, were entirely successful. William Hutt added lustre to Newton's production of Pinero's romantic comedy *Trelawny of the 'Wells'* in 1989, which Newton remounted in 1990, but to disappointing houses in both seasons (under 60 percent box office for both runs in the Festival Theatre). The only Henry Arthur Jones play ever produced at the Festival, *The Silver King* in 1993, directed by Newton, also came in at well below 60 percent, despite Jamie Portman's characterization of the play as "a rip-roaring piece of Victoriana which will give playgoers a great deal of pleasure over coming months." On the other hand, the first John Millington Synge play ever produced at the Festival, the classic *The Playboy of the Western World*, directed by Jim Mezon, did well both in its inaugural Festival production in 1996 (94 percent) and its remount in 1997 (84 percent), despite grumbles from critics and audiences alike about Elizabeth Asselstine's dim lighting and the impenetrability of the Irish accents.

FARCE Like Paxton Whitehead, Christopher Newton believed that farce was a legitimate genre to include in the Festival repertoire. He included several British and European examples in his opening seasons, and continued to schedule them throughout his years as artistic director, usually in the Festival Theatre. They sometimes sold well (*One for the Pot* virtually sold out its entire eighty-four performance run in 1985), sometimes not so well (*Célimare* in 1984 barely achieved a 50 percent box office in a modest fifty-performance run). Newton enjoyed directing them (a 1996 pre-season Toronto production of *One for the Pot*, and *Will Any Gentleman?* at the Festival Theatre in 1997), and acting in them as well (in *Charley's Aunt*, for example, in 1992 – to positive reviews).

OPPOSITE: WILLIAM HUTT AND
MARION GILSENAN IN *THE WALTZ OF
THE TORREADORS* BY JEAN ANOUILH,
1990. DIRECTED BY DAVID GILES,
SET DESIGNED BY KENNETH MELLOR,
COSTUMES DESIGNED BY CAMERON
PORTEOUS, LIGHTING DESIGNED BY
LOUISE GUINAND, MUSIC COMPOSED
BY CHRISTOPHER DONISON, SOUND
DESIGNED BY WALTER LAWRENCE.
PHOTO BY DAVID COOPER.

THIS PAGE: FIONA BYRNE, PATRICIA
HAMILTON, PATTY JAMIESON, NORA
MCLELLAN, HELEN TAYLOR, AND SUSIE
BURNETT IN *THE HOUSE OF BERNARDA
ALBA* BY FEDERICO GARCIA LORCA IN
A NEW TRANSLATION BY RICHARD
SANGER, 2002. DIRECTED BY TADEUSZ
BRADECKI, DESIGNED BY TERESA
PRZYBYLSKI, LIGHTING DESIGNED
BY KEVIN LAMOTTE. PHOTO BY
DAVID COOPER.

EUROPEAN PLAYWRIGHTS

Newton's interest in Shaw's European contemporaries was reflected in the occasional French or Russian farce, in several of the plays he chose for the Risk series (see above, page 137), and in the mainstream European plays he scheduled for both the Festival and Court House theatres, beginning with Chekhov's *The Cherry Orchard* in the Festival Theatre in his first season (see above, page 70). Others followed, some better known than others. Jean Giraudoux's *The Madwoman of Chaillot* (1985), Jean Anouilh's *The Waltz of the Toreadors* (1990), Luigi Pirandello's *Henry IV* (1991), Bertolt Brecht's *Drums in the Night* (1992), and Federico García Lorca's *The House of Bernarda Alba* (2002) were probably not familiar to most Festival patrons, and, in truth, most of them struggled at the box office. Blatant misogyny was a problem with *Waltz of the Toreadors*, prompting some hissing and uncomfortable laughter from Festival Theatre audiences at lines such as "You know, science ought to find a way of putting women permanently to sleep. We could wake them for a while at night and then they would go back to sleep again." William Hutt's performance as the aging Don Juan of the play rescued it for some, but a 50 percent box office reflected a less positive view. A widely praised performance by David Schurmann as the king couldn't push *Henry IV* above the 50 percent level either, while *Drums in the Night* plunged to 43 percent. *Madwoman* did rather better at 55.5 percent in a forty-seven performance run in the Festival Theatre, but the best among this group of less familiar European plays was *The House of Bernarda Alba*, directed by Tadeusz Bradecki in the Court House to a 73 percent box office in a run of fifty-six performances. A play of intriguing complexity – a political metaphor for Spain on the eve of Civil War, a disturbing sexual and psychological portrait of a mother's oppression of her five daughters, a universal tragedy of suppressed individuality and lost opportunity – *Bernarda Alba* posed challenges of tone and focus that, for some, Bradecki didn't entirely master. But for many others it was a moving and powerful introduction to a major but unfamiliar Spanish playwright (who was executed by Franco's fascists in 1936 shortly after completing *Bernarda Alba*).

***PEER GYNT*, 1989**   Arguably, Ibsen's *Peer Gynt* could be put in the "less familiar" category of European plays, and certainly there could have been few in the audiences that saw the 1989 Shaw Festival production who had ever seen the full six-hour version of the play. *Peer Gynt* began as a long narrative poem, first published in 1867, and then adapted for the stage in Oslo in 1876. The Festival version was in a new translation by John Lingard, one that shortened the play to about three-and-a-half hours. What remained, however, was a huge role for the actor playing Peer, in this case Jim Mezon. Directed by Duncan McIntosh in the Court House Theatre on a bare-bones set designed by Phillip Clarkson and lit by Kevin Lamotte, Mezon pulled off a towering performance as he took his character on a dizzying fantasy-filled and years-long journey through exotic locales in Norway and North Africa. Beset by adventures with trolls, lusty women, slave-traders, and madmen, Peer grows from callous youth, through arrogant middle age, to old-age mitigation of a wasted and self-indulgent life. One of the first audience members on his feet on opening night to acclaim Mezon's performance was Michael Ball, who knew a thing or two about long and demanding roles – he was performing one of the longest and most demanding of them all that season as John Tanner in *Man and Superman*.

***HEDDA GABLER*, 1991**   Ibsen's *Hedda Gabler* was better known than his *Peer Gynt*, though the Festival's 1991 production of the play was a new version, adapted and directed by Canadian playwright Judith Thompson. Thompson updated the language and idioms of the play, and added a six-minute "dream" prologue in which Hedda rejects her husband's sexual advances and threatens to shoot him. Thompson updated as well the overall presentation of Hedda (played by Fiona Reid), seeking to understand the desperation of a woman who has traded "dungeon for dungeon," from a father's control to a husband's control. So instead of seeing Hedda one-dimensionally as a destructive woman driven by hatred of the men in her life, Thompson switched the emphasis of the play, as *Hamilton Spectator* critic Stewart Brown saw it, to "a compelling indictment of the patriarchal society in which women found themselves captive and virtually helpless...put on display [by men] as prize trophies." In that sense, Hedda faced similar problems to Nora in Ibsen's earlier *A Doll's House*, though Nora ends that play by creating a new life for herself, rather than escaping from life itself, as Hedda does.

Thompson's bold effort to see a European classic in contemporary feminist terms was applauded by some critics, disparaged by others, while audience reaction was middling – a 60 percent box office in a thirty-three performance run in the Court House. Newton continued, however, to explore ways of giving a contemporary sensibility to European classics. The 1997 production of Chekhov's *The Seagull*, for example, was an adaptation by Canadian playwright David French, one that sought the comic vein in the play, a mood that director Neil Munro embraced. The result made the play something of a "low-brow American sitcom...a veritable orgy of mugging 'midst the melancholy," thought John Coulbourn in the *Toronto Sun*. Audiences seemed to prefer a more balanced Chekhov; they only half-filled the Festival Theatre for the sixty-six-performance run.

***UNCLE VANYA*, 1999**   For the Festival's next Chekhov, *Uncle Vanya* in 1999, Newton again used a version by a Canadian playwright. John Murrell had initially adapted the play for a Stratford Festival production in 1978, and he revised it for the Shaw Festival, where it was directed by Ian Prinsloo (who had been a member of the acting ensemble in 1986–87). Newton put this Chekhov in the more intimate confines of the Court House Theatre, where it did good box office (85 percent), but in a short run of only twenty-three performances. A strong cast that included Jim Mezon, Michael Ball, Bernard Behrens, and Blair Williams seemed hampered by the "deliberate sloth" (Robert Cushman's assessment) of Prinsloo's direction, a contrasting approach to Munro's more frenetic pace in *The Seagull*.

***SIX CHARACTERS IN SEARCH OF AN AUTHOR*, 2000, 2001**   Newton's third Pirandello (following *Tonight We Improvise* in 1986 and *Henry IV* in 1991) used an entirely new translation and adaptation, this one by University of Toronto scholar Domenico Pietropaolo. It turned out to be among the most successful of the adaptations that Newton had used for European plays, and, in the hands of Tadeusz Bradecki, one of the most successful productions. Judged by Newton to be "one of the seminal plays of the modern world...a kind of intellectual thriller that takes you on a wild ride into dangerous areas of the imagination," *Six Characters in Search of an Author* uses theatre as a metaphor for exploring the struggle between illusion and reality. A theatre company is rehearsing a play when six characters mysteriously intervene, "in search of an author." Metaphysical questions immediately arise: who are these characters, where are they from, who created them, are they real or illusionary, what is reality? The problem for the director of the play, as Jamie Portman put it, is how to "serve its metaphysical needs without draining it of dramatic tension." Evidence that Bradecki, the ensemble (with Kelli Fox prominent among them), and designer Peter Hartwell succeeded came from enthusiastic reviews from, among others, Portman himself ("provocative, stimulating, tantalizing in its very elusiveness") and Robert Cushman ("magnificent...bold...heart-stopping"), as well as audience demand for tickets. It was another occasion when a Festival production had clearly earned a remount, and after a short late-season run at the Court House in 2000 Newton brought *Six Characters* back for a longer run in 2001. Box office for both runs was just under an impressive 95 percent.

American plays had been integrated into the Festival mandate from as early 1972, when Donald Davis directed George S. Kaufman's and Edna Ferber's *The Royal Family* (revived by the Festival in 2003). Under Christopher Newton's artistic directorship, Neil Munro took the lead with American plays (see above, page 159), but there were plenty left for other directors in the Festival and Court House Theatres, as well as the American musicals at the Royal George Theatre (see above, page 90).

Allen MacInnis had fun with a 1987 Court House production of Ayn Rand's *Night of January 16th*, a courtroom drama where the jury is selected from members of the audience (opening night boasted a jury of Toronto celebrities). Audiences seem to have had fun as well, filling most of the fifty-five performances. They also came in large numbers to Duncan McIntosh's production of Kaufman and Hart's *Once in a Lifetime* in the Festival Theatre in 1988, despite warnings from critics such as Jamie Portman that the play was not much more than a "fragile period piece" that the Festival had "no good reason for exhuming" (except, perhaps, the welcome income from the sale of 27,627 tickets). William Gillette's *Sherlock Holmes*, directed by Newton in the Festival Theatre in 1994, sold even more tickets (45,490), and boasted a compelling Holmes in Jim Mezon and a "study in morbid villainy" (Portman) from Michael Ball as Professor Moriarty. John van Druten's romantic comedy *The Voice of the Turtle* also did well (28,153 tickets sold) at the Royal George in 1995, but Paul Lampert's production also received some critical acclaim. No one accused *The Voice of the Turtle* of being a great play, but this uncomplicated love story about an out-of-work actress and a G.I. on leave in Manhattan was welcomed by Portman (and others) as "as a small treasure" and an "enormously satisfying…affecting, unpretentious play."

There was more heft in five other American plays selected by Newton: Thornton Wilder's *The Skin of Our Teeth* in 1984, Clare Boothe Luce's *The Women* in 1985 (revived in 2010), Lillian Hellman's *The Children's Hour* in 1997 (the first Hellman play at the Festival), Wilder's *The Matchmaker* in 2000, and William Inge's *Picnic* in 2001.

***THE SKIN OF OUR TEETH*, 1984**   *The Skin of Our Teeth* production was remarkable in many ways. It was the first time that a Wilder play had been produced at the Festival; it was the first of five Festival plays memorably designed by Canadian-born and British-trained designer Michael Levine; and it was another Festival production that provoked audience walkouts.

Best known for his 1938 Pulitzer Prize-winning *Our Town* (reputed to be America's most produced play), Wilder spurned the conventional in his writing, daringly making *The Skin of Our Teeth* an epic parable of world history through the experiences of the Antrobus family of suburban New Jersey. Wilder shows the family contending with (and surviving by the skin of their teeth) the ravages of five thousand years of history – the Ice Age, the biblical flood, and war. Directed by Christopher Newton, it all happened at a madcap pace, three acts full of high-jinks and farcical goings-on (with a tour de force performance by Nora McLellan as the family maid), but never at the expense of Wilder's deep humanism and anxiety about the future of the human race. The "essential seriousness" of the play, said *Christian Science Monitor* critic Thor Eckert (apparently having forgiven Newton for the nudity in *Saint Joan* in 1981), was "unflaggingly sustained" throughout.

The Skin of Our Teeth is a challenge for any designer, particularly one working for the first time at the Shaw Festival. But Michael Levine's experience with the mostly non-naturalistic style of Glasgow's Citizens Theatre, where he was resident designer, was put to good use by the demands of Wilder's play. Levine's expressionistic design complemented the eclectic imagination of the playwright and the hectic fluidity of Newton's direction, leading to Newton's bringing him back for subsequent seasons to design *Heartbreak House* (1985), *Arms and the Man* (1986), and *The Women* and *Marathon '33* (1987).

The audience walkouts seem to have had more to do with bewilderment than with moral offence (as, for example, with *Camille* in 1981). Thirty people left before the end of the show on May 18 without comment, but the house manager's report for that day also records "intelligently inquisitive" comments and questions from audience members who stayed to the end. *The Skin of Our Teeth* was not, in any case, a show that had trouble finding an audience. In a sixty-one-performance run the box office was a solid 70 percent.

THE WOMEN, 1985 Duncan McIntosh's production of Clare Boothe Luce's excoriating satirical portrayal of Manhattan socialites in the 1930s ran for fifty-one performances in the Court House Theatre and achieved an 89.5 percent box office. With an all-female cast that included Frances Hyland, Irene Hogan, Nancy Kerr, Susan Wright, and Nora McLellan playing over forty different roles, there was plenty of interest in the play anyway, but the interest was heightened by a visit to Niagara-on-the-Lake by Luce herself (then aged eighty-two) to see it. At the end of the performance she took a curtain call, and the full house, together with cast and crew, responded, said the *Globe and Mail*, "with thunderous applause."

Prior to the performance Luce met the press in the library of the Festival Theatre, where she answered questions and gave her views on *The Women* and the issues it addresses. She pulled no punches about the kind of women she created for the play. "The women who inspired my play," she said, "deserved to be smacked across the head with a meat axe, and that is exactly what I smacked them with." The women represent, she continued, "a snob-ridden segment of society which is over-rich, over-sexed, and under-occupied."

The press (predominantly male) loved the interview and the play, one critic describing it as "an evening of quite brilliant bitchery," another confessing to "a certain sadistic pleasure in watching these loathsome women tearing each other to shreds." Less misogynistically energized views noted that the production was also "high in ensemble quality, visually stunning [in a design by Michael Levine], and beautifully paced."

THE CHILDREN'S HOUR, 1997 Newton described *The Children's Hour* in the house program as "one of the most shocking American plays of the '30s." It had been banned in Boston and Chicago, and had never had a professional production in Canada. The play tells the story of two New England teachers whose careers are destroyed by the lies of a malcontent student, who begins a rumour that the teachers are lesbian lovers. Director Glynis Leyshon used students from Niagara area schools for the students in the play, including fourteen-year-old Maggie Blake, who had previously appeared in the Festival's 1995 *Cavalcade* and (as Essie) in *The Devil's Disciple* in 1996, as well as in roles at other Ontario theatres. Blake played Mary Tilford, the malcontent student, a role central to the success of the play. She did so with great distinction, impressing, for example, Stewart Brown with her "frightening physical frenzy" as well as her "calculated ability to wheel on a dime with a new accusatory flight of fancy." Kelli Fox, as one of the accused teachers, also impressed, as did Jennifer Phipps, the grandmother who aids and abets the malicious rumour-mongering. Leyshon didn't pretend that *The Children's Hour* is essentially anything other than a melodrama, though a powerful one, deliberately emphasizing climactic moments by lighting shifts and throbbing music. Its success helped pave the way for a second Lillian Hellman play at the Festival, *The Autumn Garden* in 2005 (see below, page 235).

THE MATCHMAKER, 2000 The first Thornton Wilder play at the Festival was *The Skin of Our Teeth*, which Newton himself directed at the Festival Theatre in 1984. Newton came back to Wilder some years later with *The Matchmaker*, the play that spawned the musical comedy *Hello, Dolly!* His 2000 production, in the Festival Theatre, didn't short-change audiences on the physical comedy in the play – no shortage, Richard Ouzounian approvingly noted, of "sight gags, pratfalls and double takes" – but Newton also appreciated and respected its love stories. It is Dolly Levi, the "matchmaker," who brings the lovers together, and Newton found the perfect Dolly in Goldie Semple, praised by Buffalo critic Herman Trotter as an actress "who has always lit up every Shaw stage on which she's appeared." Her Dolly was another triumph. Ouzounian's recollection of the previous Dollys he had seen was that they concentrated on Dolly's "pushiness," ending up "seeming like teamsters in drag." Not so Goldie Semple, who exulted in her womanliness while still never missing a laugh. Here was a character, said Trotter, who knows "how to make things work in the complicated chemistry of social relationships." Semple's performance was such that for Trotter she was "a magnet for the viewer's eyes whenever she's on stage."

GOLDIE SEMPLE, JIM MEZON,
JENNIFER PHIPPS, LISA NORTON,
WENDY THATCHER, MIKE SHARA, AND
MIKE WASCO IN *PICNIC* BY WILLIAM
INGE, 2001. DIRECTED BY JACKIE
MAXWELL, DESIGNED BY CHRISTINA
PODDUBIUK, LIGHTING DESIGNED
BY ROBERT THOMSON, MUSIC BY
PAUL SPORTELLI, CHOREOGRAPHY
BY JANE JOHANSON.

OPPOSITE: WENDY THATCHER AND
FIONA BYRNE IN *PICNIC*, 2001.
PHOTOS BY DAVID COOPER.

PICNIC, 2001   Once ranked in the same league as Tennessee Williams, William Inge gradually faded from sight after enjoying a high profile in American theatre in the 1950s. The Shaw Festival's revival of *Picnic*, which had won a Pulitzer Prize in 1953, was an opportunity to reconsider Inge's work, and the verdict from audiences and critics was positive. After seeing the opening at the Court House Theatre on May 26, 2001, Richard Ouzounian confidently predicted in his review in the *Toronto Star* that the Festival had "a solid winner." And so it turned out, *Picnic* achieving an 88 percent box office in a sixty-two performance run (the longest of any of that season's Court House plays). Dealing with the impact on the lives of several people of the arrival of a drifter in a small Kansas town, *Picnic* was the first Festival play directed by Jackie Maxwell (whose appointment as Newton's successor would be announced just a few weeks after the opening of *Picnic*). The set (a front porch, where all the action occurs) and costumes were designed by Christina Poddubiuk, with lighting by Kevin Lamotte, choreography by Jane Johanson (for a dance scene), and music by Paul Sportelli. "It has everything you want to see in a production from one of our major Festivals," said Ouzounian; "superb acting in every part, no matter how small, sensitive and faithful direction, beautifully realized design, even a haunting original musical score." Among the strong cast Goldie Semple again shone, this time as the schoolteacher Rosemary, a portrait of "consummate grace and exquisite delicacy," in Ouzounian's judgment. The success of *Picnic* encouraged further exploration of Inge's plays, and Maxwell, as artistic director, followed up *Picnic* with his *Bus Stop* in 2005 (see below, page 231).

LEGACY

When Christopher Newton became artistic director of the Shaw Festival in 1980, a Canadian theatrical landscape without the Shaw Festival was conceivable. When he retired in 2002, such a situation was inconceivable. That, in a nutshell, was the measure of Newton's achievement. There was much loose and uninformed talk in the press both at the time of his appointment and at the time of his retirement of conditions at the Festival in 1980. It was not in the dire circumstances that many suggested. Indeed, the 1979 season that Newton's immediate predecessor, Leslie Yeo, had mounted was in many ways both a financial and artistic success (see above, page 63). Nonetheless, important constituencies such as government funding agencies and the Canadian cultural community showed little enthusiasm for the Festival. Immediately prior to Leslie Yeo's one year at the helm, Richard Kirschner's programming had created deep financial problems for the Festival (see above, page 60), which Yeo's season hadn't resolved, and the policies of Kirschner's predecessor, Paxton Whitehead – policies that seemed to many to give preference to a lightweight repertoire and foreign artists – had alienated bodies such as the Canada Council and the Professional Association of Canadian Theatres. Had the Festival disappeared in 1980, many local businesses, no doubt, would have regretted it, but there would also have been some rejoicing in Niagara-on-the-Lake that this spoiler of the town's genteel tranquillity had got its comeuppance. Certainly, no one was prepared to say in 1980 what was widely being said at the end of Newton's term as artistic director – that the Shaw Festival had become "an internationally renowned acting company." That was Jamie Portman's judgment, and lest it be thought that a long-term admirer of the Festival (though by no means an uncritical admirer) was displaying a nationalistic bias, it should be noted that the drama critic of London's *The Times*, reporting on the 2002 season, agreed that the Shaw Festival "has put Niagara-on-the-Lake on the international map." An American perspective – perhaps less internationally aware than Canadian and British perspectives – limited the context to North America, but still offered high praise. Newton, Buffalo critic Herman Trotter reckoned (in 2000), "has elevated the Shaw Festival to the first rank among North American repertory theaters." As regards government support, while funding remained at dismayingly low levels as far as Newton was concerned, at least the Canada Council was no longer demanding, as it had in pre-Newton years, that changes in leadership and policy needed to be made in return for higher grants. What, then, had happened to cause such a reversal of the Festival's reputation?

Central to everything was the commitment to quality. Producer Paul Reynolds explained in a 1985 interview that from the beginning of Newton's regime "the basic premise" and "the number-one goal" was "a quality product." For Newton, the context for assessing quality was not Canada, not North America, but international. His ambition, he told the Shaw Festival Guild in 1985, was to help the Festival "become great on an international level." Similarly, Reynolds spoke of the "goal of becoming a world-class theatre." To achieve this, Reynolds explained, two factors were essential: the creation of a talented ensemble of actors – Newton's responsibility – and "a talented and professional administrative team" – Reynolds' responsibility.

Newton told the Guild in his 1985 talk that the Shaw Festival exists "not to make money, but to make great theatre." But he knew very well, of course, that "great theatre," certainly the kind of great theatre that he had in mind, could not be achieved without adequate financial resources. That meant not only mounting productions that would generate good box office returns, but also attracting additional revenue from government and private sources and exercising tight control over expenditures.

The Festival's financial record under Newton was, as with all theatres, volatile, but serious crises were infrequent. In 1986 the contracts of both Newton and Reynolds were renewed for a further five years. In a press release, the board praised Newton for his "outstanding artistic vision," complemented by Reynolds' "excellent administrative direction." By then, paid attendance at Festival productions averaged around 85 percent, but towards the end of the decade – in the face of competition from the rising phenomenon of mega-musicals in the Toronto commercial theatre – the figure was declining, dropping to just over 75 percent for the 1989 season, with a disastrous impact on the budget. That season ended with a deficit of $825,000, pushing the accumulated Festival debt to over $1 million. This caused, among other expenditure

restrictions, termination of the Toronto Project (see above, page 145). The situation deteriorated still further when another big deficit in 1991 (over $400,000) increased the debt to more than $1.4 million. Things bounced back in 1992 with a large surplus of $800,000, but after a 68 percent box office return in 1993 – the lowest Newton ever experienced – the days of regular 80 percent box office returns were over, though still occasionally achieved (1998, 1999, 2001). More modest expectations were built into budget projections, administered by Elaine Calder from 1990 to 1994 and by Colleen Blake since then.

In an effort to bring some measure of stability to the budget, the Festival established an endowment fund in 1996, with an initial target of $10 million. In 2003 the Shaw Festival Theatre Endowment Foundation was created to oversee the endowed funds, which by 2010 had reached in excess of $18 million. At the discretion of the Foundation board, a portion of income earned each year by the endowment provides the Festival with revenue for operations and Festival projects such as play development and education programs. Government funding is in a fairly constant state of flux, having ranged from around 12 percent of revenue in the early 1990s to as low as 4–5 percent at the beginning of the new millennium, and, from about 2005, around 6–7 percent.

As government grants declined towards the end of Newton's term, so fundraising from private sources increased. In 1991 fundraising accounted for 12 percent of Festival revenue; by 2010 it was almost double that amount (22 percent).

Budget control over direct Festival activities – production costs in particular – was in the Festival's hands. However, the success of applications for government grants and requests for private support from individuals and corporations depended heavily not only on skilled administrators and fundraisers, but on the quality of what was presented on the Festival stages. And that quality, in turn, as Newton frequently explained, depended heavily on the acting ensemble.

In Newton's view, there are two types of performers: "one is an actor, one is a star." He made it very clear to any performers who were interested in working at the Festival that it was actors, not stars, that he was interested in. He brought trusted actors with him from Vancouver, quickly forming an ensemble that he altered each season through a process of national auditions (a process maintained by Jackie Maxwell), but always retaining a core of actors firmly committed to the ensemble philosophy. Actors habitually found themselves playing major and minor roles in any given season, or major roles in one season, minor the next. Newton used himself as an actor in this way, and he expected the same from all ensemble members. The ensemble, he would tell them, is like an orchestra, and symphonies, like plays, have different needs. "You play clarinet, and sorry, this piece isn't scored for a clarinet."

Some actors found this difficult to cope with. Tom Wood, for example, during his four seasons in the mid-1980s, found that the roles that he was being offered – after, for example, the lead in *Célimare* in 1984 – were "getting *smaller*" (his emphasis), "and I just didn't want to do them." Heath Lamberts, as well, after his great success in *Cyrano de Bergerac* and in farces such as *One for the Pot*, didn't feel that there was a good fit between his ambitions and Newton's ensemble philosophy, so there was, says Newton, a "mutual parting of the ways." Newton remained convinced, however, that no individual was more important than the ensemble, and by 1991 he was confident that he had "the best acting ensemble in North America." It was hard to find anyone willing to quarrel with that assessment.

Through the work of the ensemble and the talented directors, designers, and technical staff that he assembled at the Festival, Newton was able to demonstrate that Shaw deserved his place at the centre of the Festival's mandate. Dan Laurence's initial rancour towards Newton's approach to the plays of Shaw was replaced by unstinting admiration of Newton's ability, as Laurence saw it, "to take a fresh look at Shaw...to see beneath the frippery...peeling away the outer layers to enable us to see the passionate essentials of the work, the repressed sexuality underlying the social conventions of Shaw's day." And Newton himself had come full circle with Shaw, from treating him with disdain as just "a good coat hanger" for other playwrights of the period, to acknowledging him as, after Shakespeare, "the greatest playwright in the English language." Shaw's range of subjects, Newton argued in the 2002 Festival brochure, "is astonishing," and "his ability to create memorable characters could be happily compared to Dickens'." But above all, Newton insisted, Shaw is important because he emphasizes the importance of

thought. Ultimately it doesn't matter how much you feel if you can't articulate what you think. Shaw wants to delight, to entertain, but above all he wants to engage us in theatrical debates that reach out into the unknown, indeed "as far as thought can reach."

Newton, then, stopped treating Shaw as an obstacle to be overcome so that the wealth of talent among his contemporaries could be revealed. It was rather that Newton's, and the Festival's, rediscovery of Shaw became the inspiration for rediscovery of the work of his contemporaries – British, European, and American alike. It became a commonplace observation among audiences and critics that the Shaw Festival was the place to see plays that had long been forgotten or neglected. As Newton put it, "You'll see plays at The Shaw that you will never see anywhere else." So why stop?

Although by 2002 Newton had done virtually all the Shaw there was to do – *Buoyant Billions* was about all that was left – there was no shortage of worthwhile plays in the mandate period, especially after he had extended the mandate in 2000 to include not just plays written *during* Shaw's lifetime, but plays *set* in Shaw's lifetime. (The mandate change was announced at the 1998 annual general meeting, held in the Festival Theatre lobby on February 12, 1999.) Newton still felt, however, that 2002 was the right time to step down as artistic director. He said that he had always been confident that he knew when it was time to leave a position – from Theatre Calgary in 1971, from the Vancouver Playhouse in 1979, and from the Shaw Festival in 2002. Perhaps the beginning of the end was as early as the mid-1980s when Newton sensed what he called "a loss of nerve." He said that Cameron Porteous "had an idea around the time of *Cavalcade* that the audience decided that it *liked* us." That was a new feeling after the ordeals of the early 1980s, and he wondered if that new – and welcome! – feeling influenced him to start "doing things that would make people like us."

And, naturally, there was an age factor. He made it clear in 1998 that he planned to retire at the end of the 2002 season, by which time he would be sixty-five. A year earlier, on a trip to Australia, he had had "an epiphany," when he realized that "Oh, my God, there's a world, there's even an English-speaking world, that I have no idea about, because I've been tied to *this* work."

Newton told *The New York Times* in 2000 that "we are not terribly experimental." "We never will be," he explained, "because our audience isn't." While it is true that Newton was not able to be as experimental as he might have been with a permanent winter location for the Festival in Toronto, he was never averse to taking risks – witness the "Risk" series itself as well as ongoing risks in play selection after the series as such closed (see above, page 139). And while it may also be true that Festival audiences are less receptive of experimental work than audiences in major urban centres, there is no doubt that Newton succeeded in changing audience expectations about the Shaw Festival, and thereby changed the audiences themselves. He had said at the end of his first season that he wanted to "turn around at least 15 percent" of the audience so that they can "help us educate others who come here as to what theatre is about and what it is they are seeing: entertainment provided by a good theatre company versus merely entertaining theatre." In retrospect, that can be seen as a modest ambition. "Entertainment provided by a good theatre company" hardly captures the sustained levels of excellence achieved by the Shaw Festival under Christopher Newton's leadership, levels of excellence created and sustained by an inviolable commitment to quality, to the ensemble, to fiscal responsibility, to measured risk, and to the plays and the values of Bernard Shaw.

BRIEF ENCOUNTERS

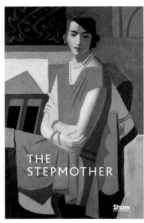

THE STEPMOTHER

THE PRESIDENT

HARVEY

A FOGGY DAY

SERIOUS MONEY

WONDERFUL TOWN

THE CRUCIBLE

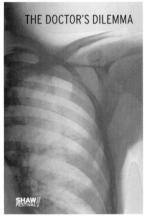

THE DOCTOR'S DILEMMA

DESIGN FOR LIVING

MRS WARREN'S PROFESSION

THE CHERRY ORCHARD

THE MAGIC FIRE

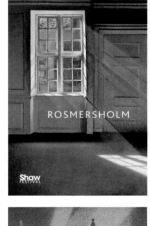

ROSMERSHOLM

the millionairess

THE DEVIL'S DISCIPLE

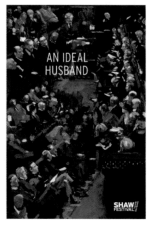

AN IDEAL HUSBAND

The Marrying of Ann Leete
Shaw Festival 1993

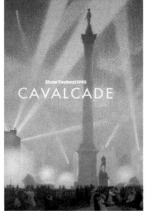

CAVALCADE

THE KILTARTAN COMEDIES

THE HEIRESS

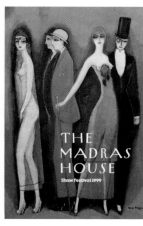

THE MADRAS HOUSE

Shaw Festival 1999

THE PHILANDERER

Shaw 07

SAINT JOAN

Shaw 07

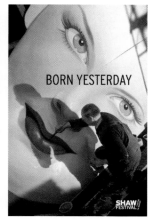

BORN YESTERDAY

THE CONSTANT WIFE

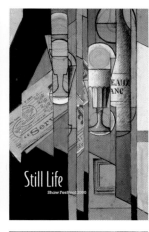

Still Life

Shaw Festival 2000

WAYS OF THE HEART

SHAW FESTIVAL

GETTING MARRIED

Shaw Festival 1999

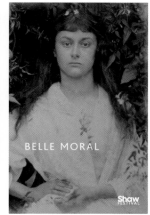

BELLE MORAL

peter pan

Shaw Festival 2001

Hobson's CHOICE

Shaw Festival 1996

fanny's first play

Shaw Festival 2001

The Chocolate Soldier

Shaw Festival 1997

picnic

Shaw Festival

TRISTAN

Shaw Festival

She Loves Me

Shaw Festival 2000

JOHN BULL'S OTHER ISLAND

SHAW FESTIVAL

ARMS AND THE MAN

Shaw Festival

Mr Cinders

Shaw Festival 1996

CHAPTER 7

JACKIE MAXWELL, 2003–

EVOLUTION, NOT REVOLUTION   In a 2005 essay in the *Canadian Theatre Review*, ensemble member Guy Bannerman described a scene that took place on the stage of the Festival Theatre on May 14, 2002. It was on the set that Cameron Porteous had designed for Neil Munro's production of Sidney Kingsley's *Detective Story*, but it was not a scene from that play.

> In a New York City precinct police station...a mysterious trench-coated figure in the obligatory slouch-brimmed fedora entered into the half-light. As the figure roamed among the desks, a second figure, similarly clad, entered behind the first: a gun blazed; the first fell victim to the second, the victim's fedora rolling away across the floor. Calmly, the newcomer stood over the body, then deliberately picked up the fallen hat. Looking it over, the murderer came to a decision. The fallen hat replaced the fedora on the head of the stranger, the rejected hat was tossed onto the floor beside the body. The murderer posed proudly in the dim room.

The audience cheered, the lights came up, the actors took their bows. The audience was made up of Shaw Festival company members; the actors were Christopher Newton and Jackie Maxwell. Maxwell, symbolically for now, had taken over from Newton as artistic director of the Shaw Festival. The reality of the transfer of power from Newton to Maxwell was, however, less dramatic and, happily, entirely bloodless.

Although Maxwell was well aware when she was at the Festival directing *Picnic* in 2001 that a search process was underway to find Newton's successor, she had no notion of applying until executive director Colleen Blake suggested it to her. Even then she hesitated. She had spent many years running theatres, and was now enjoying a busy career as a freelance director. She had a home in Stratford, where her husband was a member of the Stratford Festival company, and two young daughters in school there. After family discussions, she did, however, put her name forward. What followed, Maxwell said, was an entirely "civilized process" that quickly led to the announcement of her appointment as artistic director designate in a Festival press release on July 11, 2001. Her many accomplishments as listed in the press release included several years as artistic director of Factory Theatre in Toronto (1987–95, and as associate director from 1983), followed by five years (1996–2000) as head of new play development at the Charlottetown Festival in Prince Edward Island. (Although it was not noted in the press release, Maxwell had also, at the invitation of Christopher Newton, spent part of two summers in 1984 and 1985 at the Academy of the Shaw Festival, working with the acting ensemble on scripts she was developing at Factory Theatre.)

A native of Belfast, Northern Ireland, Maxwell grew up in a politically turbulent and dangerous environment, but also in a theatrically vibrant city. She acted with a youth group attached to the Lyric Theatre in Belfast, and, memorably, once played a corpse, a mourner, and an immigrant to Canada in a play called *Famine*, "truly one of the most depressing things ever written," according to Maxwell's mother (a drama teacher). In 1974 Maxwell left Belfast to study theatre at the University of Manchester. Like Belfast, Manchester was a theatrically exciting place, home not just to mainstream theatre, but also a venue for politically charged touring companies such as Monstrous Regiment and Joint Stock. It was from such companies that Maxwell learned that theatre "could actually change things." Manchester also happened to be the production centre for *Coronation Street,* where Maxwell was hired as an extra, working her way up on the TV soap, she recalls, "from a beer drinker to a darts player."

It was in her final year at Manchester that Maxwell met Benedict Campbell, a Canadian who had recently graduated from the Bristol Old Vic acting school. After a brief acting career in Ireland and England (the nadir of which, she says, was acting in a *Jack the Giant Killer* pantomime in Wigan, three times a day), she followed Campbell to Canada in August 1978, where, the previous January, he had been hired by the National Arts Centre (NAC) in Ottawa to play Troilus opposite a fetching Jennifer Dale as Cressida. They married (on a return trip to Manchester) and then settled in Ottawa, but while waiting for their apartment to be available they stayed in Niagara-on-the-Lake where Benedict Campbell's father, Douglas, was appearing in *Major Barbara* and *Heartbreak House.* Thus the future artistic director of the Shaw Festival, prophetically perhaps, made her first home in Niagara-on-the-Lake, and some of the first plays that she ever saw in Canada were at the Festival.

Soon hired herself by the NAC as resident assistant director, Maxwell quickly became involved in new play development, her three years at the NAC providing the genesis of her career-long "love of working with new plays and writers," as she explained in a 2001 interview with Kate Taylor.

It was abundantly clear from Maxwell's resumé that although Manchester University had given her a comprehensive education in classical and modern theatre, her interests and enthusiasms in Canada had centred on new play development and contemporary drama – largely, though not exclusively, Canadian contemporary drama. It was equally clear that these interests and enthusiasms differed markedly from Christopher Newton's. Among others, Toronto journalist Alec Scott (*Toronto Life*) pointed out other differences between them: "He's Home Counties English, she's Belfast Irish; he likes proper, brainy plays, she doesn't mind some emoting on stage; he's spent his career in the theatre mainstream, she's mainly inhabited the fringes." Given these differences, it was not surprising that there was great interest in what kind of post-Newtonian future the board and Maxwell had in mind for the Shaw Festival. In the July 2001 press release Newton was quoted as saying that "a theatre company must constantly renew itself," and that Maxwell's appointment had shown that the board had "chosen evolution rather than revolution" as the means to achieve renewal. There was no mystery in what the Festival was evolving from, but what, exactly, was it evolving *to*?

In a different context (an interview in the *National Post*), Newton anticipated and welcomed "a more Canadian and more contemporary playbill," but he expressed confidence that "the Festival will never come to the point where it is presenting plays with absolutely no connection to Shaw." The confidence turned out to be well founded, but he knew that it was inevitable that Maxwell would loosen the Shavian knot – or perhaps tie it in different ways.

Speculation and predictions were rife. *Toronto Star* critic Richard Ouzounian, for example, who described Maxwell as "an independent spirit who suffers no fools and takes no prisoners" (she had once famously "dis-invited" Ouzounian from the Factory Theatre), hoped that Maxwell, "with her proven skill at dramaturgy, will foster new scripts that will create fresh excitement for the Festival." Perhaps. But Maxwell's own statements about where the Festival would be heading were more pertinent than any amount of speculation.

Maxwell had, she said, "been allowed [by the board] to believe there's room for my ideas, for new air, for different takes on the material the Festival normally performs." She was fully aware, of course, as was everyone else in Canadian theatre, that she was the first woman to take charge of a major, internationally recognized Canadian company. However, it wasn't her sense that the board was "trying to be particularly proactive," or, through her appointment, signal a desire for radical change. "I believe I can bring something new here without upsetting the applecart," Maxwell said. It wasn't a matter of fixing problems – as Newton's task had been defined in 1980. She had attended and admired many Festival productions, ranging from *The Singular Life of Alfred Nobbs* in 1982, which she loved, to Newton's 1985 *Heartbreak House,* which "deeply" impressed her. She was, she said "taking over something in good shape, and yet trying to reinvigorate it in a way that would still be true to what it was." As Maxwell saw it, Newton had opened doors to new directions by extending the mandate in 2000 to allow for new and contemporary work in the Festival repertoire. Here, she argued, was the opportunity to make connections between Shaw and his contemporaries and new Canadian work. "I love the idea," she said, "of juxtaposing plays that were written in Shaw's lifetime with new plays that look at that period – especially new plays that capture what she saw as the "querulous and mosquito-like" spirit of Shaw. As she later (in 2005) told ensemble member Guy Bannerman, "I would be coming in to move the Shaw Festival to the next level – not in terms of quality, but opening up programming and expanding the programming ideas that Christopher Newton had started.... This would be the main focus of what I would do."

A CANADIAN VOICE   A defining feature of that focus would be a Canadian voice. Debates about the Canadian identity of the Festival were vigorous and divisive towards the end of Paxton Whitehead's term as artistic director (see above, page 55), but had waned as Christopher Newton established a distinctly Canadian ensemble and staff, supplemented from time to time by visiting directors and designers from Europe and the United Kingdom. As had been the case from the beginning, a strong American presence – essential to the success of the Festival – remained on the board and in Festival audiences. But a Canadian voice on the Festival's stages was the issue. Not that Newton could be accused of entirely ignoring Canadian plays and playwrights. He had occasionally produced Canadian plays (*Canuck* in 1980, and *Marsh Hay* in 1996, for example); he had invited Canadian playwrights to adapt plays (Sky Gilbert's *Salomé* in 1987, Judith Thompson's *Hedda Gabler* in 1991); and he had even promoted playwriting competitions (in the twenty-fifth anniversary season, 1986, for example). But Newton's record with Canadian drama could not be said to be marked either by enthusiastic commitment or conspicuous success.

Ken Gass, founder (in 1970) of Toronto's Factory Theatre (where Maxwell had successfully developed and directed many Canadian plays) saw the neglect of the Canadian voice in political terms. "By having a mandate that allowed only plays written during Shaw's lifetime," he argued, "Canadian playwrights were essentially legislated out, disenfranchised" by the Shaw Festival. "There's been this museum aspect to it. Americans come to Canada and return home having seen only what our colonial masters have written." Maxwell didn't politicize the issue, seeing it on the one hand as a mandate question (resolved by the 2000 change) and on the other simply as a reflection of Newton's interests and priorities. "New plays didn't interest Christopher," she told Guy Bannerman; "new play development was languishing in a sort of benevolent neglect."

No one could be in any doubt, then, that there would be an evolution towards a stronger Canadian voice on the stages of the Shaw Festival. But Maxwell had other programming initiatives in mind as well. She expressed a liking for American plays in general, but particularly work by Tennessee Williams, Arthur Miller, and Eugene O'Neill, "slushy, sexy, overwrought American drama" that "I absolutely adore." Irish plays, too – "hot worlds, not cool worlds. Shaw, the Anglos, operate on a cooler level."

Audiences could also anticipate changes in the way that programming was structured around the Festival's three theatres. Newton's programming had settled into a pattern of major, large-scale classical plays at the Festival Theatre, less familiar and more challenging plays at the Court House, and murder mysteries at the Royal George. While sensitive to the financial imperatives of getting the programming right in the Festival Theatre, Maxwell wanted to "deformulize" the programming. She had no interest, for example, in continuing the murder mysteries, planning instead to introduce Canadian "classics" at the Royal George. But nor did she want to "marginalize" the Canadian voice, classic or new, so Festival Theatre patrons could also anticipate changes.

While the Festival air was full of predictions, plans, expectations, speculation, guesswork, anticipation, apprehension, and excitement in 2001 and 2002 about what a Maxwellian rather than Newtonian Festival would look like, Maxwell herself was getting on with shadowing Newton as artistic director designate to learn more about the Festival. She was also busy directing *Candida* in the 2002 season, and, of course, planning the 2003 season. And as she pointed out in one interview, it's only when the season is announced that "you'll really see where my choices and Christopher's diverge."

Maxwell's 2003 season was announced on September 25, 2002. The evolution began to take firm shape. Maxwell characterized the season in the Festival's press release as one that built on Newton's exploration of "celebrated and rarely produced works from Bernard Shaw

and his contemporaries" by giving them "a new context" of contemporary plays – both international and Canadian – as well as "newly commissioned translations and some new directorial faces, providing our wonderful ensemble with an expanded world in which to play."

DIVERGENCES The divergences from Newton's programming were plain for all to see. True, some of Maxwell's 2003 selections could easily have appeared in one of Newton's seasons. Indeed, some had. Both of Maxwell's Shaw choices, *Misalliance* and *Widowers' Houses*, had been done under Newton – *Misalliance* twice (1980, 1990, both directed by Newton himself) and *Widowers' Houses* once (1992, directed by Jim Mezon). *Misalliance*, in fact, had the distinction of being in the opening seasons of both Newton and Maxwell. And while Newton had never programmed *The Royal Family* – one of Maxwell's selections – the works of George S. Kaufman had appeared in several Newton seasons. Perhaps also one of the musicals that Maxwell selected for the Royal George, *On the Twentieth Century*, would have been a comfortable fit in the musicals that Newton ran in the same theatre throughout the 1980s and 1990s. Maxwell's other musical, *Happy End* by Bertolt Brecht and Kurt Weill, linked with Newton's inclusion of Brecht in his 1980 and 1992 seasons, though neither *A Respectable Wedding* nor *Drums in the Night* were musicals. So there were certainly some compatibilities with Newton's programming. Divergences, however, trumped similarities.

The Canadian voice, for example, as anticipated, was much stronger than under Newton. Its most prominent presence was on the Festival Theatre stage, where Maxwell selected and directed a contemporary (1995) play by Quebec playwright Michel Marc Bouchard, in a translation by Linda Gaboriau. Set on an ocean liner on its way to England from Montreal in 1953 (Elizabeth II's coronation year), *The Coronation Voyage* tells a series of intense and disturbing stories about several passengers, stories showing how, as Maxwell explained in her director's notes in the house program, "any version of the truth can be challenged or revised by a simple refraction of the mirror or a slight change of focus." *The Coronation Voyage* was the first Canadian play seen at the Festival Theatre since Tony van Bridge directed Robertson Davies' *Leaven of Malice* there in 1975. By putting *The Coronation Voyage* in the Festival Theatre Maxwell was sending the message that Canadian and contemporary works would be given the kind of space and prominence normally reserved for major works of Shaw and his contemporaries. She was not about to make a "tepid or token" commitment to contemporary work, she said.

One of Maxwell's other Festival Theatre choices, Chekhov's *Three Sisters*, while much more in line with traditional Festival programming (although never before performed at the Festival), also had a strong Canadian voice. Rather than using one of the many translations already available, Maxwell commissioned a new translation by Canadian actor and playwright Susan Coyne to bring a Canadian, rather than British or European, sensibility to what Maxwell described as "my favourite play."

Complementing Canadian voices at the Festival Theatre was Sharon Pollock's *Blood Relations* at the Royal George. Based on the trial of Lizzie Borden for the murder of her parents in Fall River, Massachusetts, in 1892, Pollock's play had received many Canadian and international productions since its premiere in Edmonton in 1980. The inclusion of *The Coronation Voyage* and *Blood Relations* in the 2003 season marked the first time that two Canadian works had ever been scheduled in one Festival season.

Further divergences from Christopher Newton's programming was signalled by the first appearance at the Festival since 1965 of a Sean O'Casey play – *The Plough and the Stars* at the Court House Theatre – with an added Irish component from Brian Friel's *Afterplay*, the first time the work of one of Ireland's most celebrated contemporary playwrights had appeared at the Festival. A break from the past was also marked by the switch of this lunchtime production from the Royal George to the Court House.

A divergence, an evolution, of more fundamental significance, however, was the daring inclusion among the Court House selections of a little-known play called *Diana of Dobson's*, a 1908 romantic comedy by an actress and suffragette named Cicely Hamilton. Maxwell recognized and applauded Newton's success in "digging into the archeological end of the mandate," but she was now interested in finding the female equivalents of Harley Granville Barker and St John Hankin. *Diana of Dobson's* was the first of several important discoveries in this search.

Diana of Dobson's was directed by Alisa Palmer. New to the Festival, Palmer had directed extensively across Canada – mostly contemporary work – and had served as artistic director

of Nightwood Theatre, a women's theatre company in Toronto, from 1994 to 2001. She was one of five women making their directorial debut at the Shaw Festival in 2003. The others were Valerie Moore and Patricia Hamilton, co-directors of *On the Twentieth Century*; Martha Henry, director of *The Royal Family*; and Eda Holmes, director of *Blood Relations*. Moore and Hamilton had previous Festival experience as choreographer and actor, respectively, and Martha Henry had acted at the Festival as long ago as 1967 as Raina in *Arms and the Man*, at the beginning of a long and illustrious career as actor and director. Like Palmer, however, Eda Holmes was making her Festival debut, previously having directed at many of Canada's mainstream and alternative theatres (and having been an intern director at the Festival in 2001). Her contribution to the Festival since then has been substantial and ongoing (from 2009 as associate director).

Of the ten directors, then, in the 2003 season, six were women, the first time in Festival history that female directors had outnumbered male. With the sole exception of Daryl Cloran (*Afterplay*), the "new directorial faces" that Maxwell had referred to in the season press release were female.

There were, then, new voices aplenty in Maxwell's inaugural season. It was, Maxwell suggested, "a careful blend of the old and the new," but, like Newton's inaugural season in 1980, there could be no doubting that 2003 marked a new beginning for the Shaw Festival.

That new beginning, however – just like Newton's new beginning in 1980 – came close to being sabotaged. The circumstances were very different, but Maxwell, just like Newton, had a turbulent entrée into her new position.

SETBACKS

There were signs of problems a few weeks before the 2003 season officially began on May 20 with the opening of *Misalliance*. Advance ticket sales over the winter had been progressing well, and then in April media reports started to appear about the spread of Severe Acute Respiratory Syndrome (SARS) to Ontario. Originating in China in 2002, SARS could cause serious illness and, in about 10 percent of cases, death. Cases started to occur in Toronto in early April, and on April 23 the World Health Organization extended its travel advisory against non-essential travel to include Toronto. Tourism plummeted in Toronto (hotel occupancy rates dropped by 50 percent), and, inevitably, tourism in other parts of Ontario was affected. There was an immediate drop-off in Festival ticket sales to a level of 20 percent below sales at the same time in 2002. As the season got under way there was some recovery, aided, for example, by a special $400,000 marketing grant from the Ontario Ministry of Tourism. The grant was used by the Festival to create two mobile box offices – brightly covered vans that travelled to Canadian and U.S. cities, including Toronto, Kingston, and Montreal in Canada, and New York, Rochester, and Philadelphia in the U.S. Nonetheless, ticket sales continued to lag far behind those of 2002.

And SARS wasn't the only problem. Just a few weeks before the SARS outbreak, the war in Iraq had begun, creating an unsettling impact on leisure travel, particularly among Americans. In addition, Ontario tourism was still struggling from the effects of human West Nile Virus to which a dozen deaths had been attributed in 2002, more than in any other Canadian province. By the end of July 2002 close to four hundred probable or confirmed cases of West Nile had been reported by the Ontario Ministry of Health. And as if to add insult to injury, one of the biggest power blackouts in history hit the northeastern United States and Canada on August 14, 2003. A state of emergency was declared in Ontario, and tourism took yet another blow. It was, all in all, said Maxwell, "pretty apocalyptic," as "everything short of a collision with Mars" hit the province.

It was no consolation that the Shaw Festival was not alone in suffering these kinds of setbacks. During the summer of 2003 box office at the Stratford Festival was substantially down as well, and in Toronto the mega-musicals were either closing or having openings delayed. Closer to home, tourism in Niagara-on-the-Lake was also having a difficult time, with a drop of 30 percent in overnight accommodation bookings.

The full extent of declining ticket sales at the Shaw Festival was not apparent until after the 2003 season ended on November 30 with the final performance of *Blood Relations*. The official figures were released at the Festival's annual meeting in the lobby of the Festival Theatre

on January 30, 2004, but by then the press had already reported a fall in box office revenue from $14.5m in 2002 to just under $13.2m in 2003. In 2002, 318,838 seats were sold (76 percent of seats available), compared to 269,407 (63.5 percent) in 2003. The bottom line was a 2003 operating deficit of $3m ($500,000 of which could be attributed to a change in fiscal year end from October 31 to November 30). Thanks to income from endowment funds, the Festival, as executive director Colleen Blake reported at the annual meeting, remained "financially stable and well placed for the future." A recovery plan, she said, was in place, and at that stage advance ticket sales for the 2004 season were "in line with previous successful seasons."

The recovery plan was not publicly revealed or discussed, but the extent to which internal as well as external factors contributed to the deficit had to be considered. In particular, could any lessons be learned from the 2003 programming? A breakdown of box office figures showed that whereas the Court House and Royal George plays had done well, the Festival Theatre plays had achieved only a 52 percent box office, meaning that in excess of 100,000 seats in the company's largest theatre had gone unsold.

In terms of percentage of seats sold, the most successful productions, all achieving well in excess of an 80 percent box office, were *Widowers' Houses* and *Diana of Dobson's* (Court House) and *On the Twentieth Century* and *Happy End* (Royal George); box office for *On the Twentieth Century* was an impressive season high of 91.5 percent.

DIANA OF DOBSON'S, 2003 Joseph Ziegler's outstanding production of *Widowers' Houses* – which included what was considered by many to be one of Jim Mezon's finest Shavian performances (as Sartorious, the slum landlord) – made it clear that Shaw was alive and well at the Shaw Festival under Maxwell's direction, but it was particularly pleasing to Maxwell that her first effort at finding female voices among Shaw's contemporaries was so successful. Some critics, it is true – male critics – were lukewarm, even condescending, in their response to *Diana of Dobson's*, but Kate Taylor in the *Globe and Mail* grasped the play's meaning and importance. It was much more, Taylor recognized, than a "hand-me-down St John Hankin or Granville Barker" (Cushman), or "little more than a pleasant evening in the theatre" (Coulbourn), or "a pleasant enough two hours in the theatre" (Ouzounian). The decision of a young female worker (memorably played by Severn Thompson) in a drapery emporium (Dobson's) to spend a small inheritance on a fling in Europe rather than responsibly saving it for a more secure future, opens up new worlds to her, not just geographically speaking, but socially and morally as well. Although Diana's adventures end happily, they have reinforced for her and for the play's audiences – as Shaw's plays so often do for women in his plays, and for his audiences – the prejudices and inequalities embedded in Victorian and Edwardian society. A Canadian premiere, *Diana of Dobson's* was also, said Taylor, an "Edwardian gem," "vivid and refreshing," and "engagingly frank about social realities."

In some ways there was less at stake with the other box-office successes in Maxwell's 2003 season. Maxwell described *On the Twentieth Century* as a "hilarious, over-the-top" play, "with a sparkling, witty book and music to match," and it was there to please audiences. Which it did. Jamie Portman considered it "one of the funniest musicals ever mounted at the Shaw Festival" – and he had seen most of them. *Happy End* was a more challenging piece, but it benefited from having Tadeusz Bradecki as director. Bradecki transformed this overtly Marxist tale of unlikely encounters between gangsters and the Salvation Army in 1919 Chicago into "an exhilarating experience" for Portman, while for Richard Ouzounian Bradecki's "masterful production combined with powerhouse performances" made *Happy End* "one of the year's most exciting shows."

BLOOD RELATIONS, 2003 In terms of Maxwell's evolving agenda for the Shaw Festival, and the challenge of finding the audience for it, the other Royal George show that carried a lot of weight in 2003 was *Blood Relations*. Unlike *Diana of Dobson's*, *Blood Relations* had a strong North American production pedigree, and its subject matter – a murder in Massachusetts – had American appeal. The choice also evolved, it could be argued, from Newton's popular murder-mystery series at the Royal George. The play wasn't so much a "whodunnit" as a "why-dunnit," as Maxwell cannily put it. But it certainly had a murder-mystery feel to it. Still, there was no history of success for Canadian plays at the Festival, and no play by a

Canadian woman had ever been performed at the Festival. Maxwell didn't let these cautionary signs deter her. *Blood Relations* opened early in the season (previews from May 1) and ran for 120 performances. Maxwell's confidence in the play – and in director Eda Holmes – was rewarded. *Blood Relations* sold nearly 26,000 tickets, outselling all the other small theatre plays that season except *On the Twentieth Century*, including plays by Shaw, O'Casey, and Brecht. And for the first time at the Shaw Festival the story was being told not just by a woman in a play, but in a play by a woman, directed by a woman.

The two Irish plays – O'Casey's *The Plough and the Stars* and Brian Friel's *Afterplay* (both at the Court House) – sold least well of the small theatre plays (63 percent and 61 percent, respectively). Neil Munro's *Plough* was bogged down by difficulties many audience members (and critics) had in following the broad Irish accents that Munro encouraged his actors to use. There was no need for Irish accents in Friel's play though (directed by newcomer Daryl Cloran). Friel asks a "what if" question in *Afterplay*. What if two of Chekhov's characters, Sonia (Helen Taylor) from *Uncle Vanya* and Andrey (Simon Bradbury) from *Three Sisters*, met in a Moscow café twenty years after their plays ended? What would they have to say to each other and what would we learn about their post-play lives (a variation on the sequel that Shaw wrote for *Pygmalion*)? *Afterplay* was a natural complement to *Three Sisters* running simultaneously at the Festival Theatre. Both the heavier intellectual content and, as one critic said, "the more cerebral" location of the Court House Theatre (rather than the Royal George) marked another Maxwellian evolution, this one for the lunchtime slot.

Had the 2003 season been limited to the Court House and the Royal George the season would have been hailed as a great success, financially and critically. But as Maxwell pointed out, a full house at either the Court House or Royal George is only a 37 percent house at the Festival Theatre. Without a healthy return from the Festival Theatre plays the Festival budget is always in jeopardy. And that was the problem in 2003.

There were three plays in the Festival Theatre in 2003. Shaw's *Misalliance* opened the season on May 20 (previews from April 10), followed by the Susan Coyne adaptation of Chekhov's *Three Sisters* on May 24 (previews from April 26). Later in the season, Michel Marc Bouchard's *The Coronation Voyage* opened on July 5 (previews from June 24) and George S. Kaufman's and Edna Ferber's *The Royal Family* on August 16 (previews from August 8).

Misalliance, directed by Neil Munro (see above, page 156), had a run of 106 performances and returned a solid 66 percent box office. *The Royal Family*, directed by Martha Henry – in her first engagement with the Shaw Festival since she played Raina in *Arms and the Man* in 1967 – did rather less well at a 57 percent box office, but had a generally positive critical reception. But the two plays that represented Maxwell's decision to place Canadian voices at the centre of Festival programming both seriously disappointed at the box office.

THREE SISTERS, 2003 Chekhov's moving story of the frustrated desires of three sisters to escape from their dull country town to the excitements of Moscow, a thousand miles away, ran for fifty performances, but achieved only a 40.5 percent box office. It took Buffalo critic Richard Huntington a return visit to fully appreciate what Maxwell had achieved, which was, he judged, a genuine ensemble performance in which no individual actor "disrupts Chekhov's slow, oblique revelations of feeling by pushing too hard on the character." (In her Festival brochure note on the play Maxwell described it as "a true ensemble piece – perfect for our company.") This approach, Huntington conceded, might not appeal to those who looked for "Chekhov's meandering emotions" to be "pinned down by one or two big-scale performances," but it seemed to him – and to others – that by stressing the ensemble nature of the play Maxwell had created a "fastidiously honest and uncompromised production." Maxwell's use of silences, of stillness, of solitudes was also intrinsic to the texture of *Three Sisters*, Jamie Portman argued, and there were moments in the production "when you want to stand up and cheer, moments which, in terms of communicating the most fragile and elusive nuances of human behaviour, are as fine as anything you might hope to encounter in live theatre." Both Huntington and Portman, however, had doubts about Susan Coyne's translation, in particular her "trying too hard" to create a colloquial tone with phrases such as "I'm pooped" or "she's a piece of work." Portman wondered, too, whether the large Festival Theatre stage – despite designer Sue LePage's efforts – was the right place to capture the stifling provincial atmosphere of the play.

THE CORONATION VOYAGE, 2003 Maxwell's bold decision to put a contemporary Canadian play in the Festival Theatre didn't pay off at the box office. The sixty-four-performance run of *The Coronation Voyage* sold just over 19,000 tickets (only 34 percent of available tickets). Some positives, nonetheless, emerged. There were, to be sure, naysayers about Maxwell's strategy of putting Canadian plays on the Festival's mainstage, and there were naysayers about the play itself. Within the company, however, there was a tangible air of excitement around the production, especially on opening night with author Michel Marc Bouchard in the audience. Maxwell also received many personal messages of appreciation for making the Canadian voice more prominent at the Shaw Festival, and American critic Joel Greenberg wrote enthusiastically about the engagement of audiences with the play. At intermission at the performance he attended people were energetically discussing the play's plot and characters, and at the end, as the audience left the theatre, he detected a similar focus on discussion of the play itself, rather than the play (as he sometimes experienced) "as a respite between wineries, tea shops, and fruit stands." Audience engagement of a different kind was recorded by *National Post* critic Robert Cushman. There is a moment early in the play when a diplomat, in return for providing passports with new identities for a crime boss and his family, demands sexual access to the crime boss's thirteen-year-old son. When Cushman saw the play in Vancouver in 2000, the audience, he said, took the moment in its stride. At the Shaw Festival, however, "it produced shock waves more palpable than any I have felt in a theatre since the night the world first heard about the blinding of the horses in *Equus*."

So audiences were listening, audiences were responding, and audiences were engaging with *The Coronation Voyage*, but they were small audiences. Whatever the reason – external circumstances, programming, choice of theatres – the Festival could not prosper with such low box office returns in the Festival Theatre. That much was clear to Maxwell. But how would she respond?

HUNKERING DOWN

SARS, Maxwell said in a 2004 interview, "was a mean shock in my first year." But "we have so little control over these things" that "we have to hunker down and do as well as we can." There was no shortage of advice for Maxwell on what form the hunkering down should take. Praise for the new directions in which she was taking the Festival was tempered by well-intentioned advice on rethinking her strategies. John Coulbourn for one, in the *Toronto Sun*, applauded the introduction of Canadian plays, but suggested that *The Coronation Voyage* was "at the right Festival, but on the wrong stage." He didn't believe for one moment (as some did) that "Canadian plays just won't sell," but (citing the greater success of *Blood Relations* in the Royal George) he wasn't convinced that the Festival Theatre was the right venue.

Maxwell's dilemma was how to maintain the initiatives she had put in place for the 2003 season while responding to the obvious need to deal with the deficit from that season. Yes, she told one interviewer, "I am very aware of the bottom line, but I don't feel cowed in terms of the pieces we can do." "I do feel," she insisted, "that I can continue the exploration of the kind of juxtaposition between contemporary work and mandate work and can present more, different worlds." And, she added, "I do believe we can maintain Canadian contemporary work and can continue to do adaptations." Nor was Maxwell willing to restrict Canadian and contemporary programming to the smaller theatres.

What programming compromises, then, if any, could be expected for Maxwell's second season? Her own description of the 2004 season (in a press release, December 8, 2003) was that it represented "a carefully thought-through blend of dynamic fare from our traditional mandate plus a continuation of the initiatives we introduced last season to acclaim and enthusiasm from audiences and critics alike – contemporary programming both Canadian and international and an extra musical that pushes the genre's envelope a little further."

The selection of plays, and the theatres in which she placed them, showed that Maxwell had held firm to her principles of new directions, but with astute touches of pragmatism. Her determination to maintain Canadian work at the centre of Festival programming – i.e., at the Festival Theatre – was shown by the choice of *Nothing Sacred*, a 1988 play by George Walker. Maxwell had worked closely with Walker, one of the most successful playwrights in Canada, when she was artistic director of Factory Theatre in Toronto. The other Festival Theatre plays, however – Shaw's *Pygmalion* and *Man and Superman*, and the classic American comedy *Three Men on a Horse* by George Abbott and John Cecil Holm – were more mandate mainstream and clearly selected with at least one eye on the box office.

The Canadian element was continued at the Royal George Theatre with *Waiting for the Parade*, John Murrell's 1977 play about five women in Calgary waiting for their men to return from the Second World War, while Maxwell's interest in unearthing little-known work by Edwardian female playwrights was also continued (following *Diana of Dobson's* in 2003) by Githa Sowerby's *Rutherford and Son* (in the Court House Theatre).

Two musicals were included: the Rodgers and Hart favourite, *Pal Joey*, at the Royal George, and another American musical – this one contemporary and far less familiar – *Floyd Collins*, at the Court House.

Maxwell's enthusiasm for Irish and American plays was again reflected in her 2004 choices. *Ah, Wilderness!* (Court House) was the first O'Neill play ever produced at the Festival, while J.M. Synge's one-act play *The Tinker's Wedding* was the lunchtime performance (also at the Court House).

The 2004 season was rounded out by another potential box office hit, Oscar Wilde's *The Importance of Being Earnest*, which, surprisingly, the Festival had never produced, and a one-act farce, *Harlequinade*, by British playwright Terence Rattigan – the first appearance of a Rattigan play at the Festival. Both plays were scheduled at the Royal George.

It was an ambitious twelve-play season, the first of that size since 1999. It was also, Maxwell said, a season with a "double mission": shoring up the deficit, yes; but also making sure that artistic objectives don't "get set aside" while financial problems were addressed. Despite the 2003 deficit, then, retrenchment and reversal were not the order of the day. Advance sales for the 2004 season were encouraging, but it remained to be seen whether tourism in Ontario was recovering from the bleak situation in 2003, and whether the 2004 plays would bring back lost audiences.

NICOLE UNDERHAY; MICHAEL BALL
IN *RUTHERFORD AND SON* BY GITHA
SOWERBY, 2004. DIRECTED BY JACKIE
MAXWELL, DESIGNED BY WILLIAM
SCHMUCK, LIGHTING DESIGNED BY
LOUISE GUINAND.

OPPOSITE: PETER KRANTZ AND KELLI
FOX IN *RUTHERFORD AND SON*, 2004.
PHOTOS BY ANDREE LANTHIER.

***NOTHING SACRED, WAITING FOR THE PARADE,* 2004**   One key artistic objective for 2004 was to solidify the place of Canadian plays in the repertoire. The 2004 season produced mixed and frustrating results in this regard. The Festival Theatre's Canadian play, George Walker's *Nothing Sacred*, had a slightly higher percentage box office (38 percent) than *The Coronation Voyage* (34 percent) in 2003, but it was for a much shorter run (thirty-five performances as against sixty-four), and it sold far fewer tickets (11,526 as against 19,101). And yet much of the critical reaction was strongly positive. An adaptation of Turgenev's 1862 novel *Fathers and Sons*, *Nothing Sacred* was described by Walker as "a Canadian comedy, not a Russian tragedy," but the comedy didn't undermine the disturbing complexity of the relationships in a family attempting to come to terms with its own internal dysfunctions as well as social dysfunctions as revolution hovers. Robert Cushman, who had seen previous productions of *Nothing Sacred*, praised this new Shaw Festival production, directed by Morris Panych – the first of several Festival productions by this multi-talented actor/playwright/director – as a "brave and brilliant revival," while Richard Ouzounian was unstinting in his praise of director, designers (Ken MacDonald, set; David Boechler, costumes; Alan Brodie, lighting), and cast. "When all the elements of a production work together perfectly, you can almost hear an audible murmur of satisfaction ripple through an audience," Ouzounian wrote in the *Toronto Star*, and that is what he experienced on opening night on August 25. Among the cast, Mike Shara as Bazarov, the nihilist, and Tara Rosling as Ana, the widow, shone; but it was truly a triumph for the ensemble, which also included Jim Mezon, Patrick Galligan, Andrew Bunker, Richard Farrell, Jeff Meadows, Benedict Campbell, and Dylan Trowbridge.

Nothing Sacred was described by Ouzounian as "theatre that you really shouldn't miss." He also credited Maxwell with forging "a new house style…made up of the best of the old Shaw Festival with some refreshing additions of her own."

It was content rather than style that Maxwell was focusing on, but Ouzounian's sense of new directions at the Festival was appropriate – those new directions having also been signalled in the 2004 season by another Canadian play, *Waiting for the Parade*, directed by Festival newcomer Linda Moore in the Royal George Theatre. The production didn't receive the critical accolades enjoyed by *Nothing Sacred*, but it sold more tickets (11,892) and achieved a 60 percent box office in a sixty performance run.

***RUTHERFORD AND SON,* 2004**   Another key feature of Maxwell's evolution of the Shaw Festival – women's voices – was apparent in *Waiting for the Parade* (albeit women's voices created by a male writer), but the other important play in the 2004 season from this perspective was *Rutherford and Son*. In the 2004 season brochure Maxwell spoke of the Festival's well-established tradition of "uncovering lost gems" from the period of Shaw's life, a tradition perhaps best, but certainly not exclusively, represented by Neil Munro's series of plays by Harley Granville Barker (discussed above, page 150). The 2003 production of *Diana of Dobson's* took the tradition in a new direction, the discovery of lost gems by women writers. *Rutherford and Son* maintained that new direction, though the audience enthusiasm shown for *Diana of Dobson's* wasn't matched by *Rutherford and Son*, which in the same theatre (Court House) and with exactly the same number of performances (sixty-nine) sold nearly 9000 fewer tickets (51 percent of seats available).

Githa Sowerby's 1912 play about a failing family business in northern England, and the family divisions caused by this, enjoyed success in its own time, but had long since fallen into neglect. One or two critics felt it was a play better left buried. Most, however felt that Maxwell's direction brought out not just the best in actors such as Michael Ball (as Rutherford, the tyrannical family patriarch) and Kelli Fox (as Janet, his unmarried daughter), but also the ongoing political relevance of the patriarchy theme of the play, especially the waste that the patriarchy imposes on the life of Janet. Fox's performance as a woman whose "every aspect of living is controlled by masculine greed and stupidity" so impressed *Hamilton Spectator* critic Gary Smith that he told his readers that "if Kelli Fox isn't the great Canadian actress, I don't know who is." The whole production of *Rutherford and Son*, for Smith, was "the Shaw Festival at its finest hour."

***FLOYD COLLINS,* 2004**   Critical accolades, however, do not guarantee good box office. Another case in point in 2004 was one of the two musicals, *Floyd Collins*. This was one of those shows

that joined others (*Cyrano de Bergerac* in 1982; *Cavalcade* in 1985; and *Man and Superman*, also in 2004, for example) as among the most critically celebrated productions in Shaw Festival history.

"You wouldn't think," said Richard Ouzounian, "that a musical about a man trapped in a cave could be the most liberating event of the summer, but that's the kind of irony that great theatre thrives on. And make no mistake: *Floyd Collins* is great theatre."

Floyd Collins, with music and lyrics by Adam Guettel, is based on the true story of a caver trapped in a cave in Kentucky in 1925, an event that provoked a media circus as attempts to free him (ultimately unsuccessful) became ever more desperate. Director Eda Holmes worked with designers William Schmuck (set) and Kevin Lamotte (lighting) to turn the full Court House auditorium into performance space, with effects that included strings of bare light bulbs illuminating a cavern tunnel through the auditorium. Schmuck also made liberal and imaginative use of large mounds of newsprint to emphasize the media frenzy that engulfed the rescue attempts. The caver was played by Jay Turvey, who had been acting and singing at the Festival since 2000, but had never experienced the acclaim he received for his work in *Floyd Collins*. Turvey, said Jamie Portman, "was outstanding, running the gamut from youthful excitement to fear and disillusionment and delirium and ultimately to heart-rending resignation."

Robert Cushman's reading of the audience on opening night (August 26) was that from as early as half way through the evening it "was bursting with suppressed excitement, and when the time came to release it, they – or rather we – exploded." Richard Ouzounian was there too, and he knew that the "prolonged and spontaneous ovation" given by the audience was one of those ovations "that comes along once in a blue moon" – and the production, he said, "truly deserved it." It was "one of those truly rare occasions when everything works to perfection: brilliant staging, superb design, excellent musicianship [under the direction of Paul Sportelli], and a first-rate cast." Jamie Portman was more succinct. *Floyd Collins*, he said, was "a production which does Canadian theatre proud."

But the critical acclaim and enthusiastic audience response for *Floyd Collins* did not translate into good box office. In its thirty-nine performance run in the Court House the production sold barely half (51 percent) of available tickets. The 2004 season needed better sales than that. And, ideally, the shows that sold tickets would at one and the same time be critically acclaimed *and* reflect Maxwell's evolutionary agenda.

AH, WILDERNESS!, 2004   Part of that agenda was an increase in the number of Irish and American plays in the playbill. Maxwell's second Irish play, J.M. Synge's *The Tinker's Wedding* (following O'Casey's *The Plough and the Stars* in 2003) had only a short lunchtime run in the Court House, directed by Micheline Chevrier, who had directed *A Room of One's Own* in 2000 and *Love from a Stranger* in 2001. Not for the first time at the Festival, the production of an Irish play was hampered by the impenetrability (for some) of Irish accents, and in any event, even with reasonable sales, *The Tinker's Wedding* wasn't in a position to make much of a dent in the Festival deficit. Eugene O'Neill's *Ah, Wilderness!* (directed by Joseph Ziegler) had a longer run, however (eighty performances in the Court House), and it was well received by critics and audiences alike. O'Neill's only comedy – an elegiac coming-of-age tale that depicts O'Neill's early life as he would have wished it to be rather than the bitter mess it was – *Ah, Wilderness!* wasn't one of the "slushy, sexy" American plays that Maxwell favoured (they were to come), but it introduced one of America's most important playwrights to the Festival – and it also sold close to 20,000 tickets (76 percent box office).

THE IMPORTANCE OF BEING EARNEST, 2004   That was helpful, and the box office success of two other small theatre shows helped as well. Both *Pal Joey* and *The Importance of Being Earnest* (both at the Royal George) attracted large audiences – *Pal Joey* to the tune of 97 percent box office, *The Importance of Being Earnest*, 85 percent. Christopher Newton's production of *Earnest* (the first of several plays directed by Newton at the Festival following his retirement in 2002) sold tickets despite being one of the least funny versions of Wilde's play ever. At least that's what the critics thought, and Newton gave them good reason. It wasn't so much that Newton was against fun, but he was certainly against silliness. If, Newton argued, *The Importance of Being Earnest* is one of the greatest comedies in the English language it can't be just silly. Who are these people? What makes them so witty? What lies beneath the surface of their relationships? Getting beneath the surface was what Newton had always done with Shaw, and it's also what he did, for example – to some people's disappointment – with *Peter Pan* in 2001 (see above, page 180). Instead, then, of a silly romp, Newton gave audiences an *Earnest* that was closer to a stylized comedy of manners, thoughtful, but not ponderous, "never less than amusing, but rarely laugh-out-loud funny," said Jamie Portman. That didn't seem to trouble Festival audiences, who kept buying tickets (42,335 of them) through the seven-month run.

PAL JOEY, 2004   Audiences kept buying tickets as well for *Pal Joey*. In her second directorial appearance at the Festival (following *Diana of Dobson's* in 2003), Alisa Palmer handled Rodgers and Hart's take on sleazy Chicago nightclubs in the 1930s with panache. Although critical opinion was divided, Richard Ouzounian put *Pal Joey* "right up there with the very best musicals ever presented at the Shaw Festival," and an American critic (Herman Trotter from the *Buffalo News*) reckoned that the Festival production lifted *Pal Joey* "to new heights." William Schmuck ingeniously fitted some big sets into a small space without making everything look cramped, and the cast delivered some familiar songs such as "I Could Write a Book" (Adam Brazier) and "Bewitched, Bothered, and Bewildered" (Laurie Paton) with sensitivity and conviction. Musical director Paul Sportelli, said Ouzounian, did his "usual consummately classy job." The 97 percent box office translated into over 34,000 ticket sales for the show.

Pal Joey and *The Importance of Being Earnest* helped the Royal George plays in 2004 reach a healthy 84 percent box office. The Court House averaged 63 percent – disappointing after 2003's 77.5 percent, but not in itself disastrous. The major problem, as in 2003, was in the Festival Theatre. *Nothing Sacred* played to houses that were, on average, two-thirds empty, while what looked like a much safer choice – the 1935 Broadway comedy hit *Three Men on a Horse* – achieved only a 46 percent box office. That put the financial burden on the two Shaw

plays in the Festival Theatre. They carried it dutifully – *Pygmalion* (discussed below, page 240) was the season's bestseller at over 65,000 tickets – but at the end of the season the Festival Theatre shows were shown to have averaged a 54 percent box office, only slightly above the 2003 figure of 52 percent.

In reporting final figures for the 2004 season at the annual members' meeting on January 28, 2005, outgoing board chair Thomas Hyde and treasurer Mark Hilson put a brave face on it, but the bottom line was again troubling. Paid attendance was some 46,000 tickets short of the projected 325,000, leading to a seasonal deficit of $2.37m, and an accumulated deficit of $4.4m. The positive news was that ticket sales had increased by 10,000 over the 2003 season, and that there had been signs of a recovery in Ontario tourism in the second half of the season. Moreover, there had been critical acclaim for several productions, particularly *Nothing Sacred*, *Man and Superman*, and *Floyd Collins*. So it wasn't by any means all doom and gloom. Nonetheless, as Jackie Maxwell conceded, "there's no doubt that there is significant work to be done to rebuild attendance."

RE-STRATEGIZING

At the 2004 annual meeting, executive director Colleen Blake announced several strategies to address the deficit, including the formation of a strategic planning committee, to be headed by incoming board chair Elaine Triggs, and an internal financial review "at all levels of the organization" that would "examine every aspect for cost savings and for revenue generating opportunities." On the artistic side, Jackie Maxwell remained upbeat. "The work that we do here," she told members, "is vivid, deeply felt and far-reaching," and she eagerly anticipated the 2005 season of plays that she had announced on September 22, 2004.

In selecting the 2005 playbill Maxwell was again faced with the challenge of maintaining the new directions she had set for the Festival while rebuilding attendance. She told an interviewer in May 2005 that she had had to "back off on some of the ideas I originally had," and there were indeed some significant recalculations for her third season. The biggest single change

JULIE MARTELL; NORA MCLELLAN;
JEFF LILLICO IN *GYPSY* BY ARTHUR
LAURENTS, JULE STYNE AND STEPHEN
SONDHEIM, 2005. DIRECTED BY JACKIE
MAXWELL, MUSICAL DIRECTION AND
ORCHESTRAL ADAPTATION BY PAUL
SPORTELLI, CHOREOGRAPHY AND
ASSOCIATE DIRECTION BY VALERIE
MOORE, SET DESIGNED BY PETER
HARTWELL, COSTUMES DESIGNED
BY JUDITH BOWDEN, LIGHTING DE-
SIGNED BY KEVIN LAMOTTE, SOUND
DESIGNED BY PETER MCBOYLE.
PHOTOS BY ANDREE LANTHIER.

in 2005 was dropping a Canadian play from the Festival Theatre (where she had scheduled *Coronation Voyage* in 2003 and *Nothing Sacred* in 2004) and replacing it with a musical (*Gypsy*), the first time in Shaw Festival history that a musical had been presented in the main theatre. A Canadian play, the commissioned *Belle Moral*, was included for 2005, but Maxwell put it in the Court House. Shaw was represented by two of his best-known plays, *You Never Can Tell* and *Major Barbara*, but there was no "lost gem" by a female writer of Shaw's time (such as *Diana of Dobson's* in 2003 and *Rutherford and Son* in 2004). The 2005 season was also one in which Maxwell first revived a previous production, bringing back Tadeusz Bradecki's very successful staging of the Brecht/Weill musical *Happy End*, which had sold to 90 percent houses in 2003.

On the other hand, the inclusion of Lillian Hellman's *The Autumn Garden* and William Inge's *Bus Stop* maintained the momentum for American plays, and with the season rounded out with two Festival premieres of plays by Shaw's contemporaries (Somerset Maugham's *The Constant Wife* and R.C. Sherriff's *Journey's End*) and a lunchtime farce (*Something on the Side*) Maxwell was confident that this "truly diverse selection of worlds" would succeed artistically and financially.

GYPSY, 2005 From a financial point of view much depended on *Gypsy*, which Maxwell chose to direct herself, and on the two other plays in the Festival Theatre, *You Never Can Tell* (which opened the season on May 5) and *Major Barbara*. Maxwell needed, as she put it, "to get the Festival Theatre cooking again."

Although a musical had never before been performed in the Festival Theatre, an orchestra pit had been installed in the original 1973 building, and the time had come, Maxwell reasoned, to use it. It wasn't a matter of selecting a musical simply for its cash-cow box office potential, however. She wanted an artistic rationale as well, and with *Gypsy* she believed she had found it. A 1959 Broadway classic, with music by Jule Styne, lyrics by Stephen Sondheim, and book (based on the memoirs of the legendary burlesque performer Gypsy Rose Lee) by Arthur Laurents, *Gypsy* has plenty of great songs ("Everything's Coming Up Roses," "Some People," "Let Me Entertain You"); but it also contained a compelling storyline about the relationship between a domineering mother (Momma Rose) and her two daughters (one of whom becomes Gypsy Rose Lee).

Musical director Paul Sportelli had his work cut out to adapt the orchestration for his modest ensemble of twelve players from that for the original score for an orchestra double that size. But whatever the musical qualities of a production of *Gypsy*, success will be elusive without a powerful actress in the lead role. As John Coulbourn said in the *Toronto Sun*, "unless you have a Rose, you don't have *Gypsy*." The role had been created on Broadway by Ethel Merman. Angela Lansbury, Tyne Daly, and Bernadette Peters have been other memorable Mommas. For the Shaw Festival production Momma was played by Nora McLellan, in her twenty-first season at the Festival (beginning in 1980 in the controversial *A Respectable Wedding*). For McLellan, *Gypsy* was more than a collection of good songs; "it's gritty and it's dark," and Momma's character "is fuelled by a formidable will that rides roughshod over everybody in her path." For some critics McLellan wasn't quite pushy or "brassy" enough to capture that element of Momma Rose, and there was some disappointment as well in Peter Hartwell's spartan set, which consisted of a series of theatrical flats and rolling pieces of furniture. The point was, though, to move away from – not replicate – the excesses of Broadway mega-musicals and glitz, and, as Coulbourn noted, "return the emphasis to the story and the performers." And Coulbourn also had nothing but praise for McLellan's performance, "a personal triumph," he said, in which "she pulls out all the stops."

Maxwell did, however, make one concession for *Gypsy* that displeased Festival purists: the performers wore microphones. This had never been necessary for the musicals in the Royal George or the Court House, but in the Festival Theatre, and for actors who could sing but had never received formal training, the large Festival Theatre was a challenge. Most audiences seemed to appreciate the success of Festival technicians in enhancing voices without creating an overpowering wall of sound.

Maxwell scheduled a long run of 127 performances of *Gypsy* in the Festival Theatre, and it worked. Paid attendance was 78.5 percent; over 85,000 tickets were sold.

YOU NEVER CAN TELL, MAJOR BARBARA, 2005   A bright and breezy production of *You Never Can Tell* (the Festival's sixth of Shaw's comedy), directed by Morris Panych, designed by Ken Mac-Donald, didn't do quite as well (64 percent box office). Even so, it was a production that sparkled with inventiveness, with Beatles music, a set that resembled an art nouveau sea shell, and freewheeling performances from Nicole Underhay and Harry Judge as the twins (balanced by the cool dignity of David Schurmann's Waiter).

The third show at the Festival Theatre in 2005, *Major Barbara* was, however, one of the season's box office disappointments. Much about the production (the Festival's fifth) excelled: Joe Ziegler's nuanced direction of virtually the full text of Shaw's play; Christina Poddubiuk's distinctive and revelatory sets and costumes (emphasizing, for example, the stark contrasts between Lady Britomart's richly elegant library and the grunginess of the West Ham Salvation Army shelter); the exhilarating cut and thrust between the cynical Undershaft (Benedict Campbell) and the idealist Cusins (Ben Carlson). Diana Donnelly's Barbara was overshadowed by the stage power of Campbell and Carlson, but that was far from a fatal flaw in the production. Jamie Portman judged this *Major Barbara* a "gilt-edged triumph" that "does the Festival proud." But it nonetheless failed to build an audience, and the relatively short sixty-eight-performance run achieved only a 45 percent box office (26,109 tickets).

By the end of the season the three Festival Theatre plays had sold 66 percent (169,188) of available tickets, a big improvement (by 30,000 tickets) over 2004. But was it enough to make a dent in the deficit?

BUS STOP, 2005   Audience reaction to the plays in the two other theatres was encouraging. All the Royal George shows did well. Bringing back *Happy End* proved a happy decision, with houses averaging close to 80 percent, while the Feydeau-Desvallières farce (*Something on the Side*) achieved close to 90 percent. Maxwell's production of William Inge's *Bus Stop*, her second

Inge at the Festival (following *Picnic* in 2001), didn't achieve that level, but it ran for twice as long as the farce (ninety-one performances as against forty-six) and still managed a 73 percent box office. The success of Inge was important to Maxwell not just for box office reasons, but as evidence that Festival audiences had a taste for "hot" modern American plays. Not everything about *Bus Stop* was hot – the setting is a small-town Kansas diner where a group of bus travellers are stranded overnight by a snow storm. But the relationships in the play run hot, as the confined and restricted space (convincingly designed by Sue LePage) forces people into emotional as well as physical confrontations. For those who knew the 1956 film version of *Bus Stop* the powerful image of Marilyn Monroe's portrait of the kidnapped young woman, Cherie, would not have been easily overcome, but the success with which Nicole Underhay took hold of Cherie's innocence, vulnerability, and toughness made the character her own. At the same time the strong ensemble – Norman Browning, Guy Bannerman, Diana Donnelly, Mary Haney, Peter Krantz, Martin Happer, Michael Ball – successfully captured the aspirations and disappointments of their own disparate characters, Maxwell bringing out not just their individual identities but the coalescence of this group into a dramatic whole.

THE CONSTANT WIFE, 2005   Also successful – perhaps, indeed, exceeding expectations – in the Royal George was Somerset Maugham's *The Constant Wife*, directed by Neil Munro, and designed by William Schmuck. If not quite as shocking in its time as Ibsen's *A Doll's House*, Maugham's 1926 play about a woman disillusioned by marriage still engaged the large audiences who came to see it. Their response to the line in which a modern wife is defined as "a prostitute who doesn't deliver the goods" was an audible gasp – the line being given added punch

by the matter-of-fact way in which it was delivered by Laurie Paton as Constance, a constant wife until she recognizes the truth about her marriage to an adulterous husband. By the end of the play, Constance – even more emphatically than Ibsen's Nora – has established her independence by choosing both a lover and a profession (interior design), leaving behind those wives in her coterie whom she now sees as "chattels who sold themselves for board, lodging, and protection." Jamie Portman was one of the few critics who admired the production. He had "a marvellous evening" in contrast to the *Globe and Mail*'s Kamal Al-Solaylee, for example, who was "underwhelmed." But not for the first time the critics were at odds with the public: *The Constant Wife* averaged 93 percent houses in a long run (ninety-nine performances).

JOURNEY'S END, 2005 There was virtually no bad news, then, from the Royal George in 2005, and only one piece of it from the Court House Theatre. *Journey's End*, R.C. Sherriff's 1928 play about three days in the British trenches just before the last big German offensive of the First World War in 1918, received good notices, but didn't sell well. Under Christopher Newton's direction, and with the "claustrophobic brilliance" of Cameron Porteous's design, *Journey's End*, for Jamie Portman, amounted to "a distinguished revival of a distinguished play, and a great moment in our Canadian theatrical summer." But the great moment seemed to remain a minority taste, attracting only 47 percent houses for the seventy-four performance run.

***THE AUTUMN GARDEN*, 2005**   The other two Court House plays – *The Autumn Garden* and *Belle Moral* – did better at the box office, and they both spoke to Maxwell's new directions. Lillian Hellman's *The Autumn Garden*, like William Inge's *Picnic*, is structured to bring together a group of people in a confined space – a guest house in a small Louisiana resort in the fall of 1949 – creating the circumstances and the dynamics that bring hidden ambitions and frustrations to the surface. Often characterized as Hellman's Chekhovian play, the action is emotional, not physical, and Martha Henry – back at the Festival after directing *The Royal Family* in 2003 – again teamed up with designer William Schmuck to provide a powerful evening of theatre. *The Autumn Garden* had failed on its 1951 Broadway premiere, but Kamal Al-Solaylee argued that this Shaw Festival production demonstrated why revivals are important, providing an opportunity for re-evaluations. In this case, Henry and Schmuck, together with "a cast to die for" (according to more than one critic) left no doubt about the quality of the play, one "rich in dramatizing inner lives." Peter Hutt as Nicholas Denery, a painter who visits home with a rich wife in tow (Laurie Paton) after years away in Europe, and Sharry Flett as Constance Tuckerman, who had had a youthful romance with Denery, shone under Henry's direction. Jim Mezon, Wendy Thatcher, David Schurmann, Goldie Semple, and Mike Shara were among other ensemble members who gave the production its considerable depth.

CLOCKWISE FROM LEFT: FIONA BYRNE,
DONNA BELLEVILLE, AND JESSICA
LOWRY; JEFF MEADOWS AND DONNA
BELLEVILLE; BERNARD BEHRENS IN
BELLE MORAL: A NATURAL HISTORY
BY ANN-MARIE MACDONALD, 2005.
DIRECTED BY ALISA PALMER, DESIGN-
ED BY JUDITH BOWDEN, LIGHTING
DESIGNED BY KEVIN LAMOTTE.
ORIGINAL MUSIC COMPOSED BY
PAUL SPORTELLI. PHOTOS BY ANDREE
LANTHIER.

BELLE MORAL, 2005   As with *Gypsy* at the Festival Theatre, Maxwell had a lot of strategic investment in Ann-Marie MacDonald's *Belle Moral*, the third of the Court House plays. In its original form, with the title of *The Arab's Mouth*, *Belle Moral* had been produced at Toronto's
Factory Theatre (in 1990), while Maxwell was artistic director there. It was Maxwell's idea
to invite MacDonald to consider reworking it for the Shaw Festival. The resulting changes
amounted, in effect, to a brand-new work. *Belle Moral* was thus the first play that Maxwell
commissioned for the Festival, a strategy that became increasingly important in her planning
of subsequent seasons. *Belle Moral* also had special significance as the only Canadian play in
the 2005 season.

A celebrated novelist, actor, and broadcaster as well as playwright, MacDonald welcomed
the chance to work with the Festival. She knew it well through her partner, Alisa Palmer, who
had directed plays at the Festival in 2003 (*Diana of Dobson's*) and 2004 (*Pal Joey*), and was
also selected by Maxwell to direct *Belle Moral*. This was, however, MacDonald's first direct
Festival involvement.

Belle Moral: A Natural History takes its main title from the name of the house where the
action (set near Edinburgh, at the end of the nineteenth century) takes place, and its subtitle
from the play's subject matter – or some of it. There is certainly a major Darwinian element in
the play surrounding the mysterious provenance of a deformed canine ear, but the play's themes
and moods range much more widely than that: Freudianism, psychiatry, eugenics, nihilism,
emerging feminism, the Gothic, and much more. It's audacious writing, the eclecticism of subject matter reflecting MacDonald's view of connectivity between apparently disparate disci-
plines and philosophies. Alisa Palmer successfully held all this together, while not stifling the
intellectual energy in the production. The energy came not just from the ideas in the play, but
from the power of the acting, particularly Fiona Byrne's portrayal of the determined and independent young scientist Pearl, but also from Jeff Meadows as Pearl's eccentric and unpredictable

brother. Jamie Portman thought *Belle Moral* "overflows to a dangerous degree" with actions and ideas, but a better image of the play's excitement was conjured by the *Toronto Star*'s Robert Crew when *Belle Moral* was revived in 2008. It's a play, Crew said, "that showers you with ideas like a severed hydro line" – not, in fact, unlike a Shaw play.

And the play seemed to resonate with audiences. It was the bestselling of the Court House plays in 2005, achieving a 79 percent box office in a forty-six performance run.

2005 SEASON RESULTS When all the numbers were put together for 2005 they looked much better than they had for the two preceding seasons. Attendance rose 6 percent over 2004, and the target of 295,000 ticket sales was met, with a bit to spare. It wasn't much relative to the overall deficit, but it was with a palpable sense of relief that the Festival announced a season surplus of $52,000, first in a press release on November 30, 2005, and then, more formally, at the annual meeting on January 27, 2006. At that meeting board chair Elaine Triggs described the 2005 season as one in which "artistic bravura met careful financial planning." Jackie Maxwell – with some understandable satisfaction – said the welcome financial results were achieved "on our own artistic terms."

It was after the 2006 season, her fourth, which recorded a surplus of $714,000, that Maxwell said that she was "finally at the point where I know what makes this place tick." There are striking resemblances between the third seasons of both Christopher Newton and Jackie Maxwell (1982 and 2005). In different circumstances, and for different reasons, Newton and Maxwell both had difficult experiences in their first two seasons. They had strong agendas for change, and they both had to make compromises to make change stick. Newton said at the end of his third season that he was finally "getting it the way I wanted it to be." Maxwell waited for her fourth season before making a similar statement. But it was really that third season – 2005 – that gave Maxwell the foundation for moving ahead with the divergences that she had spoken of when first appointed. The evolution of those divergences was perhaps not as rapid as she might have wished – she likened making changes at a place like the Shaw Festival to altering the course of a monster ocean liner – but by the end of her third season she had sufficient artistic and financial confidence to keep her agenda intact.

MAXWELL AND SHAW

There was much emphasis on, and discussion of, Maxwell's new directions at the Shaw Festival, but it remained the *Shaw* Festival, and Shaw's plays remained at the core of the playbills and the spirit of the Festival. "He's a subversive, crotchety old provocateur. I take my lead from that," she said. Unlike Christopher Newton, Jackie Maxwell wasn't handicapped by an antipathy towards Shaw when she took over the Festival. She had seen, and enjoyed, Shaw at the Festival since she first came to Canada in 1978, though she didn't direct a Shaw play until 2002, the season she spent as artistic director designate in Newton's final season.

CANDIDA, 2002 The play was *Candida*, the Festival's fifth production. One of Shaw's most intimate of plays – just six characters and one set, the drawing room-cum-office of the Reverend James Morell – it was surprising to see it on the large stage of the Festival Theatre. Sue LePage's set, however, successfully focused the action on the drawing room, against a panorama of the surrounding London suburbs. As for Maxwell's direction, audiences and critics were on the lookout for new approaches to Shaw, any signs that might point towards, as it were, a Maxwellian rather than Newtonian approach to GBS.

On one level it was clear that Maxwell wanted to have fun with Shaw, and that she wanted her audiences to *enjoy* Shaw as well as appreciate him. This was most apparent in the performance of Mike Shara as the young poet Marchbanks. As John Coulbourn noted in the *Toronto Sun*, this was not a Marchbanks "rooted in an effete aristocracy" as his social background might signify, but rather "an oddly endearing man-child, almost devoid of social graces." Jamie Portman revelled in Shara's portrayal of "an awkward, un-coordinated beanpole of a romantic, crashing about the stage in a state of continuing emotional overdrive, both ludicrous and poignant in his outrageousness, and accurately communicating both the arrogance and vulnerability of youth." Shara's athleticism was evident for all to see as he hurled himself over

KELLI FOX AND BLAIR WILLIAMS IN *CANDIDA* BY BERNARD SHAW, 2002.
DIRECTED BY JACKIE MAXWELL, SET DESIGNED BY SUE LEPAGE, COSTUMES
DESIGNED BY CHRISTINA PODDUBIUK, LIGHTING DESIGNED BY KEVIN
LAMOTTE, MUSIC COMPOSED BY PAUL SPORTELLI. PHOTO BY DAVID COOPER.

JIM MEZON AND LORNE KENNEDY;
JIM MEZON AND PATRICIA HAMILTON
IN *PYGMALION* BY BERNARD SHAW,
2004. DIRECTED BY JACKIE MAXWELL,
DESIGNED BY SUE LEPAGE, LIGHT-
ING DESIGNED BY KEVIN LAMOTTE,
ORIGINAL MUSIC AND SOUND
DESIGN BY MARC DESORMEAUX.

OPPOSITE: TARA ROSLING IN *PYGMAL-
ION*, 2004. PHOTOS BY DAVID COOPER.

sofas "in ecstasies of adoration or self-abasement" – "absurd in one way," said Robert Cushman in the *National Post*, but "neither embarrassing nor unbelievable."

It was fun, then, with a meaning, an inventive way of revealing the vulnerability of one of the two men vying for Candida's love. This meshed with another sign of Maxwell's approach to Shaw – what was seen by some as a feminist perspective. It wasn't just Shara's Marchbanks who was vulnerable, but also his rival, Morell, played by Blair Williams. Williams captured his character's vulnerability in very different ways; no rolling over sofas for *him*, but still deep cracks shown in his intellectual and emotional confidence in his beliefs and in his marriage. Set against the vulnerability of these men was the serene and resourceful Candida, played by Kelli Fox, always in control, always one step ahead of the men in her life. The contrast between Candida and the men is embedded in the play, but Maxwell's production seemed to heighten that contrast to an extent that is not always evident in productions of *Candida*. Whether that pointed towards further emphasis by Maxwell on the feminist Shaw remained to be seen.

PYGMALION, 2004   There was more grist for this particular mill in Maxwell's decision to direct *Pygmalion* as her second Shaw play, which she did in 2004, her second season as artistic director. Maxwell chose to use Shaw's full text of the play – for the first time in Festival productions of *Pygmalion* – which includes scenes Shaw wrote for the 1938 film version of the play. These additional scenes – challengingly for designer Sue LePage – included, for example, a splendid ballroom setting, but also scenes that highlight Eliza as a victim rather than a glamorous debutante. In particular, the full text shows Eliza in her decrepit slum garret, and, later, against her wishes, being aggressively scrubbed clean by Higgins's housekeeper, Mrs Pearce.

Regardless of which text is used, any production of *Pygmalion* has to come to terms with the relationship between Higgins and Eliza. Tara Rosling, who played Eliza (her first Shaw play), saw Higgins "as a bit of a father figure and definitely a sexual attraction." "That's why,"

Rosling said, "she's so confused and complicated inside. She doesn't know exactly what her feelings are or what to expect from him." But Rosling knew from the early previews where audience sympathies lay in the Eliza-Higgins narrative. She heard "audible gasps" at some of Higgins's verbal abuse of Eliza, and Maxwell's choice of Jim Mezon as Higgins accentuated the abusive nature of his treatment of her. Head shaven, and loud, Mezon looked and sounded every inch the male chauvinist. As Robert Cushman neatly expressed it, this characterization "put the pig in *Pygmalion*." Mezon's Higgins, said Cushman, showed "the passion of a pedant, and the empathy of an elephant." Yes, inevitably the young and powerless Eliza would, as Rosling said, be confused in an altogether unfamiliar environment, but Maxwell wanted there to be no doubt by the end of the play that the *My Fair Lady* romantic ending was untenable. Not only did Maxwell want to honour Shaw's own views that Higgins and the increasingly independent Eliza *won't* marry, but she also insisted (in a *Globe and Mail* interview) that they "*shouldn't* be together at the end." (Bizarrely, however, Cushman read the ending as an assertion that Eliza *will* marry Higgins, and not, as Higgins himself announces, Freddy, "as surely as if they were characters in a musical.")

ARMS AND THE MAN, 2006 Maxwell took another season off (2005) from directing Shaw, but returned to him in 2006 with *Arms and the Man*. In the 1894 premiere of *Arms and the Man* Shaw was upset that the comic elements of the production obscured the serious concerns expressed in the play about the folly of romantic idealism about war. There was plenty of laughter as well in Maxwell's production, spurred by another romp from Mike Shara – this time as the very romantic idealist Shaw was criticizing, Major Sergius Saranoff, an officer in the Bulgarian army. But in the judgment of Robert Cushman and most other critics, the comic business, and not just from Shara, ended up "selling the play short." And it sold short literally as well, filling only half the seats in the Festival Theatre in a 119-performance run.

SAINT JOAN, 2007 For the following season Maxwell gave herself one of the biggest challenges as well as one of the biggest prizes available to a Shaw director – *Saint Joan*. *Saint Joan* hadn't been done at the Festival for fourteen years, when, in 1993, Neil Munro had joined forces with Cameron Porteous in a memorable production (discussed above, page 124). The Joan on that occasion had been Mary Haney. The Joan in 2007 was Tara Rosling, in only her second Shaw role. Maxwell's designer was again Sue LePage, and Kevin Lamotte did the lighting design (as he had for Maxwell's *Candida* and *Pygmalion*).

As with Munro's 1993 production, world events provided a depressing context for *Saint Joan*. In 1993 it was Bosnia, in 2007 Iraq and Afghanistan. Rosling commented just before the play opened on May 9 on how "completely appropriate" the themes of the play are for now, and, indeed, she said "for all times." As Maxwell saw them, those themes had primarily to do with the beginnings of nationalism in the fifteenth century and how nationalism was the root of the military and political traumas that we still live with. Maxwell wanted Shaw Festival audiences to be jolted, she said, "into a new awareness of the play's underlying and timeless concerns about the linkages between religion, nationalism, and war."

Like her predecessors as directors of *Saint Joan* at the Festival (Christopher Newton and Neil Munro), Maxwell also had to deal with the structure of the play. Newton (famously) had tried to restructure the play by removing the Epilogue, redundant in his view, but had been forced to submit to legal requirements to keep it (see above, page 77). Munro had reluctantly acquiesced to the same legal requirements. By the time Maxwell directed the play, however, Shaw was out of copyright in Canada, and she was free to do as she liked with the Epilogue (or anything else in the play). She partly shared Newton's and Munro's views about the Epilogue, but rather than cutting it altogether she shifted some of it to the beginning to serve as a Prologue. "Why couldn't I find a way to take all of Shaw's provocative thoughts, and use them as a way *into* the play, instead of something we listened to when it was all over," she asked herself. Thus, against a backdrop of the battlefields of the First World War, with Joan among the soldiers, audiences learned of Joan's ultimate sainthood and heard the apologia of her tormentors and erstwhile supporters, reminding the audience that Joan is now being presented and understood from a modern viewpoint. Joan's famous – and crucial – concluding lines of the Epilogue, however, were kept for the end of the play: "Oh God that madest this beautiful earth, when will it be ready to receive Thy Saints? How long, O Lord, how long?"

Tara Rosling's performance as Joan was judged by New York critic John Simon to match the finest he had ever seen, Siobhan McKenna's in Dublin in 1954. Rosling's slight physical stature made her, for some, an unlikely soldier, but the intensity of her spirituality, determination, bravery, and her essential innocence convinced most audiences and critics that they were seeing something very special. For Gary Smith in the *Hamilton Spectator* Rosling's performance was "mesmerizing"; for Richard Ouzounian in the *Toronto Star* it was "a stirring performance" whose emotional intensity "frequently brings tears to your eyes and shivers down your back"; and for Paula Citron in the *Globe and Mail* Rosling was "the perfect Saint Joan" who "burns with her mission and is impatient with the slowness of others."

Ensemble support was at its usual strength for a Shaw Festival production. One of the few scenes that doesn't feature Joan stood out as particularly compelling. Scene IV is a long debate between England's Warwick (Blair Williams) and France's Cauchon (Ben Carlson), with interventions from the bigoted English chaplain John de Stogumber (Peter Krantz) about the religious and political significance of Joan's mission to throw the English out of France. In less capable hands, the dense dialogue can be tedious; here, through deep understanding of the importance of the ideas they were debating and their consummate ability with Shavian prose, Williams, Carlson, and Krantz made it riveting.

Several members of the ensemble also skillfully handled double casting, an unusual situation at the Shaw Festival. Ric Reid, for example, played both Robert de Baudricourt, the first person in authority to take Joan seriously, and the Inquisitor at her trial. Such duality, thought Paula Citron, "reminds the audience mightily of the treacherous shifting sands of life." Perhaps, but in reality the double casting had more to do with keeping the company small enough to make a post-season tour to Chicago affordable.

Sue LePage's set had to be designed and built to accommodate a touring production. This did not, however, undermine her vibrant set design, even with the complications involved in converting the thrust stage of the Chicago host theatre (the 500-seat Courtyard Theater at the Chicago Shakespeare Theater) into a proscenium space for *Saint Joan*. A further complication was the different setting for each of the six scenes in the play, ranging from the simplicity of the banks of the river Loire outside Orléans to the magnificence of Rheims Cathedral. With the help of Kevin Lamotte's exquisite lighting, LePage achieved one of the most accomplished of her many designs for the Festival. Paul Sportelli, who wrote an original score for the production, didn't have to worry about touring (the music was recorded), but his contribution added to the richness of what Jamie Portman described as this "splendid *Saint Joan* for our time." Chicago critics were impressed, too, with praise from Barbara Vitello in the *Daily Herald* for the Festival's "triumphant Chicago debut" for Maxwell's "inspired staging," the "superb" ensemble, and Tara Rosling's "marvelous" performance. "I'm telling you," said Chris Jones in the *Tribune*, this production "is not to be missed."

MRS WARREN'S PROFESSION, 2008 As Festival audiences saw more of Jackie Maxwell's Shaw it became evident that Shaw's women were a major interest for her – Candida, Eliza, Joan. It is perhaps no coincidence that the least successful of her Shaw productions has been *Arms and the Man*, the only Shaw she has done that doesn't feature a strong leading woman. It was not surprising, then, that Maxwell chose *Mrs Warren's Profession* for her next and – as of 2011 – last Shaw play. With two strong female roles and a strong social context, *Mrs Warren's Profession* was ideal Shavian territory for Maxwell.

The Festival's fourth production of Shaw's early "unpleasant" play about prostitution in Victorian England and the economic necessities that force women into the profession, the 2008 version featured Mary Haney as Mrs Warren and Moya O'Connell as her daughter Vivie. The mother-daughter conflict is central to the play: Mrs Warren determined to continue to work (now in a managerial position) in prostitution, Vivie determined to disassociate herself from the business that, initially unbeknownst to her, has funded her Cambridge education. If disassociation from the business also involves disassociation from her mother, so be it. There are deeply emotional issues involved here, though, and it is surprising and disappointing that even veteran critics such as John Coulbourn could describe *Mrs Warren's Profession* as "a sermon masquerading as a play, with characters created simply to portray the playwright's point of view." That was far from the situation that Maxwell achieved with Mary Haney and Moya O'Connell in a production that Robert Cushman judged "her best at the Shaw Festival so far."

NICOLE UNDERHAY WITH BLAIR WILLIAMS; WILLIAM VICKERS IN *TOO TRUE TO BE GOOD* BY BERNARD SHAW, 2006. DIRECTED BY JIM MEZON, DESIGNED BY KELLY WOLF, LIGHTING DESIGNED BY ALAN BRODIE.

OPPOSITE: BLAIR WILLIAMS AND KELLI FOX IN *TOO TRUE TO BE GOOD*, 2006. PHOTOS BY ANDREE LANTHIER.

Maxwell drew from Haney, "carrot-topped and powdered" in Sue LePage's design, "the eccentric fire of one of Toulouse-Lautrec's ferocious madams," said Gary Smith in the *Hamilton Spectator*. "She storms the stage like a cat in heat, filled with feral energy, wicked to watch," Smith added. Moya O'Connell's Vivie, much cooler, more restrained, infuriatingly logical, was her mother's match. Cushman thought it "electrifying" in the way the two characters "advance, bond, and then retreat."

Like the final moments in *Pygmalion*, the ending of *Mrs Warren's Profession* is conclusive as far as Shaw was concerned – Vivie unequivocally rejects her mother. Mrs Warren's departure from her daughter's London office marks the end of their relationship. Vivie, Shaw says, gets on her with her work "with joyous content," now free of any emotional entanglements with her mother or, for that matter, with the men who have tried to enter her life. Tantalizing, though, there were hints in O'Connell's final moments alone on stage after Haney's final exit that in rejecting her mother Vivie has lost something truly valuable in her life – not dissimilar from the final moments of Christopher Newton's *Pygmalion* in 1992 when his Higgins (Andrew Gillies) hinted at loss as Eliza leaves to marry Freddy.

There are men in *Mrs Warren's Profession* – four of them (played in 2008 by Ric Reid, Benedict Campbell, Andrew Bunker, and David Jansen) – and they are important to the play. Maxwell's main focus, however, was on the exploration of a profoundly moving human story of a troubled mother-daughter relationship, even at the expense of the economic-political dimension of the play.

OTHER SHAW UNDER MAXWELL

It is sometimes assumed that the Shaw plays at the Shaw Festival more or less pick themselves each season. That is, each play comes around in rotation every few years or so. The assumption contains a modicum of truth, in that it is highly unlikely that, say, *Major Barbara*, would appear more than once every seven or eight years or so. But many other factors have to be taken into consideration: box office potential; the balance with the rest of the season; availability of the artistic director's preferred cast and director; and so on. The Shaw plays that Jackie Maxwell and her predecessors have chosen for the Festival reflect factors such as these.

NEIL MUNRO, JIM MEZON, TADEUSZ BRADECKI, CHRISTOPHER NEWTON   A major difficulty faced by Christopher Newton when he came to the Shaw Festival was the paucity of directors in Canada who had any experience of directing Shaw. Maxwell, on the other hand, had a considerable body of experience and talent readily available, including three of the foremost Shaw directors in the world: Neil Munro, Jim Mezon, and Newton himself. She could – and did – also call on Polish director Tadeusz Bradecki, another accomplished and experienced director of Shaw. It was also part of Maxwell's evolutionary strategy when she took over the Festival to bring in new directors, which she has regularly and productively done for Shaw.

NEIL MUNRO   Maxwell chose Neil Munro to direct *Misalliance*, the opening show of her first (2003) season, and in the following season he directed *Man and Superman* (both productions are discussed above, page 156). But for his untimely death in 2009, Munro would surely have directed more Shaw.

JIM MEZON   Jim Mezon, whose several Shaw productions under Christopher Newton are discussed above (page 122) has been used sparingly by Maxwell as a Shaw director, but his 2006 production of *Too True to be Good* was a hit at the Court House Theatre (91 percent box office). It featured, said Kamal Al-Solaylee in the *Globe and Mail*, "half a dozen drop-dead ferocious performances" (not surprisingly in a cast that consisted of William Vickers, Nicole Underhay, Mary Haney, David Jansen, Kelli Fox, Blair Williams, Benedict Campbell, Andrew Bunker, Graeme Somerville, and Norman Browning). Robert Cushman's characterization of the production of this wordy and complex 1932 "political extravaganza" (Shaw's subtitle) as "a cast-iron example of what this institution [the Shaw Festival] is for" bore an uncanny resemblance to Herbert Whittaker's assessment of the Festival premiere of *Too True* in 1974 as "coming close to being a model for what the Shaw Festival should be trying to accomplish" (see above, page 37).

OPPOSITE: EVAN BULIUNG WITH
CRAIG PIKE, RICHARD STEWART, AND
ALI MOMEN IN *THE DEVIL'S DISCIPLE*
BY BERNARD SHAW, 2009. DIRECTED
BY TADEUSZ BRADECKI, DESIGNED BY
PETER HARTWELL, LIGHTING DESIGN-
ED BY KEVIN LAMOTTE. PHOTO BY
DAVID COOPER.

THIS PAGE: PATRICK MCMANUS,
RIC REID, GUY BANNERMAN, THOM
MARRIOTT, BENEDICT CAMPBELL, AND
GRAEME SOMERVILLE IN *JOHN BULL'S
OTHER ISLAND* BY BERNARD SHAW,
2010. DIRECTED BY CHRISTOPHER
NEWTON, DESIGNED BY WILLIAM
SCHMUCK, LIGHTING DESIGNED BY
LOUISE GUINAND. PHOTO BY DAVID
COOPER.

TADEUSZ BRADECKI   Maxwell has twice invited Tadeusz Bradecki to direct Shaw – for *Candida* in 2011 (see below, page 290) and *The Devil's Disciple* in 2009, the Festival's fourth production of Shaw's take on the American Revolution. As he explained in a note in the house program, Bradecki was intrigued by the historical events depicted by Shaw in *The Devil's Disciple* and the history of Niagara-on-the-Lake, which might never have existed, he argued, if the War of Independence hadn't prompted the migration of thousands of Empire loyalist north to what was then Upper Canada. Bradecki incorporated parts of Shaw's preface into his production to provide historical context, and also added new dialogue of his own to make the Niagara-on-the-Lake connection. The show itself was another Festival ensemble triumph, led by Evan Buliung as the charismatic rebel Dick Dudgeon and Jim Mezon as the superbly droll British General Burgoyne.

CHRISTOPHER NEWTON   Christopher Newton has directed at the Shaw Festival in all but two seasons (2003, 2006) since his retirement. Two of his productions have been Shaw plays: *John Bull's Other Island* in 2010 (the Festival's fourth production), and *Heartbreak House* in 2011 (the Festival's sixth production).

Previous Festival productions of *John Bull's Other Island* (1964, 1985, 1998) were against a backdrop – however remote from Niagara-on-the-Lake – of political turbulence in Ireland. By 2010 the turbulence had, happily, dissipated, but other issues, ones directly related to the play, had emerged. The plans of cocksure English businessman Tom Broadbent (Benedict Campbell) to invest in resort and golf course developments in pristine Irish landscapes beg questions about the impact of economic development on environmental quality and cultural values, as well as the willingness of affected communities to embrace – or not – such development. Add a range of characters and situations that create comic mayhem, a love story that goes awry, dialogue (sensibly and sensitively cut by Newton) that brims with wit and ideas, and an ensemble, director, and designer (William Schmuck) that can give shape to Shaw's Irish mosaic, and you have the

OPPOSITE: BEN CARLSON AND DEBORAH HAY IN *THE PHILANDERER* BY BERNARD SHAW, 2007. DIRECTED BY ALISA PALMER, DESIGNED BY JUDITH BOWDEN, LIGHTING DESIGNED BY LOUISE GUINAND. PHOTO BY EMILY COOPER.

THIS PAGE: PETER MILLARD, FIONA BYRNE, KRISTA COLOSIMO, PETER KRANTZ, DAVID SCHURMANN, NICOLA CORREIA-DAMUDE, AND MARTIN HAPPER; NICOLA CORREIA-DAMUDE IN *GETTING MARRIED* BY BERNARD SHAW, 2008. DIRECTED BY JOSEPH ZIEGLER, DESIGNED BY SUE LEPAGE, LIGHTING DESIGNED BY LOUISE GUINAND. PHOTOS BY DAVID COOPER.

makings of a successful production – which is what critical and audience reaction judged this *John Bull* to be. "If anyone ever claims," wrote Lawrence Switzky in *Curtain Up*, "that Shaw couldn't write with his heart and his brain, they need only be referred here."

ALISA PALMER, JOSEPH ZIEGLER, EDA HOLMES, AND MORRIS PANYCH   The new directors brought in by Maxwell to direct Shaw came nowhere near matching the collective experience of Munro, Mezon, Bradecki, and Newton with GBS. But they quickly fulfilled Maxwell's hopes that they would bring energy and insight to Shaw's plays as well as being the foundation for a new generation of Shavian directors.

ALISA PALMER   Alisa Palmer had directed three plays at the Festival (*Diana of Dobson's*, 2003; *Pal Joey*, 2004; and *Belle Moral*, 2005) before Maxwell offered her a Shaw. It was *The Philanderer*, the Festival's fifth production of Shaw's early (written in 1893) comedy of the sexes, in which his own turbulent relationships with women is reflected in the character he called Leonard Charteris. This production of *The Philanderer* marked the first time that a full-length Shaw play had been performed in the Royal George. As was the case with Jim Mezon's production in 1995 (see above, page 122), Palmer included Shaw's original, but discarded, third act of the play in a limited number of performances (fifteen). But whether in the shorter or longer version of the play, it was refreshing to see a Shaw play that so unambiguously reminded critics and audiences – as Christopher Newton had been saying for years – that Shaw was keenly interested in sex. We are only twenty minutes into the play, having already witnessed Charteris's (Ben Carlson) frantic attempts to disentangle himself (literally) from a double-dealing fiasco, before it's clear, said Jamie Portman, that "those critics, led by the late Kenneth Tynan, who insisted that Shaw was sexless had rocks in their head." Palmer kept the shenanigans going at full throttle as sexual freedom clashed with sexual hypocrisy, and, reported Gary Smith in the *Hamilton Spectator*, "had the theatre rocking with laughter." Smith didn't entirely approve of this, worrying that Palmer's "rambunctious production" came close to resembling "a frantic comedy by Feydeau."

Concerns about undervaluing the seriousness in Shaw were not new at the Festival (Paxton Whitehead had faced it in the 1970s), but they became prominent again with the younger directors. Morris Panych, for example, was accused of not taking Shaw seriously enough in some of his productions of Shaw (e.g., *The Doctor's Dilemma*, below, page 254). One of the qualities, however, of Shaw Festival ensembles has been their ability to integrate the comic with the serious. In Palmer's *Philanderer*, for example, the interaction between the fathers (Norman Browning and Peter Hutt) of the women in Charteris's life was as funny as anything ever seen on the Royal George stage, with Browning "growling through his whiskers" and Peter Hutt "sputtering with apoplectic fury." But as Jamie Portman recognized, what the audience got here was not hilarity for its own sake, but "an hilarious contribution to the image of the late Victorian father." Similarly, the rest of the ensemble – Ben Carlson, Deborah Hay, Nicole Underhay, Peter Krantz, Nicolá Correia-Damude, and Michael Strathmore – knew full well, as did Alisa Palmer, that they were in a Shaw comedy, not a Feydeau farce, and that language, sentiment, and ideas were where their focus should be – and was.

JOSEPH ZIEGLER   Joseph Ziegler – no stranger to the Shaw Festival, having first acted in the company in Christopher Newton's first season in 1980 – was entrusted with two Shaws in Maxwell's difficult early years. His *Widowers' Houses* in 2003 was a great success critically and at the box office (see above, page 214). His *Major Barbara* in 2005 was a critical success, but disappointed at the box office (see above, page 231). He then took on, in 2008, one of Shaw's wordiest "discussion plays," *Getting Married*, last seen at the Festival in 1999 in a strong production directed by Jim Mezon (see above, page 124). The critics were again dubious about the merits of a play that, for example, Canadian Press reviewer John Law described as "a long-winded rant" about marriage and divorce, "just a constant stream of arguments tripping over each other." But Law, like others, was full of praise for Ziegler's production, which took full advantage of another great ensemble to maintain a pace and a clarity that allowed Shaw's always witty and frequently startling perceptions about marriage to hold the audience's attention. And while Ziegler recognized the need for laughs (there were plenty of them), he didn't shortchange what he described in the house program as the play's "deep understanding of the need for love, companionship and children." With a cast of thirteen on a small stage (the Royal George), Ziegler and designers Sue LePage (set and costumes) and Louise Guinand (lighting) also had their work cut out to manage the traffic; happily, on LePage's two-tiered stage order triumphed over chaos.

EDA HOLMES   It was a mark of Jackie Maxwell's great confidence in Eda Holmes that she gave her *In Good King Charles's Golden Days* as her first Shaw play. By 2009 Holmes had more than proved her worth to the Festival with productions of *Blood Relations* in 2003, *Floyd Collins* in 2004, *Love Among the Russians* in 2006, *Tristan* in 2007, and *Little Foxes* in 2009 (the year in which she was also appointed associate director of the Festival). But for a first Shaw play, *In Good King Charles's Golden Days* was something of a challenge. Only twice done at the Festival (1981 and 1997), and rarely anywhere else, it is, like *Getting Married*, a discussion play. Whereas the discussion in *Getting Married* has a recognizable and limited focus, however, the discussions (plural) in *In Good King Charles's Golden Days* are – to put it mildly – eclectic, roaming over a range of topics, some germane to the play's Restoration period setting, some not. Politics, science, economics, art, literature, geography, mathematics, and, yes, marriage, are all there as people famous (including King Charles II) and not-so-famous gather, mostly uninvited, at the home of Isaac Newton.

Although Holmes's production failed to convince everyone of the vitality of the play, there was sufficient energy and conviction in the performances of, for example, Benedict Campbell as Charles, Graeme Somerville as Newton, and Ric Reid as George Fox to persuade Robert Cushman, for one, that he had seen the Festival's "best Shaw in a number of years." *In Good King Charles's Golden Days* is, to be sure, a play that demands good listeners and concentration, but Shaw Festival audiences have become very good at that, and Holmes, to her credit, trusted them. Nonetheless, there was clearly an issue around this production relating to audience accessibility to Shaw's more complex plays. The discussions among Maxwell, and her colleagues about how to resolve this in more creative ways than simply cutting the text heavily eventually resulted in the approach taken with Shaw's *On the Rocks*, produced in 2011 (see below, page 290).

CLAIRE JULLIEN; GRAEME SOMERVILLE; LISA CODRINGTON IN *IN GOOD KING CHARLES'S GOLDEN DAYS* BY BERNARD SHAW, 2009. DIRECTED BY EDA HOLMES, SET DESIGNED BY CAMELLIA KOO, COSTUMES DESIGNED BY MICHAEL GIANFRANCESCO, LIGHTING DESIGNED BY BONNIE BEECHER.

OPPOSITE: BENEDICT CAMPBELL IN *IN GOOD KING CHARLES'S GOLDEN DAYS*, 2009. PHOTOS BY DAVID COOPER.

MORRIS PANYCH   Unlike Joseph Ziegler, Morris Panych had not worked at the Shaw Festival under Newton, his first Festival assignment coming in 2004 when Maxwell invited him to direct George Walker's *Nothing Sacred*. This was followed in 2005 by his first Shaw, *You Never Can Tell* (see above, pages 222 and 231). Panych's *Doctor's Dilemma* was as inventive as his *You Never Can Tell*, again complemented by Ken MacDonald's stunning design, with huge x-rays, a Van Gogh-inspired painting of tuberculosis bacilli, and, in the artist Dubedat's studio, a giant suspended paintbrush. There were some who felt that the set overpowered the play – it "dwarfs the cast at almost every turn," John Coulbourn thought – but it is difficult to overpower actors such as Patrick Galligan, Michael Ball, Patrick McManus, Ric Reid, Jonathan Widdifield, and – especially – Thom Marriott, the doctors whose ethics and competencies are mocked so mercilessly by Shaw. Coulbourn also thought that Panych's audacious use of Rolling Stones music (he had used The Beatles in *You Never Can Tell*) telegraphed that he wasn't taking the play seriously. Panych's house program notes, however, in which he argued vigorously for "the primacy of the common good over individual profit" as the fundamental basis for medical policy and practice showed just how seriously he took the play's underlying issues.

It is no doubt an over-simplification to say that the "breezy, fast-paced style" that Robert Crew detected in Panych's *The Doctor's Dilemma* represented a new approach to Shaw by a group of young directors. And it is probably an even bigger stretch to suggest that the new directors took their cue from Maxwell's diverting approach to her first Shaw play, *Candida* in 2002. But there certainly was a marked absence of reverence (which is not the same as a lack of respect) in the approach of Panych and others, signifying a willingness to find the fun in Shaw as well as the seriousness. Maxwell took risks in giving them the opportunity to try their hand at Shaw. The risk paid off handsomely not just in the quality of individual productions but in ensuring that the Festival would have the new generation of directors that it needed to keep Shaw alive on stage.

MAXWELL OUTREACH

As explained above (page 213), Jackie Maxwell's first season as artistic director of the Shaw Festival was disrupted by a number of factors beyond her control, including SARS, the West Nile Virus, outbreak of war in Iraq, and widespread power failures – "everything but locusts," she told the *National Post* in November 2010. There was one other disruptive factor that was, paradoxically, welcome.

THE PRODUCTION CENTRE   Immediately after the close of the 2002 season work had begun on a large building project, the biggest since the 1972–73 construction of the Festival Theatre. The objective of the The Festival Theatre Project was to refurbish the Festival Theatre and to build a new Production Centre. Areas of the theatre to be renovated included the lobby, shop, and box office, and the Production Centre was to be built at the south end of the theatre. Periods of intense cold during the winter of 2002–3 caused construction delays in the refurbishment of the Festival Theatre, so that by the time the 2003 season opened work hadn't quite been completed. Audiences arrived to find doors missing from the entrance of the theatre, but Jackie Maxwell took to the stage to assure them that the doors would be in place by the time they left. And indeed they were.

The Production Centre (subsequently named the Donald and Elaine Triggs Production Centre) provided much-needed new rehearsal spaces (three), a green room (subsequently named the Christopher Newton Green Room), administrative offices, an Academy suite, a recording studio and music rehearsal rooms, and an audience reception lounge (subsequently named the Macdonald Heaslip Lounge).

Officially opened on June 20, 2004, the Production Centre was designed by Lett/Smith Architects, under the leadership of Peter Smith, who had been site architect for the original Festival Theatre construction. It was Smith's intention to preserve the integrity of Ron Thom's building, and his success in achieving this was recognized by his peers with an Award of Excellence in 2005 from the Ontario Association of Architects.

JONATHAN GOULD AND KRISTA COLOSIMO IN *THE DOCTOR'S DILEMMA* BY BERNARD SHAW, 2010. DIRECTED BY MORRIS PANYCH, SET DESIGNED BY KEN MACDONALD, COSTUMES DESIGNED BY CHARLOTTE DEAN; LIGHTING DESIGNED BY ALAN BRODIE.

OPPOSITE: PATRICK GALLIGAN AND MICHAEL BALL IN *THE DOCTOR'S DILEMMA*, 2010. PHOTOS BY EMILY COOPER.

FUNDRAISING   The Festival Theatre Project, which also included acquisition of a new properties shop in nearby Virgil (also the location of the scene construction shop, opened in 1989), cost $20.25 million. This funding came from a mix of private, corporate, and government sources, and that cost was just part of a larger $50 million capital and endowment "Campaign for the Shaw Festival." The increasing importance of fundraising to the financial and artistic health of the Festival is reflected in the big rise in the proportion of annual revenue derived from this source – around 10 percent at the beginning of the 1990s to over 20 percent in 2010. Thousands of Shaw Festival members contribute to fundraising efforts, but Festival fundraising events such as the annual boxing night (see above, page 147), support from corporate sponsors and foundations, and generous and ongoing support from board members, major donors, and the Governors International Advisory Council (formed in 2008) are crucial. There have also been several extraordinary gifts from which the Festival has benefited in a number of ways. The $1 million donation in 2005 from vintners Donald and Elaine Triggs assisted with costs of building the Production Centre, and 2009 was a bumper year: a $3.1 million bequest from philanthropist Mona Campbell helped retire the Festival's deficit; the Slaight Family gave $5 million to support the Academy (founded in 1985 while Allan Slaight was board chair); and Valerie Pascal Delacorte, wife of the late Gabriel Pascal, producer of several films of Shaw's plays, bequeathed income from movie rights to the plays and from the film of *My Fair Lady* to set up the Gabriel Pascal Memorial Fund to support Festival productions. Special government grants such as $2.5 million (provincial) towards the Production Centre, and marketing grants of, for example, $2.1 million (federal) and $800,000 (provincial) in 2009, and $2.6 million (federal) in 2010 have supplemented annual operating grants.

EDUCATION   The Slaight family grant to the Academy (henceforth known as The Slaight Family Academy) provided a major boost for the Festival's education objectives, sustaining and enriching training programs for new and returning members of the acting ensemble, and enabling the establishment of the Shaw Theatre School, a fall drama program for young people in areas such as voice, movement, stage combat, choreography, and scene study. Particularly important for the Festival was the opportunity provided by the Slaight family grant to establish the Mandate Intensive, an annual program in which the company's apprentice and young actors immerse themselves in the world of Shaw and his contemporaries. First held in February 2010, the Mandate Intensive consists of two weeks of text and scene study, lectures and discussions on the cultural history of the mandate period, and dialect, voice, and movement work. "The result," Maxwell said of the 2010 program, "was sixteen young actors ready to dive into the season with a strong sense of, and much more comfort in, the worlds they are about to enter."

Festival training activities also include the long-established Intern Directors Project (named since 2009 The Neil Munro Intern Directors Project in honour of the former Festival associate director) in association with Theatre Ontario, training opportunities for apprentice stage managers and design assistants, and a burgeoning Music Intern Program under the guidance of Paul Sportelli.

Other education programs continued to thrive as the Festival approached its fiftieth anniversary season. The annual seminars, established in 1965 (see above, page 144), maintained their momentum under the leadership of Academy co-director Denis Johnston, supported by Corresponding Scholars Dan Laurence, Ronald Bryden, Leonard Conolly, Dennis Kennedy, Ann Saddlemyer, Don Wilmeth, and (post-Johnston) Craig Walker. The seminars were complemented from 2004 by an annual Shaw Symposium, initiated by Johnston and Conolly, and co-sponsored by the Festival and the International Shaw Society. Johnston was also instrumental in giving the Festival's house programs greater educational substance, with background essays, production histories, and extensive historical illustrations (researched and selected by program designer Scott McKowen and Christina Poddubiuk). The first of the Festival's several book publications, Tony van Bridge's memoirs *Also in the Cast*, appeared in 1995 under Johnston's editorship. After Johnston left the Festival in 2005, literary manager Joanna Falck (appointed in 2007) and publications co-ordinator Jean German edited the house programs, maintaining the reputation of the programs as being among the best anywhere. (Buffalo critic Terry Doran praised them in 1997 as "models of information and insight," with period photographs and illustrations that "are a marvel of scholarly acuity.")

An important contributor to the house programs and seminars, as well as to the Festival generally, was Ronald Bryden, a distinguished literary editor, dramaturge, and critic in England until coming to Canada in 1976 to teach at the University of Toronto. In 1992 Christopher Newton invited Bryden to become literary adviser to the Festival, a post he held until Newton retired in 2002. Bryden then continued to serve the Festival as a Corresponding Scholar until his death in 2004. Some of Bryden's program essays were co-published by the Festival and Mosaic Press in 2002 as *Shaw and His Contemporaries: Theatre Essays*.

The Festival's commitment to education, particularly focusing on efforts to introduce young people to the Festival, was reflected not only in the Shaw Theatre School, but in other youth programs such as Shaw Summer Camps, and workshops for teachers. Key administrators of these and similar programs in the 2000s were Carolyn Mackenzie, Rod Christensen, and Suzanne Merriam. University connections were maintained with Brock, Guelph, and Queen's (a summer university credit course).

THE LOCAL COMMUNITY   During the 1990s and the early 2000s relationships with the local Niagara-on-the-Lake community remained free from the turbulence that marked some earlier decades, but the Festival was ever alert to potential problems. Care was taken, for example, to keep the community well informed through newsletters and press releases of the Festival Theatre renovations and the construction of the Production Centre in 2002–4. The Festival also continued to promote good community relationships by organizing events that contributed to Niagara area charities. These included, for example, the annual Village Fair and Fête (since discontinued) and the Town Previews that give local residents the opportunity to purchase discounted tickets for selected previews, the proceeds all going to charities. The community also benefits from Festival offers such as the Niagara Neighbours Program, which provides discounted tickets for selected Festival shows. Such measures, explains executive director Colleen Blake, are "a thank-you to our neighbours, in acknowledgement of their ongoing support for The Shaw."

Although area residents were by no means exclusive beneficiaries of prominent speakers who came to the Shaw Festival throughout the early 2000s, they had more frequent opportunities to attend them than visitors in town for just a few days. A 2002 series of lectures in honour of Christopher Newton's retirement as artistic director featured four speakers who shared many of Bernard Shaw's passions: social and environmental activist Maude Barlow, human rights advocate Stephen Lewis, writer and social critic John Ralston Saul, and Shaw biographer Michael Holroyd. Stephen Lewis returned in 2009 to speak on "Gender Equality: The Single Most Important Struggle on the Planet," and other speakers who came in 2007 and 2008 (in series funded by the Government of Ontario) included acclaimed novelist Salman Rushdie, American journalist Seymour Hersh, and Canadian playwright Tomson Highway.

Off-season use of the Festival Theatre includes a film series, which began in 2006, and, on one remarkable occasion, the theatre was the venue for a live four-hour broadcast on a 25-foot screen of the inauguration of President Barack Obama (January 20, 2009). The Festival press release announcing this event pointed out that almost 40 percent of Festival audiences are American, and that the Festival "has a strong history of producing American plays."

THE THEATRE COMMUNITY   Through a limited number of tours, Jackie Maxwell has kept the Shaw Festival well connected with other theatres in Canada and the United States. The tour of *Candida* to the National Arts Centre in Ottawa in 2002 maintained links with the NAC that began in 1969. And the Festival was back at the NAC in 2004 with *Rutherford and Son*. The *Candida* tour established a new link for the Festival with the Meadow Brook Theatre in Rochester, Michigan, where there were twenty-seven well-received performances following the NAC run. In the fall of 2007 there was a tour to several Canadian and U.S. locations of a reading of Shaw's *Village Wooing* by Jim Mezon and Catherine McGregor, followed in January 2008 by a major touring production of *Saint Joan* in another new location for the Festival, the high profile Chicago Shakespeare Theater (see above, page 245).

In the early years of her appointment Maxwell spoke of the importance of a Toronto winter season for the Shaw Festival, though like much else at the Festival the thinking around the idea changed as her programming evolved. Christopher Newton saw a Toronto presence as a vital means of giving the acting ensemble experience with new and contemporary plays, plays that,

he believed, would never get to the Festival itself. But as Maxwell broke new ground by bringing contemporary work to the Festival stages, so the need for the ensemble to go elsewhere for that kind of experience lessened. Maxwell's rationale for getting the company to Toronto had more to do thereafter with showcasing the quality of the Festival's productions in one of North America's most active theatre communities and making sure that Toronto theatregoers were aware of the changes that were taking place at the Festival. She had in mind plays such as *Floyd Collins* and *Belle Moral*. While the costs of co-productions with Toronto companies thwarted those possibilities, a co-production arrangement was nonetheless successfully negotiated with Toronto's Obsidian Theatre Company for the Festival's 2011 production of *Topdog/Underdog*; this agreement will take the production to Toronto after it closes in Niagara-on-the-Lake. Maxwell also continues to explore opportunities for tours to major regional theatres in the United States and – her "ultimate dream" – taking a Shaw play from the Festival to Shaw's hometown of Dublin and the theatre that both accepted and rejected Shaw, the Abbey.

Maxwell's prominence in the Toronto theatre community has enabled her to attract several playwrights and directors from Toronto to the Shaw Festival. That same prominence, however, has also meant that her decisions and policies as artistic director have been carefully scrutinized, sometimes with unforeseen consequences. The only serious controversy in which Maxwell and the Festival became embroiled during her first eight seasons as artistic director was initiated by a member of the Toronto theatre community, playwright and actor Andrew Moodie.

Globe and Mail critic Kelly Nestruck noted in his review of the Festival's 2008 production of Lillian Hellman's *The Little Foxes* that the only two actors of colour in the show were playing servants. That got him thinking "how overwhelmingly white the Festival's acting company is," and that "colour-blind casting has yet to reach Niagara-on-the-Lake." The preponderance of white actors at the Shaw Festival was not news to Maxwell, nor was it a new issue at the Festival. Christopher Newton had cast a black actor (Roy Lewis) in the Festival's 1987 production of Noel Coward's *Hay Fever*, and had received hostile letters from what Newton judged to be still a "very conservative" audience. And when Maxwell took over the Shaw Festival in 2003 she commented (in an interview with Kate Taylor) on the "almost uniformly white face of the Shaw Festival," expressing the hope that "the company will become more multiracial as more contemporary programming appears on the playbill." But progress wasn't fast enough for Moodie and others. In an open letter to Maxwell on August 5, 2008 (posted on Facebook) Moodie claimed that an (unnamed) employee of the Festival had told him that a play Moodie had submitted had been rejected because it contained "too many people of colour."

In his letter Moodie said he wasn't interested in "name calling," he just wanted to find a way "to tear down barriers of discrimination" that he believed existed at the Shaw Festival. He invited anyone who supported more diversity at the Festival to join his Facebook campaign called "Share the Stage."

Maxwell responded to a flurry of emails – some constructive, some abusive – generated by Moodie's letter by offering to meet him to discuss the issues he was raising. The meeting took place in Toronto on August 15, 2008. It was, Maxwell, thought, "a really civil and very heartfelt exchange of ideas and thoughts," but she was disappointed by Moodie's "editorializing" account of the meeting (posted on August 15). In her response to Moodie (posted on August 16), Maxwell explained that the ensemble was built not by hiring leads, or bringing in an actor for one particular part, but by building a company of actors deeply committed to the ensemble principle over the long term. There was, then, no quick fix to the diversity issue. It would take time. And discussions on Facebook and by email were proving counterproductive. There had been many constructive comments about the issue, but a great deal of personal invective directed towards Maxwell in what she later (in 2010) described as "one of the most truly upsetting times in my professional life." The conversation would continue, she said, but not in the public forum of Facebook. "There will be results from all of this, but not as a knee-jerk response to ultimatums." An immediate result was the casting of Lisa Codrington – one of the servants in *The Little Foxes* referred to by Nestruck – in Shaw's *In Good King Charles's Golden Days* and Coward's *Ways of the Heart* in 2009, but that was just one example of a steadily increasing emphasis by Maxwell on diversity in both the repertoire and the ensemble (see below, page 294).

One other controversy – happily, short-lived – that involved the wider professional theatre community occurred in 2010. As momentum was gathering for the opening of the 2010 season, negotiations for new contracts with members of IATSE (the International Alliance of Theatrical

Stage Employees) broke down. At issue was the Festival's right to contract out some services. On March 10, 2010, the Festival implemented a lockout of sixteen employees represented by IATSE, and the next day 150 audience services and production facilities staff went on strike. For the first time in Festival history picket lines were seen around the Festival's theatres. With the first preview of the season (*Harvey*) scheduled to open at the Royal George on April 1, marathon bargaining sessions soon got underway, and a tentative agreement, subsequently ratified by both sides, was reached on March 19.

ONGOING EVOLUTION

The adjustments made by Maxwell for her third season playbill (2005) helped create a small budget surplus for the season. There followed a financial roller coaster of seasons, ranging from a deficit of $927,000 in 2007 to a surplus of $1.7 million in 2009 (the year in which the accumulated deficit was retired), and back to a deficit of $1.3 million. External factors continued to hamper ticket sales: the global economic crisis that began in 2008, ongoing security issues that hindered travel between the United States and Canada, the growing strength of the Canadian dollar that made Canada a less attractive destination for Americans. Through it all, Maxwell remained focused on taking the Festival forward in ways she had identified at the time of her appointment as artistic director, even if, as she conceded in a May 2007 interview with Gary Smith, the pace of change might have to be more measured that she had once envisaged.

MANDATE FAMILIAR   Whatever changes she was implementing, however, Maxwell remained firmly committed to traditional features of the Festival's mandate. There remained, then, through the 2006–11 seasons, a selection of plays by Shaw, of course (see above, page 238), but also by several of his contemporaries: Coward (*Design for Living*, 2006, and *Tonight at 8:30*, 2009), Hankin (*The Cassilis Engagement*, 2007), Maugham (*The Circle*, 2007), Priestley (*An Inspector Calls*, 2008), Rattigan (*After the Dance*, 2008), Wilde (*An Ideal Husband*, 2010), and Barrie (*Half an Hour*, 2010; *The Admirable Crichton*, 2011).

The Circle (1967), *Tonight at 8:30* (1971), *The Admirable Crichton* (1976), *An Inspector Calls* (1989), and *An Ideal Husband* (1995, 1996) had all been previously produced at the Festival (though not the full cycle of plays in *Tonight at 8:30*).

While the general tenor, style, and manner of these plays would have been familiar to regular Festival theatregoers, Maxwell made sure – as Christopher Newton had always done – that there always remained in the mix elements of surprise. For example, the one St John Hankin play previously produced at the Festival, *The Return of the Prodigal* in 2001–2, had been a great success despite its unfamiliarity (see above, page 184). However, the next – *The Cassilis Engagement* – was even less familiar than that one. *The Return of the Prodigal* had been directed by Newton, and he also directed *The Cassilis Engagement* in a production that again convincingly showed that the neglect of the play was undeserved. The duelling mothers of Goldie Semple (the aristocratic Mrs Cassilis) and Mary Haney (the very lower middle-class Mrs Borridge), one fighting against, one fighting for, the unlikely marriage of their socially mismatched children, displayed – often hilariously, but also terrifyingly – the wicked power and determination of maternal love. Their children (David Leyshon and Trish Lindström) were squeezed helplessly between unforgiving family and social forces. The production was one of those blue ribbon Shaw Festival occasions when acting, direction, script, and design (William Schmuck) blended perfectly.

Equally unfamiliar was Rattigan's *After the Dance*, set in 1939, on the eve of the Second World War. A cynical portrait of a generation more concerned with self-indulgence than facing reality, the play's disappointing reception by critics and audiences (it achieved only a 56 percent box office) was perhaps in part the result of a late switch of director (Christopher Newton replacing an ill Neil Munro), perhaps in part because of intrinsic weaknesses in the play itself.

The Circle, too, could hardly have been known to many Festival theatregoers. It had been forty years since the first Festival production, and there had been few opportunities anywhere else to see it, even if this witty but wise exploration of the tensions and harmonies of married life is generally considered to be Maugham's best play. Happily, Neil Munro's production proved popular. Scheduled to end its 115-performance run at the Royal George Theatre on October 28, 2007, it was given a two-week extension to November 11.

Sheer curiosity helped generate interest in these neglected plays by little-known playwrights, and Maxwell was sensitive to the need to find ways of generating at least matching interest in more familiar works. Audience members didn't need help in recognizing the importance of Noel Coward, for example. Not only was Coward frequently produced in North American theatres, but the Festival itself had regularly featured Coward in its repertoire (second only to Shaw in frequency). *Design for Living*, however, was one of the few Coward plays that had not been produced at the Festival, and in Morris Panych's 2006 production it proved a great hit with Festival audiences. The ménage-à-trois around which the play is built – an interior decorator (Nicole Underhay), an artist (Graeme Somerville), and a playwright (David Jansen) – provided the intellectual and sexual fireworks that illuminated Coward's take on 1930s' decadent self-indulgence, while Panych's direction allowed audiences to enjoy the often raucous comedy without sacrificing the emotional intensity of the relationships.

***TONIGHT AT 8:30*, 2009**   But whereas *Design for Living* was new to the Festival, Coward's *Tonight at 8:30* had previously been produced – or, at least, *parts* of it had. Maxwell's innovative approach to Coward's cycle of ten one-act plays, written in 1935–36 as star vehicles for himself and Gertrude Lawrence, was to bring all ten plays together, for the first time, in repertory. She grouped together three sets of three thematically related plays (giving them the composite titles *Brief Encounters*; *Play, Orchestra, Play*; and *Ways of the Heart*), and kept one – *Star Chamber* – by itself for a lunchtime production (in a Canadian premiere). They were spread among three theatres (*Brief Encounters* in the Festival; *Play, Orchestra, Play* in the Court House; and *Ways of the Heart* and *Star Chamber* in the Royal George), and the openings were staggered throughout the season. Once *Ways of the Heart* was in preview from July 21, it was possible to see all ten plays over the space of a few days. In addition, on three occasions during the season (August 8, August 29, and September 19), audiences had the opportunity to see the full cycle in one day (marketed as "Mad Dogs and Englishmen – A Coward Marathon"). Reminiscent of previous one-day marathons at the Festival (*Back to Methuselah* in 1986 and *Man and Superman* in 1977, 1989, and 2004), the *Mad Dogs* day began earlier than any of the previous ones, with a 9:30 start in the morning with *Star Chamber*, followed by *Ways of the Heart* (11 am), *Play, Orchestra, Play* (3 pm), and *Brief Encounters* (8 pm). Maxwell directed *Brief Encounters*; the other directors were Blair Williams (*Ways of the Heart*), Christopher Newton (*Play, Orchestra, Play*), and Kate Lynch (*Star Chamber*).

Apart from the fascination of witnessing the astonishing breadth of dramatic situations and moods that Coward created in *Tonight at 8:30* – from, say, the moving intimacy of *Still Life* in the very public space of a railway station waiting room, to a Victorian family in mourning (or supposedly so) for their late patriarch in *Family Album*, to the unexpected outcome of the working-class domestic strife of *Fumed Oak* – there was the attraction of seeing members of the ensemble move among wildly contrasting roles in the space of an evening's (or matinee's) performance. It was, Maxwell said, a wonderful opportunity to "show off" the acting ensemble. Examples of ensemble versatility abounded in *Tonight at 8:30*, but Goldie Semple's trio of roles in *Brief Encounters* was typical of many bravura performances: from interfering busybody in *Still Life*, to outraged mother-in-law in *We Were Dancing*, to sozzled socialite in *Hands Across the Sea*.

Tickets for the *Mad Dogs* days were as hard to find as vermouth in a Noel Coward martini, and although the regular performances were met with uneven critical reaction they collectively sold close to 80,000 tickets.

Goldie Semple's appearance in *Tonight at 8:30*, her seventeenth season at the Shaw Festival, was the last of her career. She died in December 2009 at the age of fifty-six. Her life and her career as one of Canada's most loved and renowned actors were celebrated by friends and family (including her husband Lorne Kennedy) at the Festival Theatre on March 28, 2010.

***AN IDEAL HUSBAND*, 2010**   Maxwell's other challenge with the relatively familiar came from Wilde's *An Ideal Husband*. As with Coward, Festival patrons didn't need reminding who Wilde was, and many who attended the 2010 production of *An Ideal Husband* – directed by Maxwell – would likely have seen Duncan McIntosh's production from 1995 and 1996 (see above, page 176). McIntosh's decision to stress the darker side of Wilde's social satire was not universally

admired by critics, and Maxwell's determination – not unlike Christopher Newton's approach to *The Importance of Being Earnest* in 2004 – to dig beneath the surface wit to find the moral compass of the play met with similar critical resistance in some quarters. What was more widely recognized and appreciated, however, was the way in which Maxwell's direction, Judith Bowden's imposing two-tiered set and stylish though modernized costume designs, and Kevin Lamotte's operatic-like lighting reflected the essence of a play that is, after all, about blackmail and political corruption (as well as repentance and forgiveness). What a relief it was, said Robert Cushman in the *National Post*, to meet Wilde characters who, while funny, "are more than walking epigrams." Not that the production lacked wit and passion, the combined talents of Steven Sutcliffe (Viscount Goring), Patrick Galligan (Sir Robert Chiltern), Catherine McGregor (Lady Chiltern), and Moya O'Connell (Mrs Cheveley, the blackmailer), and the strong ensemble – Lorne Kennedy, Marla McLean, and Wendy Thatcher prominent among them – made sure of that (with a little help from Oscar Wilde).

Other contemporaries – British and European – of Shaw found their way into Maxwell's playbills including *The Invisible Man*, an adaptation of the H.G. Wells novel by Michael O'Brien, directed by Neil Munro at the Royal George Theatre in 2006. The same season also saw Munro's adaptation of Ibsen's *Rosmersholm*, which Munro also directed (at the Court House Theatre).

EUROPEAN FARCE Maxwell also included European farces by two authors who had been included in previous Festival seasons, Georges Feydeau and Ferenc Molnár. Paxton Whitehead and Christopher Newton had both scheduled Feydeau (*The Chemmy Circle*, 1968, and *A Flea in Her Ear*, 1980), and in 2005 Maxwell had chosen *Something on the Side*. She turned to Feydeau again in 2007 with an adaptation of *L'Hôtel du Libre-Échange* by Morris Panych, renamed *Hotel Peccadillo*. Panych introduced Feydeau himself into *Hotel Peccadillo*, played by Lorne Kennedy as "a graveyard ghoul in a three-piece suit." With an updated text as well (Botox and Viagara allusions, for example), a live orchestra, and a zany forced-perspective set design by Ken MacDonald (a series of doors that became smaller and smaller), the show deserved better than the 47 percent box office it managed in the Festival Theatre.

But that disappointment was eased somewhat by the great success of Molnár's *The President* for the 2007 season. Molnár's *The Guardsman* had been included by Whitehead in his 1969 season. Maxwell's choice was *The President*, in an adaptation by Canadian playwright Morwyn Brebner, who gave the play a North American milieu. A variation on the Pygmalion story, the plot of *The President* revolves around the frantic efforts of a New York bank tycoon (Norrison) to turn an oafish Communist taxi driver (Tony Foot) into a well-bred, well-spoken young man who might pass for a capitalist. Norrison's problem is that wealthy clients (from Iowa) have entrusted their daughter (Lydia) to his care, but she has secretly married Tony, a choice hardly likely to meet with her parents' approval. And they are about to arrive in New York. Norrison has an hour to transform Tony.

On his Festival directorial debut, Blair Williams kept the twenty-two characters (played by fifteen actors) moving at the dizzying pace (on Cameron Porteous's accommodating set) that the action requires – it takes place in real time – but never losing control. At the centre of it all was Lorne Kennedy's Norrison, a tour de force performance of immense technical skill and sustained energy. Richard Ouzounian wanted to award Kennedy "ten dozen roses, the Order of Canada, and a lifetime gift certificate to Tim Hortons for his astonishing performance." They were awards that Kennedy would surely have wanted to share with Williams, with Chilina Kennedy (as Lydia), Jeff Meadows (Tony), and the whole ensemble.

The President sold over 90 percent of available tickets in its fifty-five performance run at the Royal George, and was revived for the 2011 season, again directed by Williams and designed by Porteous with Lorne Kennedy as Norrison.

AMERICAN MUSICALS Few would have been surprised to see any of these plays by Shaw's contemporaries in a Christopher Newton season, but there were many ways in which the divergences from the kind of programming that Newton preferred were being consolidated during these years.

Working closely with music director Paul Sportelli, Maxwell ensured that the Festival mounted a broad range of musicals, from big Broadway shows in the Festival Theatre to smaller or more contemporary work in the Royal George and Court House theatres.

As explained above (page 229), the programming of a musical (*Gypsy*) in the Festival Theatre in 2005 marked a major divergence from past practice. The success of that change gave Maxwell confidence to continue selecting Broadway musicals for the Festival Theatre: *High Society* in 2006, *Mack and Mabel* in 2007, *Wonderful Town* in 2008, and *My Fair Lady* in 2011.

In the Royal George Theatre Maxwell scheduled *Sunday in the Park with George* in 2009 and *One Touch of Venus* in 2010, and in the Court House Theatre *A Little Night Music* in 2008. (Maxwell also built a Canadian voice into Festival musicals through two Paul Sportelli-Jay Turvey collaborations, *Tristan* in 2007, and *Maria Severa* in 2011.

Among the Festival Theatre musicals, *High Society*, based on Philip Barry's 1939 play *The Philadelphia Story* by way of the 1956 movie adaptation with music and lyrics by Cole Porter (and starring Bing Crosby, Frank Sinatra, and Grace Kelly), did as well as *Gypsy* at the box office (78 percent), despite some harshly negative reviews of Kelly Robinson's production (designed by William Schmuck). There was some sniping as well at Maxwell for allegedly putting box office returns ahead of artistic quality. Maxwell had decided, charged Gary Smith in the *Hamilton Spectator*, that big musicals are "a quick way to make a buck," and Robert Cushman (*National Post*) concluded that *High Society* was chosen simply because "it's a famous title." Such theories were quickly disproved next season by *Mack and Mabel*, which received a good

deal of critical acclaim but disappointed at the box office. Like *High Society*, *Mack and Mabel* had flopped on Broadway, but Molly Smith's Shaw Festival production, "defied the odds," said Jamie Portman, in "a slick, assured, and exhilarating revival" of the Michael Stewart (book) and Jerry Herman (music and lyrics) play about silent film star Mack Sennett and his lover Mabel Normand. As Mack, Benedict Campbell was welcomed by critics as a "dazzling new star" of musical theatre, and Paul Sportelli was hailed as "the musical fairy god-mother" for giving "joyous life" to Herman's score. An American critic – Tony Brown in the Cleveland *Plain Dealer* – judged this production the best he had ever seen of *Mack and Mabel*. But where were the audiences? Box office plummeted from the 78 percent of *Gypsy* and *High Society* to 57 percent, a drop of about 20,000 tickets.

Maxwell persevered, however, with putting a musical in the Festival Theatre, choosing Leonard Bernstein's *Wonderful Town* for the 2008 season. Unlike *High Society* and *Mack and Mabel*, *Wonderful Town* had enjoyed a long Broadway run (559 performances in 1953–54), as well as a successful Broadway revival in 2003. The Shaw Festival production, directed by Roger Hodgman, with a design team of William Schmuck (set), Judith Bowden (costumes), and Louise Guinand (lighting), was the Canadian premiere of this story of two Ohio sisters (an actress and a writer) seeking fame in New York. There were many standout performances in the production – Chilina Kennedy as the voluptuous actress sister, Thom Marriott as the domesticated football player, William Vickers as an Irish cop, and the whole ensemble – but *Wonderful Town* still didn't take off at the box office, selling a modest 62.5 percent of tickets.

STEPHEN SONDHEIM   Maxwell's production of *Merrily We Roll Along* in the Royal George Theatre in Christopher Newton's final season (2002) had introduced Stephen Sondheim to the Shaw Festival. Despite the problematic past of *Merrily* – it managed only sixteen performances on Broadway in 1981 – Maxwell and Newton figured that it was a good fit for the Shaw's ensemble. "Here is a musical," said Newton, "about the traps and triumphs of the modern world that might have been written especially for our company." But would Festival audiences respond

OPPOSITE: GOLDIE SEMPLE IN *A LITTLE NIGHT MUSIC* BY STEPHEN SONDHEIM AND HUGH WHEELER, 2008. DIRECTED BY MORRIS PANYCH, MUSICAL DIRECTION BY PAUL SPORTELLI, CHOREOGRAPHY BY VALERIE MOORE, SET DESIGNED BY KEN MACDONALD, COSTUMES DESIGNED BY CHARLOTTE DEAN, LIGHTING DESIGNED BY ALAN BRODIE.

THIS PAGE: JUSTIN STADNYK, GEORGE MASSWOHL AND ROBIN EVAN WILLIS IN *A LITTLE NIGHT MUSIC*, 2008. PHOTOS BY MICHAEL COOPER.

to what Maxwell conceded was a "more urban, more sassy" musical than the norm at the Shaw Festival? The answer was a resounding "yes." *Merrily* was one of the hits of the season, hitting close to 93 percent in ticket sales.

Sondheim had to wait, though, until 2005 for his next Festival appearance, this time as lyricist for *Gypsy* (see above, page 229), and then Maxwell pleased Sondheim enthusiasts by scheduling *A Little Night Music* for the Court House Theatre in 2008. She invited audiences "to look at it anew in the intimate setting of the Court House," giving director Morris Panych, designer Ken MacDonald, and musical director Paul Sportelli the challenge of downsizing a Broadway-sized show into a pocket-sized space. Sportelli used an orchestration by Shaw Festival music intern Jason Jestadt for a chamber quintet, and although that meant some loss of the swell of a full orchestra for big numbers like "A Weekend in the Country," there were also some welcome gains. Robert Cushman, for example, realized that the famous "Send in the Clowns" "can bring on as much sweet sorrow when sounded by a clarinet as by a full complement of strings." There was the added pleasure in the Court House of hearing the cast – featuring Goldie Semple as Desirée Armfeldt and George Masswohl as Fredrik Egerman – sing acoustically. MacDonald's imaginative set design featured several trees that moved on wheels around the stage to create a changing series of acting spaces and vistas, used deftly by Panych and the cast to shape relationships as well as spaces – albeit also sometimes making it difficult for the audience to see clearly what was happening through the foliage. But that didn't seem to be an obstacle to popular success; *A Little Night Music* was another Sondheim hit (93 percent box office).

In addition to *A Little Night Music*, Sondheim's *Follies* was presented in 2008 in four concert performances in the Festival Theatre, with a full orchestra, followed the next season by *Sunday in the Park with George* in the Royal George, one of Sondheim's collaborations with James Lapine. With growing experience of producing Sondheim, Maxwell by now was convinced that "the sophisticated, literate yet heartfelt worlds created by Stephen Sondheim and his collaborators" were "a perfect match for the deftness, clarity and great heart of our ensemble." Critics were beginning to agree, particularly Cushman, for whom Alisa Palmer's production of *Sunday in the Park*, though "uneven," was "the most satisfying" he had ever seen. Audiences continued to be satisfied as well. In double the number of performances compared to *A Little Night Music* (sixty-six for *A Little Night Music* in the Court House, 130 for *Sunday in the Park* in the Royal George), *Sunday in the Park* still reached a 69 percent box office.

Paul Sportelli has been musical director for all of the Festival's Sondheim productions, and his sensitivity to the complexities of Sondheim's music has been crucial. (Richard Ouzounian said of Sportelli's work in *Sunday in the Park* that he seems to have "an almost psychic feel for Sondheim.") Around Sportelli, Maxwell has been building a group of artists equally in synch with Sondheim's work: herself, designer Judith Bowden, and choreographer Valerie Moore prominent among them. Whatever the fate of traditional Broadway musicals in the Festival Theatre, the Shaw Festival has created the artistic strength to be a leading interpreter (in any of its theatres) of Sondheim in the coming years, with major works such as *Sweeney Todd*, *Company*, and *Into the Woods* all waiting enticingly in the wings. Sondheim's "mixture of intelligence and heart suits us perfectly," Maxwell has said.

AMERICAN PLAYS   Inclusion in the 2005 Festival playbill of Lillian Hellman's *The Autumn Garden* and William Inge's *Bus Stop* (see above, pages 235 and 231) signalled Maxwell's intention to explore the emotionally and politically intense side of modern American drama. That focus continued into subsequent seasons. Three plays in particular captured this evolution: Arthur Miller's *The Crucible*, Hellman's *The Little Foxes*, and Eugene O'Neill's *A Moon for the Misbegotten*.

THE CRUCIBLE, 2006   Prior to *The Crucible*, the Shaw Festival had staged only one Arthur Miller play, *All My Sons* in 1999, directed by Neil Munro. The better known *Crucible* ranks high on anyone's list of great American plays of the twentieth century, and its deeply moving and yet politically charged subject matter made it a perfect fit for Maxwell's American drama agenda. She gave the play – astutely – to Tadeusz Bradecki, with a cast (led by Benedict Campbell, Jim Mezon, and Kelli Fox) and a design team (Peter Hartwell, set; Teresa Przybylski, costumes; and Kevin Lamotte, lighting) that helped create a memorable production.

Miller's tale of witch hunts in late seventeenth-century Massachusetts famously allowed Miller to express his outrage at the parallel political witch hunts mounted by Senator Joseph McCarthy in the United Sates in the early 1950s. Campbell gave a searing performance as John Proctor, one of the victims of the witch hunt, while Kelli Fox, as Proctor's wife, torn between anger (at her husband's infidelity) and charity, was equally gripping. The two, said Robert Cushman in the *National Post*, played the Proctors "as finely as I have ever known them to be played." As Deputy Governor Danforth, Jim Mezon, Cushman added, presented "a terrifying image of a calm judicial mind turning itself into a one-man lynch mob."

Some of the intimacy of relationships in the play – the final meeting between Proctor and his wife, for example, in Proctor's cell – was diminished by the size of the Festival stage, but Peter Hartwell's gaunt, hinged wooden-panelled set, aided by Lamotte's lighting, served a variety of settings well.

In his program note Bradecki argued that "the evils of mindless persecution and the terrifying power of false accusations have repeatedly scythed their bloody crops." The point, it seems, got through for most of the critics, tellingly for Cleveland critic Tony Brown, who felt that Bradecki's production "gathers even more steam in light of disclosures of inhumane treatment of prisoners in U.S. custody and the U.S. government's use of domestic spying in the hunt for terrorists." The Festival's production of *The Crucible*, said Brown, "is just about everything anyone could hope for theater to ever be." Sadly, it played to half-empty houses, with only a 46 percent box office in a run of sixty-three performances.

THE LITTLE FOXES, 2008   Both Lillian Hellman plays at the Festival prior to *The Little Foxes* – *The Children's Hour* in 1997 and *The Autumn Garden* in 2005 – had done well critically and at the box office, so Maxwell's choice of another Hellman play for the 2008 season was not surprising. As with her choice of *The Autumn Garden*, *The Little Foxes* met two of Maxwell's priorities: more female playwrights and more emotionally intense American drama in Festival playbills.

Both of the previous Hellman plays had been staged in the Court House Theatre. *The Little Foxes*, however, features a grand staircase in a southern mansion as an integral part of the set and action of the play, ruling out the Court House Theatre for even the most creative of designers. Maxwell opted for the Royal George over the Festival Theatre, still giving set designer Cameron Porteous some challenges (stylishly negotiated) with fitting the staircase and the elegant furnishings of a wealthy family into a small space.

The family in question, though – or at least some members of it – are not as wealthy as they would like to be, so plans are afoot to do a deal with a Chicago industrialist to build a textile mill on the family's cotton plantation. The obstacle to the plan is the principled family patriarch, and it's up to his wife – the formidable Regina Giddens – to dispose of the obstacle. She does so with a shocking ruthlessness, refusing to come to his help as he lies dying on the staircase.

The success of a production of *The Little Foxes* doesn't depend entirely on the actress playing Regina, but she carries a lot of responsibility. It's a role that has attracted (on stage and on film) renowned actresses such as Tallulah Bankhead, Anne Bancroft, Bette Davis, and Elizabeth Taylor, so the Festival's Regina – Laurie Paton – was in good company. Some critics found Paton short on nastiness, but Herman Trotter in the *Buffalo News* thought her "as dastardly a Regina as one could want," Paton playing the role "with superb, supercilious aloofness." Robert Cushman detected a Lady Macbeth-like "creamy malice" beneath the superficially endearing external features of Paton's performance.

Paton was supported by a strong ensemble that included David Jansen, Ric Reid, Peter Krantz, Gray Powell, Sharry Flett, and Krista Colosimo.

The cast also included two black actors, Lisa Codrington and Richard Stewart, who played domestic servants, appropriate casting in the context of early twentieth-century social structures in the southern United States. It was this casting, however, that prompted *Globe and Mail* critic Kelly Nestruck to comment that "colour-blind casting has yet to reach" the Shaw Festival, a casual remark (he put it in brackets in his review) that triggered the brief but difficult debate discussed above (page 260).

Nestruck was also one of the few critics who accused director Eda Holmes of bowdlerizing Hellman's text. It was a carefully considered decision by Holmes (supported by Maxwell) to replace "nigger" with "coloured" (as, for example, in Regina's line "I think you should either be a nigger or a millionaire"). When faced with the same issue in his 1994 production of *The Front Page* (see above, page 161), Neil Munro had opted to keep the offensive word, but after consulting a number of theatre professionals, some white, some of colour, Holmes chose to change it. It was not, she argued, only a matter of the offence caused by the word, but the worry that its inclusion would detract from the main theme of the play, which is not about race, but about greed.

A MOON FOR THE MISBEGOTTEN, 2009   Maxwell brought the plays of Eugene O'Neill to the Shaw Festival audiences in 2004 with Joseph Ziegler's production of *Ah, Wilderness!* A comedy, *Ah, Wilderness!* doesn't pack the emotional punch of later O'Neill plays such as *Long Day's Journey Into Night* and its sequel, the less well known *A Moon for the Misbegotten* (first performed in 1947). Joseph Ziegler directed this first heavyweight O'Neill play at the Shaw Festival in the Court House Theatre, with a cast headed by Jenny Young, Jim Mezon, and David Jansen.

A Moon for the Misbegotten is set in 1923 in a dilapidated farm house in Connecticut on barren land from which Phil Hogan (Mezon) and his daughter Josie (Young) eke out a living. Their landlord, James Tyrone (Jansen), visits, but the emotional bond that develops between Josie and James as they face their respective demons (hers a deep lack of self-respect, his alcohol) ultimately evaporates in the haze of James's alcoholism.

There is deep pain in the turmoil endured by Josie and James, but the Shaw Festival production of *A Moon for the Misbegotten* was dominated by a towering performance from Jim Mezon as Josie's ruthlessly devious, selfish, swaggering, drunken father. Mezon stormed and

bellowed and connived his way around Christina Poddubiuk's convincing set with the power of a hurricane and the wiliness of a fox. It was one of the most vital performances of the 2009 season, and of a Shaw Festival career that has hardly been short of highlights since Mezon's first appearance at the Festival as Yasha in *The Cherry Orchard* in 1980.

A *Moon for the Misbegotten* was far less popular with audiences than *Ah, Wilderness!* (45 percent box office as against 76 percent), but, as with Sondheim, Maxwell has opened the door to other intriguing O'Neill possibilities.

Maxwell's exploration of major American plays continued into 2011 with *Cat on a Hot Tin Roof*, the second Tennessee Williams play to be staged at the Festival. Her interest in American drama has been widespread, however, encompassing less familiar plays such as Ruth and Augustus Goetz's *The Heiress*, a 1947 adaptation of Henry James's novel *Washington Square* (directed by Joseph Ziegler at the Royal George in 2006), and big comedies such as Garson Kanin's 1946 *Born Yesterday*, brilliantly directed (in her Shaw Festival debut) by Gina Wilkinson in Sue LePage's luxury hotel suite setting in the Festival Theatre in 2009, with consummate performances by Deborah Hay and Thom Marriott, supported by another blue-chip ensemble. Another individual performance in an American play that will long be remembered was Peter Krantz's portrayal of Elwood Dowd in Mary Chase's *Harvey* at the Royal George Theatre in 2010, directed by Ziegler. One of the most popular plays of the season, *Harvey*'s run was extended for fourteen performances after the scheduled close, for a total of 141 performances, one of the longest in Festival history. (The record is held by *She Loves Me*, which ran at the Royal George in 2000 for 169 performances.) Comedy – with an edge – is also the prevailing tone of Clare Boothe Luce's 1936 play *The Women*. First produced at the Festival in 1985 (see above, page 196), the second production in 2010, directed by Alisa Palmer, again provided the opportunity to celebrate, as Maxwell put it, "the extraordinary actresses in our company."

OPPOSITE, CLOCKWISE FROM TOP:
MOYA O'CONNELL AND JENNY YOUNG
WITH THE ENSEMBLE IN *THE WOMEN*
BY CLARE BOOTHE LUCE, 2010.
DIRECTED BY ALISA PALMER, DESIGN-
ED BY WILLIAM SCHMUCK, LIGHT-
ING DESIGNED BY KEVIN LAMOTTE,
ORIGINAL MUSIC BY LESLEY BARBER.
PHOTO BY EMILY COOPER.

JEFF MEADOWS AND NICOLE
UNDERHAY IN *SUMMER AND SMOKE*
BY TENNESSEE WILLIAMS, 2007.
DIRECTED BY NEIL MUNRO, SET
DESIGNED BY PETER HARTWELL,
COSTUMES DESIGNED BY CHRISTINA
PODDUBIUK, LIGHTING DESIGNED
BY ALAN BRODIE, ORIGINAL MUSIC
BY MARC DESORMEAUX. PHOTO
BY DAVID COOPER.

PETER KRANTZ IN *HARVEY* BY MARY
CHASE, 2010. DIRECTED BY JOSEPH
ZIEGLER, DESIGNED BY SUE LEPAGE,
LIGHTING DESIGNED BY LOUISE
GUINAND. PHOTO BY DAVID COOPER.

THIS PAGE: TARA ROSLING AND MIKE
SHARA IN *THE HEIRESS* BY RUTH GOETZ
AND AUGUSTUS GOETZ, 2006. DIRECT-
ED BY JOSEPH ZIEGLER, DESIGNED
BY CHRISTINA PODDUBIUK, LIGHT-
ING DESIGNED BY LOUISE GUINAND.
PHOTO BY DAVID COOPER.

THE IRISH STRAIN   Maxwell had said when she was appointed artistic director that she would bring a stronger Irish voice to the Shaw Festival, reflecting, of course, her own background (and Shaw's), but also an enthusiasm for numerous Irish plays and playwrights whose work had not yet been included in Festival playbills. Early Irish choices by Maxwell were Brian Friel's *Afterplay* and Sean O'Casey's *The Plough and the Stars* in 2003, and John Millington Synge's *The Tinker's Wedding* in 2004. There was an Irish hiatus in 2005 and 2006, but a double presence in 2007.

A MONTH IN THE COUNTRY, 2007   The first might better be termed semi-Irish. It was a 1992 adaptation by Brian Friel of Ivan Turgenev's *A Month in the Country* set, Chekhov-like, in the wasteland of provincial Russia in the 1840s. Although Maxwell had always felt an affinity between the Russians and the Irish ("love of drink and melancholy humour," she suggested), in this instance crossing a Russian playwright with an Irish playwright wasn't a good idea according to John Coulbourn in the *Toronto Sun*. It yields a play "that seems to drag on forever," he said. Director Tadeusz Bradecki saw it differently, finding in this blend of "Chekhovian atmosphere and Irish melancholy" life aplenty. There is a legitimate ennui in the play as characters struggle to find purpose and meaning in their lives, but there is also a good deal of sexual tension as a married woman (Natalaya Petrovna) and her teenage ward compete for the same young man. Fiona Byrne gave what many considered to be one of her finest performances as the self-indulgent Natalya, at once suffering pain in herself and causing deep pain for others. Friel's adaptation and Bradecki's staging also created more humour than found in the original – in Ric Reid's emotionally dyspeptic doctor (Robert Cushman's term), for example, and in Blair Williams' whiny and insecure husband, much more interested in his threshing machine than in his wife (until consumed by jealousy).

THE KILTARTAN COMEDIES, 2007   The Irishness of *A Month in the Country* was subtle and inconspicuous, but there was no missing the Irishness of *The Kiltartan Comedies*. This lunchtime production (in the Court House Theatre, directed by Micheline Chevrier) consisted of two short contrasting plays by Irish nationalist Lady Augusta Gregory. The first, *The Rising of the Moon*, has an overt political context in pre-independence Ireland – it is built around a confrontation between a sergeant of the Royal Irish Constabulary (played by Douglas E. Hughes) and an Irish rebel (Patrick McManus) – but Chevrier's light-handed approach kept the politics in the background and the humanity in the foreground. The second play, *Spreading the News*, is a cautionary and rambunctious tale about the dangers of village gossip. A less restrained Chevrier gave free rein to the cast to revel in Irish stereotypes and slapstick humour.

THE CHERRY ORCHARD, 2010   More Irishness emerged in 2010, and, as with *A Month in the Country*, it came indirectly, again in the form of an adaptation of a nineteenth-century Russian play by a contemporary Irish playwright. The pairing this time was Anton Chekhov's *The Cherry Orchard* with Tom Murphy, like Brian Friel one of Ireland's leading playwrights. An added Irish component was that the director selected by Maxwell for the production was a Dubliner, Jason Byrne, whose work Maxwell had seen and admired in several of his previous productions in Canada.

John Coulbourn didn't much care for the Russian/Irish blend in *A Month in the Country*, but this time he thought the Festival "had come up with a pretty tasty bit of theatrical fusion." Not that there was an obvious Irishness about Murphy's adaptation – a few colloquialisms in the dialogue, perhaps, but no change in the familiar plot or setting. Nor did Murphy or Jason Byrne have a particular agenda for the play or the production. This troubled some audiences and critics, as did other aspects of the production: the slow pace of the dimly lit (by Kevin Lamotte) opening scene, Byrne's willingness to trust in long silences, his confidence in the ensemble to shape their own stage movements (which differed from production to production), the naturalism of the dialogue (overlapping speeches making it difficult to follow every word). There was much here both to engage and to flummox.

But even the flummoxed could hardly fail to appreciate the quality of the ensemble performance, and, even in the context of an ensemble focus, the outstanding performances of, for example (and among many), Benedict Campbell as the nouveau-riche businessman Lopakhin;

OPPOSITE: BENEDICT CAMPBELL IN *THE CHERRY ORCHARD* BY ANTON CHEKHOV, A VERSION BY TOM MURPHY, 2010. DIRECTED BY JASON BYRNE, DESIGNED BY PETER HARTWELL, LIGHTING DESIGNED BY KEVIN LAMOTTE.

THIS PAGE: GABRIELLE JONES; GORD RAND; AL KOZLIK IN *THE CHERRY ORCHARD*, 2010. PHOTOS BY DAVID COOPER.

Jim Mezon as the grave but ridiculous Gayev; Laurie Paton as the stoically but naively detached Ranyevskaya; and Al Kozlik as the servant Firs, the fading symbol of a Russian aristocratic past that must now give way to a new political and social order.

Campbell's drunken whirling dervish speech of triumph and exultation after he has become the new owner of Ranyevskaya's estate was extraordinary, contrasting dramatically with the deeply moving performance of Kozlik as Firs, alone and dying at the end of the play as sounds of axes chopping down the cherry trees are heard outside.

The Irish voice was back in full force in 2011 with Lennox Robinson's *Drama at Inish*. Like Shaw, Robinson (1886–1958) was an Irish Protestant, but unlike Shaw he became actively involved in Irish theatre, managing the Abbey Theatre in Dublin for several years. He also wrote a number of plays, several of which deal with Irish political issues. He became best known as a playwright, however, for his comedies, including *Drama at Inish*. First produced in 1933, *Drama at Inish* concerns the reactions of the citizens of Inish to a visiting theatre group and their productions of Ibsen, Strindberg, and Chekhov – with unanticipated outcomes for the community. Maxwell described Robinson – new to the Shaw Festival – as "a well kept Irish secret," and *Drama at Inish* as "a little seen Irish gem."

NEW ROOTS

Irish plays, American plays, a wide range of musicals, including new and contemporary work: these have been, and will continue to be, features of Jackie Maxwell's Shaw Festival playbills. They mark change, they reflect evolution. But something that Maxwell said in an interview with Melissa Leong in the *National Post* in November 2010 highlighted a more fundamental change that has taken place under her leadership. "Once I hit my seventh year [2009]," she told Leong, "that was when I felt that my early ideas of Canadian programming and women's voices had really taken root."

After a further two seasons, the evidence was even firmer. Two of Maxwell's major priorities had been accomplished. Canadian and women's voices had been fully integrated into the mainstream of Shaw Festival programming.

CANADIAN VOICES   Maxwell's seventh season included *Albertine in Five Times* by Quebec playwright Michel Tremblay. *Albertine* was the eighth Canadian play that Maxwell had programmed, at least one in every season she had been artistic director – not to mention translations and adaptations by Canadian writers and directors such as Susan Coyne, Neil Munro, Morwyn Brebner, and Maureen LaBonté. After only very occasional programming of Canadian plays in the forty-one seasons before Maxwell arrived, there could be no doubt by 2009 that Canadian plays – new plays and revivals – were at the Festival to stay.

Through her difficult first three years, Maxwell had held firm to programming Canadian plays: *The Coronation Voyage* and *Blood Relations* in 2003; *Nothing Sacred* and *Waiting for the Parade* in 2004; *Belle Moral* in 2005 (revived in 2008). After *The Invisible Man* in 2006 there was the world premiere of *Tristan* in 2007, a musical by Paul Sportelli and Jay Turvey based on a short story by Thomas Mann that ran for forty-one performances in the Court House Theatre, directed by Eda Holmes. (The work of Sportelli and Turvey appeared again in 2011 in another musical world premiere, *Maria Severa*, a work based on the real-life story of a prostitute in early nineteenth-century Lisbon.)

ALBERTINE IN FIVE TIMES, 2009   In 2008 *Belle Moral* (see above, page 237) was revived, and then, in 2009, came *Albertine in Five Times*. First produced in French (*Albertine en cinq temps*) in Ottawa in 1984, an English version of *Albertine* followed at Toronto's Tarragon Theatre a year later, in a translation by Bill Glassco and John van Burek. The Shaw Festival production (in the Court House Theatre) was in a new translation by Linda Gaboriau. At the Tarragon Theatre Patricia Hamilton was one of the five Albertines who appear in the play. Hamilton was also cast in the Shaw Festival production: in Toronto she played Albertine at age fifty; at the Festival she excelled in the pivotal role of Albertine at seventy. The other Albertines were played by Marla McLean (thirty), Jenny L. Wright (forty), Mary Haney (fifty), and Wendy Thatcher (sixty). At seventy, in a seniors' home – unwillingly – Albertine is looking back at various stages of

WENDY THATCHER, MARLA MCLEAN,
PATRICIA HAMILTON, JENNY L. WRIGHT,
NICOLA CORREIA-DAMUDE, AND MARY
HANEY IN *ALBERTINE IN FIVE TIMES* BY
MICHEL TREMBLAY, 2009. DIRECTED
BY MICHELINE CHEVRIER, DESIGNED
BY TERESA PRZYBYLSKI, LIGHTING
DESIGNED BY ERECA HASSELL, ORIG-
INAL MUSIC COMPOSED BY MARC
DESORMEAUX. PHOTO BY EMILY
COOPER.

DONNA BELLEVILLE IN *AGE OF AROUSAL*
BY LINDA GRIFFITHS, 2009. DIRECTED
BY JACKIE MAXWELL, DESIGNED BY SUE
LEPAGE, LIGHTING DESIGNED BY ALAN
BRODIE, ORIGINAL MUSIC AND SOUND
DESIGNED BY JOHN GZOWSKI, MOVE-
MENT BY VALERIE MOORE. PHOTO BY
DAVID COOPER.

her tough and troubled life, presented by the other Albertines mostly in a series of monologues. Albertine's sense of being trapped and isolated at seventy was powerfully represented by Teresa Przybylski's set of iron bars and a staircase that seemed to lead nowhere. Critic Lawrence Switzky (*Curtain Up*) read the set as "a cage simultaneously blowing apart and caving in." It "splendidly captured," he said, "the dynamism of Tremblay's haunted character." Director Micheline Chevrier used the set's abstract images to shape the presentation of Albertine, despite her many personal flaws, as essentially a victim of patriarchal society. The play was not a great favourite with audiences (a 54 percent box office in a forty-nine-performance run) or, for the most part, with critics. But Switzky, for one, was alert to the implications of Maxwell having chosen a Tremblay. "Let's hope," he said, "that the Shaw plumbs more of Canada's rich franco-phone drama in the near future."

AGE OF AROUSAL, 2010 *Albertine in Five Times* is about the life of one woman in five phases; Linda Griffiths' 2007 play *Age of Arousal*, selected and directed by Maxwell for the 2010 sea-son, is about five women in one phase. Another distinguished Canadian playwright – anglo-phone, though, like Tremblay, born in Montreal – Griffiths took her inspiration for *Age of Arousal* from George Gissing's 1893 novel, *The Odd Women*. The woman are "odd" in the sense that a population imbalance in late Victorian England – half a million more women than men – left many women unmarried, and therefore faced with both the challenge and the op-portunity of forging a life and an identity of their own, in, of course, a male dominated society. In *Age of Arousal* Griffiths focuses on the efforts of one such woman to help herself and other women respond to their social context. Mary Barfoot has established a school for typists, which she runs with her partner and lover Rhoda Nunn. At Rhoda's invitation, three sisters join the school, and the five women – with the involvement of one man – then begin a journey of self-exploration that is variously sexual, economic, and cultural.

CLOCKWISE FROM LEFT: CLAIRE JULLIEN; BLAIR WILLIAMS; JENNIFER PHIPPS IN *THE STEPMOTHER* BY GITHA SOWERBY, 2008. DIRECTED BY JACKIE MAXWELL, SET DESIGNED BY CAMELLIA KOO, COSTUMES DESIGNED BY WILLIAM SCHMUCK, LIGHTING DESIGNED BY LOUISE GUINAND. PHOTOS BY EMILY COOPER.

The play's late-Victorian context was familiar to Shaw Festival audiences, but as Maxwell put it, Griffiths' perspective on that context was "a provocative and exhilarating leap" for them. The exploration of sexual identity was more open than Shaw and his contemporaries would have dared (or been allowed by censorship laws), and Griffiths' dramaturgical strategy of "thoughtspeak" was entirely new to Festival audiences. "Thoughtspeak" constituted spoken subtext – heard by the audience, but not by other characters on stage – where, as Maxwell explained in program notes, "suppressed desires, fears, hope burst to the surface." Characters speak their most private thoughts even as they hide them from one another. This "moving from polite dialogue to a 'thoughtspeak' aria of volcanic sexual desire and back again," Maxwell posited, requires from the actors "an extraordinary combination of emotional accessibility and extreme technical precision." In her cast – Donna Belleville, Jenny Young, Kelli Fox, Sharry Flett, Zarrin Darnell-Martin, and Gray Powell – Maxwell found the necessary qualities.

Sue LePage's ingenious set – in which antique typewriters played a starring role – John Gzowski's original music, and Valerie Moore's choreography enriched a production that spoke to the "new" Shaw Festival – insights into the traditional mandate period from multiple perspectives: contemporary, Canadian, and female.

WOMEN'S VOICES   In her November 2010 interview with Melissa Leong, Jackie Maxwell said that she believed that by 2009 "women's voices," as well as Canadian programming, had "taken root" at the Shaw Festival. In truth, the two areas overlapped to a considerable degree. Much of the Canadian programming – playwrights, themes of plays, directors, designers – had given voice to female perspectives. Prominent among such productions were *Blood Relations*, *Waiting for the Parade*, *Belle Moral*, *Albertine in Five Times*, and *Age of Arousal*. In addition, Maxwell's continuing exploration of plays by women among Shaw's contemporaries (what she has called her "archaeological" programming) produced interesting results. After *Diana of Dobson's* in 2003 and *Rutherford and Son* in 2004, Maxwell programmed *The Stepmother* in 2008.

***THE STEPMOTHER*, 2008**   *The Stepmother* arrived at the Shaw Festival courtesy of Jonathan Bank, artistic director of the Mint Theatre in New York. Bank had come across this forgotten play in the basement of a London publishing house and, on a visit to the Niagara-on-the-Lake, had handed a copy of the faded typescript to Maxwell. The play had been written by Githa Sowerby, whose *Rutherford and Son* Maxwell had included and directed in her second (2004) season (see above, page 222). So the playwright wasn't new to Maxwell, but the play certainly was. This was hardly surprising since *The Stepmother* had never been published and had been performed only once, in a private production in London in 1924.

Maxwell says she "nearly passed out" when she grasped the significance of Jonathan Bank's discovery. Here was an opportunity to mount the first professional production of a play by a woman prominent in her time – a writer and, like Shaw, a member of the Fabian Society – whose work was slowly beginning to emerge from obscurity. She decided to direct it herself (in the Court House Theatre), and the Festival also took steps to publish the play (in collaboration with Women's Press in Toronto in 2008, edited by Joanna Falck, with an introduction by Maxwell).

The stepmother in *The Stepmother*, Lois Relph (played by Claire Jullien in her Shaw Festival debut), a gifted dress designer who successfully runs her own business, is not the stereotypical "wicked stepmother." She is in fact loved and appreciated by her two stepdaughters. But that is almost incidental to the main action of the play, which concerns Lois's need to free herself from her bullying and financially irresponsible husband (the father of her stepdaughters) who has married her only to gain access to her inherited money. It is a Shavian-like theme, but Sowerby's approach is much less cerebral, much more emotional than Shaw's.

Maxwell's production refused to play down the emotion; rather Blair Williams as Lois's husband, was allowed to revel in his villainy, prompting boos both during the play and at the curtain call for his malevolent scheming against his wife. For some audience members this was a chance to play their "hiss the villain" role in an Edwardian melodrama; for others there seemed to be a genuine sense of outrage at the blatant demonstration of marital abuse. And satisfaction as well when *The Stepmother* ends not as Ibsen ended his *A Doll's House*, with the exit of a wife to a precarious future, but with the forced exit of Lois's husband to a precarious exile, leaving his wife in control of their home and, more importantly, of her own independent future.

"Archaeological" plays, Canadian plays, American plays by women (Lillian Hellman and Clare Boothe Luce, for example): all strengthened women's voices at the Shaw Festival. And so did Maxwell's choice of directors and designers. Of the ninety-six productions in Maxwell's first nine seasons, forty-two were directed by women. And sixty-nine of the productions were fully or partially designed by women (set, costumes, or lighting).

NEW DIRECTIONS

While the directions that Maxwell had set for the Festival in 2003 had been vigorously followed, other programming issues had – inevitably – arisen, issues that had not been at the forefront of Maxwell's thinking when she took over the Festival. They were and are issues that will shape the evolution of the Festival in the years to come.

A NEW APPROACH TO SHAW   There is, for instance, the issue of Shaw himself. When the Shaw Festival began in 1962, Shaw had been dead for a mere twelve years. He was still a famous figure, known around the world through his widely performed plays and well-remembered essays, speeches, and broadcasts. His plays were also still taught in schools, colleges, and universities. Two generations later, Shaw is no longer a household name, and his works are far less frequently read and studied. It has become increasingly difficult to sustain long runs of even his better known plays in the large Festival Theatre, and the complexities and – for modern audiences – opaqueness of some of his lesser known plays render them inaccessible for many theatregoers. Maxwell has taken the view, then, that it cannot be business as usual with Shaw. The onus, she says, is on the Festival "not only to continue to revitalize this brilliant provocateur's work, but also to show that he does not exist in a bubble of his own." Shaw, Maxwell argued, "is part of a continuum of writers, who, to this day continue to subvert and question the status quo, and challenge the assumptions that rule our lives."

There are, then, as Maxwell sees it, two kinds of challenges with Shaw: revitalizing and contextualizing his own plays, and finding the continuum that links him to more contemporary writers.

The 2011 season showed how Maxwell planned to approach the first challenge. Lest anyone doubted her commitment to Shaw, she scheduled three of his plays (*Heartbreak House*, *Candida*, *On the Rocks*) and a musical, *My Fair Lady*, based on a fourth Shaw play, *Pygmalion*.

The last time there had been three Shaw plays in a Festival season was in 1999, also the year that *Heartbreak House* had last been performed. Maxwell invited the hugely experienced Christopher Newton to direct *Heartbreak House*. He had directed it in 1985 (see above, page 103), a production that Maxwell had seen and had greatly admired. She was, she said, "eager to see what new insights he will now bring to this extraordinary play."

Contrasting with her strategy to give an experienced Shaw director the opportunity to revisit one of Shaw's plays was her invitation to Gina Wilkinson to direct *Candida*. Wilkinson had taken the Festival by storm with her production of *Born Yesterday* in 2009, but had never directed a Shaw play. *Candida* was the first Shaw play to be given a full production at the Shaw Festival (in the inaugural season of 1962), and was also the first Shaw play that Jackie Maxwell directed (in the Festival's 2002 season). Here, then, was the potential for fresh insights into a classic Shaw play from a demonstrably accomplished but, from a Shavian perspective, ingenue director. (Sadly, Gina Wilkinson died early in December 2010. "A brilliantly bright light has gone out in Canadian theatre," Maxwell said. Maxwell chose the experienced Tadeusz Bradecki to replace Wilkinson as the director of *Candida*.)

As for *On the Rocks*, this late and complex political play, produced only once at the Festival (in 1986: see above, page 117), while very funny, poses particular problems of audience accessibility and understanding. "There is no doubt," Maxwell said, "that some of Shaw's later plays are extremely dense, *full* of arcane references, demanding a level of informed focus that can be difficult for many to maintain." Discarding such plays was not an option, for they are, she acknowledged, "full of extraordinary ideas, some still so pertinent that it takes your breath away." Maxwell's solution to the dilemma was to invite playwright and actor Michael Healey to "re-envision" *On the Rocks* for a contemporary audience, giving him carte blanche to adapt the play. This "dynamic pairing" between Shaw and Healey, "a playwright of similar wit and provocative politic," was to be the first of a series of such pairings so that contemporary playwrights could give their "singular take" on some of Shaw's less performed plays. John Murrell, for example, whose adaptation of *Uncle Vanya* and his play *Waiting for the Parade* were produced at the Festival in 1999 and 2004, respectively, has been commissioned to adapt *Geneva*, another of Shaw's late political plays.

There is, then, a new strategy in place for keeping the full range of Shaw's plays in the Festival repertoire, the results of which won't be apparent for some years. In the meantime, the results of Maxwell's related strategy of defining a continuum between Shaw and contemporary playwrights are already beginning to emerge.

"CONTEMPORARY SHAVIANS" IN THE STUDIO THEATRE Although a performance space in the Production Centre that opened in 2004 was not in the original plans for the Centre, a lighting rig and control booth were included in the design. When Maxwell toured the space with Colleen Blake while it was still under construction she saw the potential for performances, but it wasn't until three or four years later that the idea began to take shape.

The idea developed around the continuum between Shaw and contemporary playwrights, playwrights that Maxwell began referring to as "Contemporary Shavians" – that is, playwrights committed to the "provocative, spirited, cranky exploration of the status quo that is Bernard Shaw and the spirit that pervades this place." She saw such playwrights, at least initially, as appealing to a relatively small proportion of Festival audiences, and, therefore, better suited to a new, smaller, and more flexible space than any of the three existing Festival theatres. Over time, Maxwell hoped, Festival audiences would come to welcome contemporary work written in the spirit of Shaw, and, moreover, that contemporary work would bring in new audiences.

The new performance space in the Production Centre was to be the venue for the contemporary Shavians. It was called the Studio Theatre, where plays would open late in the season – when all the other Festival plays were on stage – for a short run. Seating would be on risers, which could be arranged in a variety of configurations. Seating capacity, depending on the configuration, was around 200, about two-thirds the size of the Court House and Royal George Theatres.

The first play to be performed in the Studio Theatre was *The Entertainer*, by British playwright John Osborne (1929–94). Directed by Maxwell, it began previews on July 31, 2009, and had a limited run of twenty-five performances. Maxwell said that "the idea was to pack the houses and really create a buzz around this new idea." With an 82 percent box office and keen interest in the new venture from the company, audiences, and the press, *The Entertainer* came close to meeting these aspirations.

The Entertainer was an interesting choice. Written in 1957, it followed Osborne's sensational *Look Back in Anger* (1956), the play that immediately established Osborne as the original "angry young man" of British theatre. The central character of *The Entertainer* is a musical hall performer named Archie Rice (played in the original production by Laurence Olivier and in the Festival production by Benedict Campbell), whose talents and whose profession are in terminal decline. Archie is the conduit through which Osborne mounts a blistering criticism of an England blighted by postwar political and social decay. As *Guardian* critic Michael Billington pointed out in his house program essay, Osborne had no time for Shaw – his plays were "posturing wind and rubbish," Osborne said – but Osborne's views on British ineptitude, prejudice, and inflated sense of importance in the world matched Shaw's in many respects.

And so did the views and values of the author of the Festival's second contemporary Shavian, Caryl Churchill. A prolific playwright, Churchill (born in 1938) has followed a political and feminist agenda throughout her career, most famously perhaps in her anti-Thatcherite play *Top Girls* in 1982. She wrote *Serious Money*, Maxwell's choice for the 2010 Studio Theatre play, in 1987 in response to the scandals on the London stock market in the 1980s, scandals driven, the play charges, by greed and corporate excess.

Serious Money was a much riskier choice than *The Entertainer*. Structurally it is a good deal more complex, with no clear-cut plot line in a series of rapidly changing scenes. It is, moreover, written in rhyming verse, and, freed from the censorship (not abolished in England until 1968) that restricted the language that Osborne could give his characters, Churchill doesn't spare her audiences the offensive language that comes naturally to the predominantly young and crass people that populate her play (eighteen actors played fifty roles).

Kelly Wong, a cast member, was not alone in wondering how audiences would react to *Serious Money.* "Would they understand what's going on? Were people going to be offended by the language?" Unsurprisingly, some people didn't get it, and some were indeed offended by the language. (Robert Cushman noted empty seats after the intermission even on opening night.) But under Eda Holmes' inventive but focused direction on Peter Hartwell's fluid set (Hartwell had also designed the London premiere of the play), the ensemble came through with a performance that combined massive kinetic energy with intellectual conviction. In another limited run (twenty performances), *Serious Money* didn't do as well at the box office as *The Entertainer*, but it came close to 70 percent.

British contemporary Shavians Osborne and Churchill were followed in 2011 by an American, Suzan-Lori Parks, and an Australian, Andrew Bovell.

American playwright August Wilson once argued that Parks' plays "subvert theatrical convention and produce a mature and inimitable art that is as exciting as it is fresh" – which is an excellent way of describing Shaw's plays as well. Parks' *Topdog/Underdog* premiered at the New York Shakespeare Festival in 2001 and went on to win a Pulitzer Prize. The Shaw Festival production was both a Canadian premiere and the first ever Festival production of a work by a playwright of colour. The play concerns the struggles of two brothers to come to terms with their current relationship – reflected in the title – and their family history. Described by Parks as "a play about family wounds and healing," *Topdog/Underdog* impressed Maxwell as "full of passion and poetry," "harsh and humane" at one and the same time.

Andrew Bovell's *When the Rain Stops Falling* marked another first – the first play by an Australian writer at the Shaw Festival. It premiered in Adelaide in 2008, in London in 2009, and in New York in 2010, when *Time* critic Richard Zoglin judged it the best new play of the year. The Festival production was its Canadian premiere. With a complicated structure based on several time-shifts (the action opens in the year 2039), *When the Rain Stops Falling* is a challenging play for audiences, for which Bovell has been unapologetic – "I guess what I was

interested in doing is giving the audience a bit of work to do," he said prior to the New York opening. There is nothing easy about the theme, either. Like *Topdog/Underdog*, it has to do with struggling to come to terms with the past, the play as a whole, said Zoglin, serving as "a powerful metaphor for the impossibility of escaping the past."

The 2011 season was the first in which *two* plays by contemporary Shavians had been scheduled in the Studio Theatre (for runs of seventeen and twenty performances, respectively). It is conceivable that such plays might eventually migrate to one or more of the Festival's other theatres, but the significance of the new theatre and its playbills as things stood in 2011 was that Maxwell had opened up what she rightly described as a "rich vein of programming" for the Festival, "one that will add immeasurably to our future seasons."

PLAY DEVELOPMENT   Although the first full Festival production of *Serious Money* was at the Studio Theatre in 2010, its first appearance at the Festival was actually in 2008, when it was part of the Reading Series. The Reading Series was initiated by Christopher Newton and Denis Johnston in 1996 as a venue for rehearsed readings of plays of the mandate period (several of which were broadcast), but soon after her arrival at the Festival, Maxwell began to see the potential of the Reading Series for trying out plays that might be in the running for a full production in a later season. Thus it was with *Serious Money* and, in 2009, with *Topdog/Underdog*. She also saw the potential for using the series for play development. Two Paul Sportelli/Jay Turvey musicals, for example, *Tristan* (2005 Reading Series) and *Maria Severa* (2009) made their way into full productions in 2007 and 2011 via this route.

Play development is seen by Jackie Maxwell as "a vital part of our company's work." It is something that has a very public face in arenas such as the Reading Series, for which productions are advertised and tickets purchased in the normal way, but there is much important work that goes into play development out of the public eye. Both Jackie Maxwell and literary manager Joanna Falck work closely with Canadian playwrights, several of whom have enjoyed residencies at the Festival, learning more about the Festival and getting feedback on their work from Maxwell and Falck. Accustomed to writing plays for much smaller companies, some playwrights are surprised (and delighted) to learn that they don't have to limit their plays to four or five characters. From Falck's perspective, a clear message has been sent across Canada that the Festival is making a strong commitment to new plays by Canadian writers. Their work, Maxwell and Falck have told provincial and federal funding agencies, is set to play "a vital role on the stages of the Shaw Festival."

DIVERSITY   At the same time, Maxwell is determined to diversify Shaw Festival playbills, "pushing the geographical and cultural boundaries of the mandate." The 2006 production of *The Magic Fire* (directed by Maxwell) took Festival audiences into the devastated world of European émigrés in Argentina in the 1950s, one example of Maxwell's move towards a less Anglo-European feel about the Shaw Festival. Her November 2010 interview with Melissa Leong is again revealing. "I feel now," Maxwell said, "that I'm focusing on diversifying the worlds that we go to. I've been looking at some plays from South America. I've been looking at some African plays, and wonderful historical plays from women of colour." Asian plays are also in her sights.

Maxwell's embracing of diversity extends as well to the acting ensemble. In the discussions around colour-blind casting in 2008 (see above, page 260) she promised change in the ethnic diversity of the ensemble. As we saw above, she also insisted that change could not be instantaneous. Two years later, however, she could point to young actors in the ensemble "of many ethnicities," while established actors such as Nigel Shawn Williams (appearing in 2011 with Kevin Hanchard in *Topdog/Underdog* and as the Reverend James Morell in Shaw's *Candida*) take lead roles. The co-production of *Topdog/Underdog* with Toronto's Obsidian Theatre, which describes itself as "Canada's leading culturally diverse theatre company," also addresses Maxwell's commitment to diversity.

Jackie Maxwell's changes at the Shaw Festival have sometimes been referred to as her "elastic mandate." And, indeed, there is, by 2011, much more flexibility to the mandate than ever before. But Maxwell has never lost sight of the core of the mandate. Every play that she programs,

PATRICIA HAMILTON, RIC REID,
WANETA STORMS, MICHAEL BALL,
GOLDIE SEMPLE, LILA BATA-WALSH,
JENNIFER PHIPPS, DONNA BELLEVILLE,
AND SHARRY FLETT IN *THE MAGIC FIRE*
BY LILLIAN GROAG, 2006. DIRECTED
BY JACKIE MAXWELL, DESIGNED BY
SUE LEPAGE, LIGHTING DESIGNED BY
LOUISE GUINAND, SOUND DESIGNED
BY JOHN GZOWSKI. PHOTO BY DAVID
COOPER.

she says, "necessitates engagement" by the audience. "Why," she always asks, "does this play deserve to be in a Shavian environment?" Thus the issue debated at the "Speed of Ideas" forum in 2011 by playwrights Tony Kushner, Suzan-Lori Parks, and critic Michael Billington is "the necessity of provocative ideas" as the essence of the Shaw Festival mandate, a necessity as important in 2011 as it was at the Festival's founding fifty years ago.

In her introduction to the 2011 Festival brochure, Maxwell writes of the "passion" of a local lawyer, Brian Doherty, that brought the Shaw Festival into being. That passion and the achievements it generated are worthy of expansive celebration and homage. But the Festival must also, Maxwell says, look forward to the next fifty years, bringing audiences "new worlds, new playwrights, and new visions of Shaw himself."

Having signed a new contract as artistic director at the end of the 2010 season, Jackie Maxwell made it clear that she anticipates spending several more seasons bringing those new experiences to the Shaw Festival, thereby ensuring that the second half-century of the Festival's history will begin on a very different footing from the first.

APPENDIX A

ARTISTIC DIRECTORS AND BOARD CHAIRS

ARTISTIC DIRECTORS

Andrew Allan 1963–65

Barry Morse 1966

Paxton Whitehead 1967–77

Tony van Bridge (Acting) 1975

Richard Kirschner 1978

Leslie Yeo (Guest) 1979

Christopher Newton 1980–2002

Jackie Maxwell 2003–

BOARD CHAIRS

Calvin Rand 1965–1977

John P.S. Mackenzie 1978–1980

George H. Montague 1981–82

Gary F. Burroughs 1983–84

Allan Slaight 1985–86

John H. Clappison 1987–88

J. Howard Hawke 1989–90

Bernard Ostry 1991–92

Joseph M. Pigott 1993–94

Anthony R. Graham 1995–96

Brian Segal 1997–98

Richard H. McCoy 1999–2000

Lorne R. Barclay 2001–2

Thomas R. Hyde 2003–4

Elaine G. Triggs 2005–6

Richard D. Falconer 2007–8

Janet McKelvey 2009–10

Gary Comerford 2011–

APPENDIX B

SHAW FESTIVAL PRODUCTION RECORD

1962
COURT HOUSE THEATRE

Don Juan in Hell (from *Man and Superman*) by Bernard Shaw

Candida by Bernard Shaw

1963
COURT HOUSE THEATRE

You Never Can Tell by Bernard Shaw

How He Lied to Her Husband by Bernard Shaw

The Man of Destiny by Bernard Shaw

Androcles and the Lion by Bernard Shaw

1964
COURT HOUSE THEATRE

Heartbreak House by Bernard Shaw

Village Wooing by Bernard Shaw

The Dark Lady of the Sonnets by Bernard Shaw

John Bull's Other Island by Bernard Shaw

1965
COURT HOUSE THEATRE

Pygmalion by Bernard Shaw

The Millionairess by Bernard Shaw

The Shadow of a Gunman by Sean O'Casey

1966
COURT HOUSE THEATRE

Man and Superman by Bernard Shaw

Misalliance by Bernard Shaw

The Apple Cart by Bernard Shaw

1967
COURT HOUSE THEATRE

Arms and the Man by Bernard Shaw

Major Barbara by Bernard Shaw

The Circle by Somerset Maugham

1968
COURT HOUSE THEATRE

Heartbreak House by Bernard Shaw

The Importance of Being Oscar by Micheál MacLiammóir

The Chemmy Circle by Georges Feydeau

1969
COURT HOUSE THEATRE

The Doctor's Dilemma by Bernard Shaw

Back to Methuselah (Part I) by Bernard Shaw

Five Variations of Corno di Bassetto by Louis Applebaum and Ronald Hambleton

The Guardsman by Ferenc Molnár

1970
COURT HOUSE THEATRE

Candida by Bernard Shaw

Forty Years On by Alan Bennett

1971
COURT HOUSE THEATRE

The Philanderer by Bernard Shaw

O'Flaherty, V.C. by Bernard Shaw

Press Cuttings by Bernard Shaw

Summer Days by Romain Weingarten

Tonight at 8:30 by Noel Coward

A Social Success by Max Beerbohm

1972
COURT HOUSE THEATRE

Getting Married by Bernard Shaw

Misalliance by Bernard Shaw

The Royal Family by George S. Kaufman and Edna Ferber

1973
FESTIVAL THEATRE

You Never Can Tell by Bernard Shaw

Fanny's First Play by Bernard Shaw

The Brass Butterfly by William Golding

COURT HOUSE THEATRE

Sisters of Mercy: A Musical Journey into the Words of Leonard Cohen by Gene Lesser

1974
FESTIVAL THEATRE

The Devil's Disciple by Bernard Shaw

Too True to be Good by Bernard Shaw

Charley's Aunt by Brandon Thomas

COURT HOUSE THEATRE

The Admirable Bashville by Bernard Shaw

Rosmersholm by Henrik Ibsen

1975
FESTIVAL THEATRE

Pygmalion by Bernard Shaw

Caesar and Cleopatra by Bernard Shaw

Leaven of Malice by Robertson Davies

COURT HOUSE THEATRE

The First Night of Pygmalion by Richard Huggett

GKC: The Wit and Wisdom of Gilbert Keith Chesterton by Tony van Bridge

1976

FESTIVAL THEATRE

Mrs Warren's Profession
by Bernard Shaw

Arms and the Man
by Bernard Shaw

The Apple Cart by Bernard Shaw

The Admirable Crichton
by J.M. Barrie

COURT HOUSE THEATRE

Arms and the Man
by Bernard Shaw

1977

FESTIVAL THEATRE

Man and Superman
by Bernard Shaw

The Millionairess
by Bernard Shaw

Thark by Ben Travers

COURT HOUSE THEATRE

Great Catherine
by Bernard Shaw

Widowers' Houses
by Bernard Shaw

1978

FESTIVAL THEATRE

Major Barbara by Bernard Shaw

Heartbreak House
by Bernard Shaw

John Gabriel Borkman
by Henrik Ibsen

COURT HOUSE THEATRE

Lady Audley's Secret: A Musical Melodrama by Mary Elizabeth Braddon, George Goehring, and John Kuntz

1979

FESTIVAL THEATRE

You Never Can Tell
by Bernard Shaw

Captain Brassbound's Conversion by Bernard Shaw

The Corn is Green
by Emlyn Williams

Dear Liar by Jerome Kilty

COURT HOUSE THEATRE

Village Wooing by Bernard Shaw

Blithe Spirit by Noel Coward

My Astonishing Self
by Michael Voysey

1980

FESTIVAL THEATRE

Misalliance by Bernard Shaw

The Cherry Orchard
by Anton Chekhov

A Flea in Her Ear
by Georges Feydeau

The Grand Hunt
by Gyula Hernády

COURT HOUSE THEATRE

The Philanderer by Bernard Shaw

Overruled by Bernard Shaw

A Respectable Wedding
by Bertolt Brecht

Canuck by John Bruce Cowan

ROYAL GEORGE THEATRE

Puttin' on the Ritz the music and lyrics of Irving Berlin

Gunga Heath by Heath Lamberts

1981

FESTIVAL THEATRE

Saint Joan by Bernard Shaw

Tons of Money by
Will Evans and Valentine

The Suicide by Nikolai Erdman

Camille by
Robert David MacDonald

COURT HOUSE THEATRE

In Good King Charles's Golden Days by Bernard Shaw

The Magistrate
by Arthur W. Pinero

ROYAL GEORGE THEATRE

The Man of Destiny
by Bernard Shaw

Rose Marie by Rudolf Friml

1982

FESTIVAL THEATRE

Pygmalion by Bernard Shaw

See How They Run by Philip King

Camille by
Robert David MacDonald

Cyrano de Bergerac
by Edmond Rostand

COURT HOUSE THEATRE

Too True to be Good
by Bernard Shaw

The Singular Life of Albert Nobbs by George Moore

ROYAL GEORGE THEATRE

The Music-Cure
by Bernard Shaw

The Desert Song
by Sigmund Romberg

HERB FOSTER IN *CAESAR AND CLEOPATRA*, 1983. PHOTO BY DAVID COOPER.

1983

FESTIVAL THEATRE

Caesar and Cleopatra
by Bernard Shaw

Cyrano de Bergerac
by Edmond Rostand

Rookery Nook by Ben Travers

Private Lives by Noel Coward

COURT HOUSE THEATRE

The Simpleton of the Unexpected Isles by Bernard Shaw

Candida by Bernard Shaw

The Vortex by Noel Coward

ROYAL GEORGE THEATRE

O'Flaherty, V.C.
by Bernard Shaw

Tom Jones by
Sir Edward German

1984

FESTIVAL THEATRE

The Devil's Disciple
by Bernard Shaw

Private Lives by Noel Coward

The Skin of Our Teeth
by Thornton Wilder

Célimare by Eugène Labiche

COURT HOUSE THEATRE

Androcles and the Lion
by Bernard Shaw

The Vortex by Noel Coward

The Lost Letter by Ion Caragiale

ROYAL GEORGE THEATRE

The Fascinating Foundling
by Bernard Shaw

How He Lied to Her Husband
by Bernard Shaw

Roberta by Jerome Kern

1984 by George Orwell

1985

FESTIVAL THEATRE

Heartbreak House
by Bernard Shaw

The Madwoman of Chaillot
by Jean Giraudoux

One for the Pot by
Ray Cooney and Tony Hilton

Cavalcade by Noel Coward

COURT HOUSE THEATRE

John Bull's Other Island
by Bernard Shaw

The Women by Clare Boothe Luce

Tropical Madness No.2: Metaphysics of a Two-Headed Calf by Stanisław Witkiewicz

ROYAL GEORGE THEATRE

The Inca of Perusalem
by Bernard Shaw

Murder on the Nile
by Agatha Christie

Naughty Marietta by
Victor Herbert

1986

FESTIVAL THEATRE

Arms and the Man by
Bernard Shaw

Back to Methuselah
by Bernard Shaw

Banana Ridge by Ben Travers

Cavalcade by Noel Coward

COURT HOUSE THEATRE

On the Rocks by Bernard Shaw

Holiday by Philip Barry

Tonight We Improvise
by Luigi Pirandello

ROYAL GEORGE THEATRE

Passion, Poison, and Petrifaction by Bernard Shaw

Black Coffee by Agatha Christie

Girl Crazy by George and Ira Gershwin

1987
FESTIVAL THEATRE

Major Barbara by Bernard Shaw

Hay Fever by Noel Coward

Marathon '33 by June Havoc

Peter Pan by J.M. Barrie

COURT HOUSE THEATRE

Fanny's First Play by Bernard Shaw

Night of January 16th by Ayn Rand

Playing with Fire by August Strindberg

Salomé by Oscar Wilde

ROYAL GEORGE THEATRE

Augustus Does His Bit by Bernard Shaw

Not in the Book by Arthur Watkyn

Anything Goes by Cole Porter, Guy Bolton, and P.G. Wodehouse

1988
FESTIVAL THEATRE

You Never Can Tell by Bernard Shaw

Peter Pan by J.M. Barrie

War and Peace by Leo Tolstoy

Once in a Lifetime by Moss Hart and George S. Kaufman

COURT HOUSE THEATRE

Geneva by Bernard Shaw

The Voysey Inheritance by Harley Granville Barker

He Who Gets Slapped by Leonid Andreyev

ROYAL GEORGE THEATRE

The Dark Lady of the Sonnets by Bernard Shaw

Hit the Deck by Vincent Youmans

Dangerous Corner by J.B. Priestley

1989
FESTIVAL THEATRE

Man and Superman by Bernard Shaw

Berkeley Square by John L. Balderston

Once in a Lifetime by Moss Hart and George S. Kaufman

Trelawny of the 'Wells' by Arthur W. Pinero

COURT HOUSE THEATRE

Getting Married by Bernard Shaw

Peer Gynt by Henrik Ibsen

Nymph Errant by Cole Porter

ROYAL GEORGE THEATRE

Shakes versus Shav by Bernard Shaw

The Glimpse of Reality by Bernard Shaw

An Inspector Calls by J.B. Priestley

Good News by Ray Henderson, Laurence Schwab, B.G. DeSylva, and Lew Brown

1990
FESTIVAL THEATRE

Misalliance by Bernard Shaw

Trelawny of the 'Wells' by Arthur W. Pinero

The Waltz of the Toreadors by Jean Anouilh

Present Laughter by Noel Coward

COURT HOUSE THEATRE

Mrs Warren's Profession by Bernard Shaw

Nymph Errant by Cole Porter

Ubu Rex by Alfred Jarry

ROYAL GEORGE THEATRE

Village Wooing by Bernard Shaw

Night Must Fall by Emlyn Williams

When We Are Married by J.B. Priestley

1991
FESTIVAL THEATRE

The Doctor's Dilemma by Bernard Shaw

A Cuckoo in the Nest by Ben Travers

Lulu by Frank Wedekind

COURT HOUSE THEATRE

The Millionairess by Bernard Shaw

Henry IV by Luigi Pirandello

Hedda Gabler by Henrik Ibsen

ROYAL GEORGE THEATRE

Press Cuttings by Bernard Shaw

A Connecticut Yankee by Richard Rodgers, Lorenz Hart, and Herbert Fields

This Happy Breed by Noel Coward

1992
FESTIVAL THEATRE

Pygmalion by Bernard Shaw

Counsellor-at-Law by Elmer Rice

Charley's Aunt by Brandon Thomas

COURT HOUSE THEATRE

Widowers' Houses by Bernard Shaw

Drums in the Night by Bertolt Brecht

Point Valaine by Noel Coward

ROYAL GEORGE THEATRE

Overruled by Bernard Shaw

On the Town by Leonard Bernstein, Betty Comden, and Adolph Green

Ten Minute Alibi by Anthony Armstrong

1993
FESTIVAL THEATRE

Saint Joan by Bernard Shaw

The Silver King by Henry Arthur Jones

Blithe Spirit by Noel Coward

COURT HOUSE THEATRE

Candida by Bernard Shaw

The Unmentionables by Carl Sternheim

The Marrying of Ann Leete by Harley Granville Barker

ROYAL GEORGE THEATRE

The Man of Destiny by Bernard Shaw

Gentlemen Prefer Blondes by Jule Styne, Leo Robin, Anita Loos, and Joseph Fields

And Then There Were None by Agatha Christie

1994
FESTIVAL THEATRE

Arms and the Man by Bernard Shaw

The Front Page by Ben Hecht and Charles MacArthur

Sherlock Holmes by William Gillette

COURT HOUSE THEATRE

Too True to be Good by Bernard Shaw

Eden End by J.B. Priestley

Ivona, Princess of Burgundia by Witold Gombrowicz

ROYAL GEORGE THEATRE

Annajanska, the Bolshevik Empress by Bernard Shaw

Lady, Be Good! by George and Ira Gershwin, Guy Bolton, and Fred Thompson

Busman's Honeymoon by Dorothy L. Sayers and M. St Clare Byrne

Rococo by Harley Granville Barker

1995
FESTIVAL THEATRE

You Never Can Tell by Bernard Shaw

The Petrified Forest by Robert Sherwood

Cavalcade by Noel Coward

COURT HOUSE THEATRE

The Philanderer by Bernard Shaw

An Ideal Husband by Oscar Wilde

Waste by Harley Granville Barker

ROYAL GEORGE THEATRE

The Six of Calais by Bernard Shaw

The Voice of the Turtle by John van Druten

Ladies in Retirement by Edward Percy and Reginald Denham

The Zoo by Arthur Sullivan and Bolton Rowe

1996
FESTIVAL THEATRE

The Devil's Disciple by Bernard Shaw

Rashomon by Fay and Michael Kanin

Hobson's Choice
by Harold Brighouse

COURT HOUSE THEATRE

The Simpleton of the Unexpected Isles by Bernard Shaw

An Ideal Husband
by Oscar Wilde

The Playboy of the Western World by J.M. Synge

Marsh Hay by Merrill Denison

ROYAL GEORGE THEATRE

Mr Cinders by Vivan Ellis, Richard Myers, Clifford Grey, and Greatrex Newman

The Hollow by Agatha Christie

Shall We Join the Ladies?
by J.M. Barrie

The Conjuror by David Ben and Patrick Watson

1997

FESTIVAL THEATRE

Mrs Warren's Profession
by Bernard Shaw

Hobson's Choice
by Harold Brighouse

Will Any Gentleman?
by Vernon Sylvaine

The Seagull by Anton Chekhov

COURT HOUSE THEATRE

In Good King Charles's Golden Days by Bernard Shaw

The Playboy of the Western World by J.M. Synge

The Children's Hour
by Lillian Hellman

The Secret Life by
Harley Granville Barker

ROYAL GEORGE THEATRE

The Chocolate Soldier
by Oscar Straus

The Two Mrs Carrolls
by Martin Vale

The Conjuror, Part 2 by
David Ben and Patrick Watson

Sorry, Wrong Number
by Lucille Fletcher

1998

FESTIVAL THEATRE

Major Barbara by Bernard Shaw

You Can't Take It With You
by George S. Kaufman and
Moss Hart

Lady Windermere's Fan by Oscar Wilde

COURT HOUSE THEATRE

John Bull's Other Island
by Bernard Shaw

The Lady's Not for Burning
by Christopher Fry

Joy by John Galsworthy

ROYAL GEORGE THEATRE

Passion, Poison, and Petrifaction by Bernard Shaw

A Foggy Day by George and Ira Gershwin

The Shop at Sly Corner
by Edward Percy

Brothers in Arms
by Merrill Denison

Waterloo by
Arthur Conan Doyle

1999

FESTIVAL THEATRE

Heartbreak House
by Bernard Shaw

You Can't Take It With You by George S. Kaufman and Moss Hart

Easy Virtue by Noel Coward

All My Sons by Arthur Miller

COURT HOUSE THEATRE

Getting Married by Bernard Shaw

The Madras House by
Harley Granville Barker

S.S. Tenacity by Charles Vildrac

Uncle Vanya by Anton Chekhov

ROYAL GEORGE THEATRE

Village Wooing by Bernard Shaw

Rebecca by Daphne du Maurier

A Foggy Day by George and Ira Gershwin

Waterloo by Arthur Conan Doyle

2000

FESTIVAL THEATRE

The Doctor's Dilemma
by Bernard Shaw

Easy Virtue by Noel Coward

Lord of the Flies adapted for the stage by Nigel Williams from the novel by William Golding

The Matchmaker
by Thornton Wilder

COURT HOUSE THEATRE

The Apple Cart by Bernard Shaw

A Woman of No Importance
by Oscar Wilde

A Room of One's Own adapted by Patrick Garland from the essay by Virginia Woolf

Six Characters in Search of an Author by Luigi Pirandello

ROYAL GEORGE THEATRE

Time and the Conways
by J.B. Priestley

She Loves Me by Joe Masteroff, Jerry Bock, and Sheldon Harnick

Still Life by Noel Coward

2001

FESTIVAL THEATRE

The Millionairess
by Bernard Shaw

Peter Pan by J.M. Barrie

The Man Who Came to Dinner by Moss Hart and George S. Kaufman

COURT HOUSE THEATRE

Fanny's First Play
by Bernard Shaw

Picnic by William Inge

Six Characters in Search of an Author by Luigi Pirandello

The Return of the Prodigal
by St John Hankin

ROYAL GEORGE THEATRE

The Mystery of Edwin Drood
by Rupert Holmes

Laura by Vera Caspary and George Sklar

Love from a Stranger
by Frank Vosper

Shadow Play by Noel Coward

2002

FESTIVAL THEATRE

Caesar and Cleopatra
by Bernard Shaw

Candida by Bernard Shaw

Detective Story by Sidney Kingsley

Hay Fever by Noel Coward

COURT HOUSE THEATRE

The Return of the Prodigal
by St John Hankin

The House of Bernarda Alba
by Federico García Lorca

His Majesty by
Harley Granville Barker

Chaplin by Simon Bradbury

ROYAL GEORGE THEATRE

The Old Ladies
by Rodney Ackland

Merrily We Roll Along
by Stephen Sondheim and George Furth

The Old Lady Shows Her Medals by J.M. Barrie

2003

FESTIVAL THEATRE

Misalliance by Bernard Shaw

Three Sisters by Anton Chekhov

The Coronation Voyage
by Michel Marc Bouchard

The Royal Family
by George S. Kaufman and Edna Ferber

COURT HOUSE THEATRE

Widowers' Houses
by Bernard Shaw

Diana of Dobson's
by Cicely Hamilton

The Plough and the Stars
by Sean O'Casey

Afterplay by Brian Friel

ROYAL GEORGE THEATRE

On the Twentieth Century
by Betty Comden, Adolph Green, and Cy Coleman

Blood Relations
by Sharon Pollock

Happy End by Bertolt Brecht and Kurt Weill

2004

FESTIVAL THEATRE

Pygmalion by Bernard Shaw

Man and Superman
by Bernard Shaw

Three Men on a Horse by John Cecil Holm and George Abbott

Nothing Sacred
by George F. Walker

COURT HOUSE THEATRE

Ah, Wilderness!
by Eugene O'Neill

Rutherford and Son
by Githa Sowerby

The Tinker's Wedding
by J.M. Synge

Floyd Collins by Adam
Guettel and Tina Landau

ROYAL GEORGE THEATRE

*The Importance of Being
Earnest* by Oscar Wilde

Pal Joey by Richard
Rodgers, Lorenz Hart,
and John O'Hara

Waiting for the Parade
by John Murrell

Harlequinade
by Terence Rattigan

2005
FESTIVAL THEATRE

You Never Can Tell
by Bernard Shaw

Major Barbara by Bernard Shaw

Gypsy by Arthur Laurents,
Jule Styne, and Stephen Sondheim

COURT HOUSE THEATRE

Belle Moral: A Natural History
by Ann-Marie MacDonald

Journey's End by R.C. Sherriff

The Autumn Garden
by Lillian Hellman

ROYAL GEORGE THEATRE

The Constant Wife
by Somerset Maugham

Happy End by Bertolt
Brecht and Kurt Weill

Something on the Side
by Georges Feydeau and
Maurice Desvallières

Bus Stop by William Inge

2006
FESTIVAL THEATRE

Arms and the Man
by Bernard Shaw

The Crucible by Arthur Miller

High Society by Cole
Porter and Arthur Kopit

COURT HOUSE THEATRE

Too True to be Good
by Bernard Shaw

Rosmersholm by Henrik Ibsen

Love Among the Russians
[*The Bear* and *The Proposal*]
by Anton Chekhov

The Magic Fire
by Lillian Groag

ROYAL GEORGE THEATRE

The Invisible Man
by Michael O'Brien

The Heiress by Ruth Goetz
and Augustus Goetz

Design for Living
by Noel Coward

2007
FESTIVAL THEATRE

Saint Joan by Bernard Shaw

Mack and Mabel by Michael
Stewart and Jerry Herman

Hotel Peccadillo based on
L'Hôtel du Libre-Echange
by Georges Feydeau and
Maurice Desvallières

COURT HOUSE THEATRE

The Cassilis Engagement
by St John Hankin

Tristan by Paul Sportelli
and Jay Turvey

The Kiltartan Comedies
[*The Rising of the Moon*
and *Spreading the News*]
by Lady Augusta Gregory

*A Month in the Country
(after Turgenev)* by Brian Friel

ROYAL GEORGE THEATRE

The Philanderer
by Bernard Shaw

The Circle by
Somerset Maugham

Summer and Smoke
by Tennessee Williams

JULIE MARTELL IN *A LITTLE NIGHT MUSIC*,
2008. PHOTO BY DAVID COOPER.

2008
FESTIVAL THEATRE

An Inspector Calls
by J.B. Priestley

Wonderful Town by
Leonard Bernstein, Betty
Comden, and Adolph Green

Mrs Warren's Profession
by Bernard Shaw

Follies: In Concert
by James Goldman
and Stephen Sondheim

COURT HOUSE THEATRE

The Stepmother
by Githa Sowerby

A Little Night Music by Hugh
Wheeler and Stephen Sondheim

Belle Moral by
Ann-Marie MacDonald

ROYAL GEORGE THEATRE

Getting Married by Bernard Shaw

The Little Foxes by Lillian Hellman

After the Dance
by Terence Rattigan

The President by Ferenc Molnár

2009
FESTIVAL THEATRE

Brief Encounters [*Still Life*,
We Were Dancing, and *Hands
Across the Sea*] by Noel Coward

Born Yesterday by Garson Kanin

The Devil's Disciple
by Bernard Shaw

COURT HOUSE THEATRE

Ways of the Heart [*The
Astonished Heart*, *Family
Album*, and *Ways and Means*]
by Noel Coward

A Moon for the Misbegotten
by Eugene O'Neill

Albertine in Five Times
by Michel Tremblay

ROYAL GEORGE THEATRE

Play, Orchestra, Play [*Red
Peppers*, *Fumed Oak*, and
Shadow Play] by Noel Coward

*Sunday in the Park with
George* by Stephen Sondheim
and James Lapine

*In Good King Charles's Golden
Days* by Bernard Shaw

Star Chamber by Noel Coward

STUDIO THEATRE

The Entertainer by John Osborne

2010
FESTIVAL THEATRE

An Ideal Husband by Oscar Wilde

The Women by Clare Boothe Luce

The Doctor's Dilemma
by Bernard Shaw

COURT HOUSE THEATRE

The Cherry Orchard
by Anton Chekhov

John Bull's Other Island
by Bernard Shaw

Age of Arousal by Linda Griffiths

ROYAL GEORGE THEATRE

Harvey by Mary Chase

One Touch of Venus by
Kurt Weill, Odgen Nash,
and S.J. Perelman

Half an Hour by J.M. Barrie

STUDIO THEATRE

Serious Money
by Caryl Churchill

2011
FESTIVAL THEATRE

My Fair Lady by Alan Jay
Lerner and Frederick Loewe

Heartbreak House
by Bernard Shaw

The Admirable Crichton
by J. M. Barrie

COURT HOUSE THEATRE

Drama at Inish – A Comedy
by Lennox Robinson

On the Rocks by Bernard Shaw

Maria Severa by
Paul Sportelli and Jay Turvey

ROYAL GEORGE THEATRE

Cat on a Hot Tin Roof
by Tennessee Williams

Candida by Bernard Shaw

The President by Ferenc Molnár

STUDIO THEATRE

When the Rain Stops Falling
by Andrew Bovell

Topdog/Underdog
by Suzan-Lori Parks

SHAW FESTIVAL
TOURING PRODUCTIONS

A SCENE FROM *BERKELEY SQUARE*, 1989. PHOTO BY DAVID COOPER.

Full details of the dates and locations of all Festival touring productions up to and including 2007 can be found in *The Shaw Festival Production Record*, edited by L.W. Conolly and Jean German (Oakville and Niagara-on-the-Lake: Mosaic Press and the Shaw Festival, 2008). Numbers in parantheses in the list below indicate the number of performances in each location.

1967

Major Barbara, Montreal (8), Winnipeg (22).

1969

The Guardsman, Ottawa (7).

1970

Candida, Kingston (4), Ottawa (12).

1971

The Philanderer, Kingston (5), Montreal (5), Ottawa (20), Rochester (2).

Summer Days, Ottawa (16).

1972

Misalliance, Ottawa (16), Rochester (2), Kingston (4), Montreal (5), Washington DC (16).

1973

The Philanderer, Washington DC (15).

You Never Can Tell, Ottawa (20), Winnipeg (27), Detroit (8), New Haven (8), Ann Arbor (6).

1974

The Devil's Disciple, Halifax (18), Truro (1), Yarmouth (1), Charlottetown (2), St John's (3), Fredericton (4), Belleville (2), Kingston (2).

Too True to Be Good, Cambridge, Mass (8).

Charley's Aunt, Cambridge, Mass. (8), Ottawa (24), Philadelphia (16).

1975

Caesar and Cleopatra, Ottawa (24), Philadelphia (16).

The Devil's Disciple, Philadelphia (16), Washington DC (16), Toronto (8).

1978

Thark, Ottawa (24), Montreal (8).

Heartbreak House, Ottawa (24).

1979

Blithe Spirit, Corning (1), Rochester (2), Oswego (1), Montreal (8), and several locations throughout Ontario (19).

1980

The Grand Hunt, Ottawa (23), Seattle (31).

1982

The Desert Song, Montreal (25), and several locations throughout Ontario (21).

1983

Tom Jones, several locations throughout Ontario (21).
Candida, Victoria (23).

1984

Roberta, several locations throughout Ontario (19).

Célimare, Ottawa (20), London (24).

Cyrano de Bergerac, Toronto (40).

1985

Heartbreak House, Ottawa (20).

1987

One for the Pot, Ottawa (21).

The Women, Toronto (4).

Hay Fever, Ottawa (19).

1988

You Never Can Tell, Winnipeg (29), Calgary (31).

1989

An Inspector Calls, Philadelphia (7).

Berkeley Square, Ottawa (20).

1990

Night Must Fall, Philadelphia (8).

1991

The Doctor's Dilemma, Ottawa (20).

1994

Arms and the Man, Ann Arbor (5).

The Front Page, Ann Arbor (3).

1996

One for the Pot, Toronto (51) [a Mirvish Productions remount at the Royal Alexandra Theatre].

2001

A Room of One's Own, London (1), Ottawa (14), Winnipeg (20).

2002

Candida, Ottawa (19), Rochester, Michigan (27).

2004

Rutherford and Son, Ottawa (19).

2007

Village Wooing, Hamilton (1), Guelph (1), Toronto (1).

2008

Saint Joan, Chicago (16).

SOURCES

FIONA BYRNE IN *THE HOUSE OF BERNARDA ALBA*, 2002. PHOTO BY DAVID COOPER.

In 1983 the Shaw Festival and the University of Guelph reached an agreement to make the University the official repository of the company's archives. All materials that the Festival had accumulated up to 1983 were transferred to Guelph, and annual deposits have been made every year since then to what have been known since 1999 as the L.W. Conolly Theatre Archives (www.lib.uoguelph.ca). Archival materials include a wide range of administrative and production records, and it is these records that have provided the primary research resource for this book. The reviews and articles on each season have been particularly helpful (call number XZ1 MS A217, arranged chronologically by season), as have production photographs (XZ1 MS A001), which Scott McKowen has drawn on extensively for illustrations in this book. A number of important primary sources are also held in the Festival's own library, including the transcripts of interviews conducted by Nancy Butler and others with many Festival volunteers and company members, among them Calvin Rand, Barry Morse, Paxton Whitehead, Tony van Bridge, Leslie Yeo, Christopher Newton, and Jackie Maxwell.

Other valuable unpublished sources include two doctoral dissertations: Arthur Day, *The Shaw Festival at Niagara-on-the-Lake in Ontario, Canada, 1962–1981: A History* (Bowling Green State University, 1982), and Margaret Elizabeth Rae, *The Christopher Newton Years at the Shaw Festival, 1980–1993* (University of Toronto, 1995).

Indispensable published sources include Brian Doherty's own account of the founding and the early years of the Shaw Festival in his book *Not Bloody Likely: The Shaw Festival, 1962–1973* (Toronto: J.M. Dent & Sons, 1974) and *Shaw Festival Production Record, 1962–2007*, edited by L.W. Conolly and Jean German (Oakville and Niagara-on-the-Lake: Mosaic Press and The Academy of the Shaw Festival, 2008). Building on the work of editors of earlier editions – Dan H. Laurence, Denis Johnston, and Jean German – the *Record* gives detailed information on forty-six seasons of Festival productions, as well as related activities such as the Reading Series, the Toronto Project, and the Directors Project.

Barry Morse gives an engaging account of his experiences with the Shaw Festival as artistic director and actor in his memoirs (written with Anthony Wynn and Robert E. Wood), *Remember with Advantages: Chasing the Fugitive and Other Stories from an Actor's Life* (Jefferson, NC, and London: McFarland and Co., 2006), and Tony van Bridge reflects on his many years at the Festival in *Also in the Cast: The Memoirs of Tony van Bridge* (Oakville and Niagara-on-the-Lake: Mosaic Press and The Academy of the Shaw Festival, 1995).

Two books edited by Katherine Holmes, former Director of Communications for the Shaw Festival, in celebration of the Festival's twenty-fifth anniversary in 1986, provide valuable pictorial materials: *The Pictorial Stage: Twenty-Five Years of Vision and Design at the Shaw Festival* (Niagara-on-the-Lake: The Shaw Festival Theatre Foundation, 1986) and *Celebrating! Twenty-Five Years on the Stage at the Shaw Festival* (Erin, Ontario: The Boston Mills Press, 1986). Arnold Edinborough's *The Festivals of Canada* (Toronto: Lester and Orpen Dennys, 1981) also contains numerous production photographs and other images of the Festival. The work of former Head of Design Cameron Porteous at the Festival (and at other theatres) is depicted in *Risking the Void: The Scenography of Cameron Porteous* (Toronto: Theatre Museum of Canada and the University of Guelph, 2009), the catalogue of an exhibition curated and designed by Sean Breaugh and Patricia Flood, and seen in Niagara-on-the-Lake, Toronto, and Guelph.

Selections from the theatre essays of former Festival Literary Adviser and Corresponding Scholar Ronald Bryden, many written for Festival house programs, were published in *Shaw and His Contemporaries: Theatre Essays* (Oakville and Niagara-on-the-Lake: Mosaic Press and The Academy of the Shaw Festival, 2002), and program essays and director's notes (by Neil Munro) for the Festival's groundbreaking productions of the plays of Harley Granville Barker were collected in *Granville Barker at the Shaw Festival* (Niagara-on-the-Lake: The Academy of the Shaw Festival, 2002), edited by Denis Johnston. Johnston also edited *Shaw and His Contemporaries: Four Plays* (Oakville and Niagara-on-the-Lake: Mosaic Press and The Academy of the Shaw Festival, 2001), containing the texts of four plays from the 2001 season (Shaw's *The Millionairess* and *Fanny's First Play*, J.M. Barrie's *Peter Pan*, and St John Hankin's *The Return of the Prodigal*). In *George Bernard Shaw and Christopher Newton: Explorations of Shavian Theatre* (Oakville: Mosaic Press, 1993), Keith Garebian gives a biographical and critical account of Christopher Newton's career in Canada, focusing on his productions of Shaw plays at the Shaw Festival.

The Oxford Companion to Canadian Theatre, edited by Eugene Benson and L.W. Conolly (Toronto: Oxford University Press, 1989), and the online *Canadian Theatre Encyclopedia* (www.canadiantheatre.com), under the editorial supervision of Anne Nothof, have provided useful information on the broad context of Canadian theatre in which the Shaw Festival is situated.

INDEX